Supervisory Management

Supervisory Management

W. Bolton

HEINEMANN : LONDON

William Heinemann Ltd
10 Upper Grosvenor Street, London WIX 9PA

LONDON MELBOURNE TORONTO
JOHANNESBURG AUCKLAND

First published 1986

British Library Cataloguing in Publication Data
Bolton, W. (William), *1933–*
  Supervisory management.
  1. Supervision of employees
  I. Title
  658.3'02   HF5549

ISBN 0 434 90159 8

Set by Graphicraft Typesetters Ltd, Hong Kong
Printed in Great Britain by
Redwood Burn Ltd, Trowbridge, Wilts

Contents

Preface

This book has been written for those who require an introduction to management studies and are, or aim to be, supervisors, i.e. first line managers. It is an appropriate text for those studying on courses in supervision offered by the National Examinations Board for Supervisory Studies (NEBSS), on courses for the Business and Technician Education Council (BTEC), Higher National Certificate (HNC) and Higher National Diploma (HND) courses – in particular for Mechanical and Production Engineering as it more than covers the units Management and Communication Studies IV and Production Planning and Control IV – on courses of the Association of Supervisory and Executive Engineers, and a wide variety of others.

The book has been written in five parts: Part One Principles and practice of supervision, Part Two Industrial relations, Part Three Communications, Part Four Economic and financial aspects of supervision and Part Five Technical aspects of production. Within each part the material is further subdivided into chapters, each chapter including revision questions and assignments and further questions.

Acknowledgements

The author and publisher are grateful to the following for permission to quote material:

Alexandra Workwear plc
Employment Relations: Resource Centre
Engineering Industry Training Board
Harper & Row Publishers Inc.
Her Majesty's Stationery Office
David S. Lake Publishers
McGraw-Hill Book Company
MIT Press
The Open University
Routledge and Kegan Paul
Scott Greenham Group plc
Tavistock Publications
Wardle Storeys plc

Part One Principles and practice of supervision

This part of the book consists of five chapters on the principles and practice of supervision.

Chapter 1 Organisations. This chapter looks at the various ways organisations can be classified and the effect of size on an organisation.

Chapter 2 Structure organisations. The reasons for having an organisational structure and some of the forms it can take form the basis of this chapter. The work of Woodward, and Burns and Stalker are considered in relation to structure and the question of the 'right' structure raised.

Chapter 3 Managers and supervisors. This chapter is concerned with a first look at the functions of managers and supervisors and takes a specific look at the role of the supervisor in the production industry.

Chapter 4 Management theories. This chapter outlines some of the main contributions to management theory; the work of Fayol, Taylor, Mayo, Maslow, McGregor and Argyris being discussed and extracts from their writings included. This can be considered to be the basic reference/background chapter for Part One.

Chapter 5 Functions of management. This follows on from Chapter 3, drawing on Chapter 4, with a more detailed look at management functions: planning, organising, leading, controlling, motivating and making decisions.

1 Organisations

Classification by primary objectives

Business organisations can be classified by their organisational goals, i.e. what they are trying to achieve. There are two types of organisation by this classification:

1 Those having the primary objective of the maximisation of profit.
2 Those having the objective of the maximisation of national welfare and interests.

Examples of organisations having the maximisation of profit as their main concern are those which are involved in taking raw materials or components and producing products which are sold at a higher price than the total costs, e.g. the Ford Motor Company when they take raw materials and components and turn them into cars. Other types of profit-led organisations are those which provide a service to other organisations or individulas, e.g. an insurance company, and those which buy completed items and resell them at a price greater than their cost, e.g. shops. Examples of organisations which have the maximisation of national welfare and interests are schools, colleges, hospitals, the fire service and the police. These organisations are generally financed by the state to provide a service to the community.

Classification by ownership

The following represents a classification of organisations by the ownership:

1 Private sector business organisations.
2 Public sector business organisations.
3 Public sector administrative organisations.

Within each of the above classifications there are a number of different types of organisation. The following illustrates the main types of such organisations.

1   *Private sector business organisations*

(a) *The sole trader*

This is the most common form of private business organisation in Britain. Essentially a single person provides the capital, takes the decisions and assumes the risks involved in running the business. Such a sole trader has legally unlimited liability for all the debts of the business, up to the limit of his or her personal estate. Small local retail outlets and services are examples of such organisations, e.g. local newsagents, plumbers, corner shops, etc.

(b) *The partnership*

This form of organisation consists of between two and twenty people, referred to as the partners, combining to provide the capital. In the ordinary or general partnership all the partners should share the profits and losses equally, have equal rights in the running of the organisation and have unlimited liability for the debts of the business. In the limited partnership there are active and sleeping partners, the active partners running the organisation while the sleeping partners play no part in this. Sleeping partners however do have, unlike the active partners, limited liability in that they are only liable for the debts of the business up to the extent of the capital they have put into the business.

(c) *The private joint stock company*

This type of organisation consists of between two and fifty people who each contribute towards a joint stock of capital through the ownership of shares. There is limited liability for the debts of the organisation, the limit being just what each shareholder has put into the organisation. There are two main types of shares, ordinary and preference, the difference between them being the degree of risk associated with them. The ordinary share is the most risky in that the dividends accruing to the shareholder depend on the profitability of the organisation, while the preference shares carry fixed dividends which are paid before the ordinary share dividend is fixed. Because of the greater risk attached to the ordinary shares such shareholders have voting rights (which generally do not occur with the preference shares) in the election of the directors of the organisation. The overall control and management of the organisation is in the hands of these directors. There are a number of legal requirements, based on the Companies Acts, that must be satisfied before an organisation can operate as a private joint stock company. Such companies are usually small family companies.

(d) *The public joint stock company*

This differs from the private joint stock company in having no upper limit on the number of shareholders, the company offering its shares to the general public. There is a minimum number of seven shareholders required. Again there are legal requirements that have to be satisfied before an organisation can operate as this type of company. The advantage of this type of company is the very large capital that can be raised, such companies often having gross trading incomes of millions of pounds per year.

(e) Multinational companies

These are organisations which own or control facilities, such as factories, distribution outlets and offices, in more than one country. The interests of such organisations are not generally bound up with the interests of any one country, the organisation pursuing its own interests independent of any national considerations. Their operations in any one country are however restricted by the constraints imposed on them by the country concerned. Royal Dutch Shell and General Motors are examples of such multinationals. A very large percentage of the world's output stems from a relatively small number of these multinationals.

(f) Co-operatives

Co-operatives are organisations formed by a number of people joining together to share in some business activity. Producers' co-operatives may be, for instance, a group of farmers joining together to buy and then share the use of expensive pieces of farm machinery or perhaps collectively market their produce. Co-operative retail societies have members, who are also customers. The members have shares and obtain a return in the form of fixed interest on capital and a dividend on purchases. The members elect the directors of the society.

Within the public sector organisations there are a number of different types of organisation. The following illustrates the main types of organisation in the public sector business sphere.

2 Public sector business organisations

(a) Public corporations

These are the nationalised industries and are organisations created by an Act of Parliament and under the general direction of the government. The Post Office, National Coal Board and the British Gas Corporation are examples of such organisations. The nationalised industries are responsible for a very large slice of the economic activity of the country, employing very large numbers of people.

(b) Mixed enterprises

These are organisations which are basically joint stock companies but have the state as a shareholder. Examples of such organisations are British Petroleum and Rolls Royce, though there are many smaller companies in which the state is a shareholder. The National Enterprise Board, set up in

1975, acts as a holding company to which the government entrusts its shares. This body is also responsible for helping with the provision of finance. The National Enterprise Board is answerable to the government. In most instances the state does not hold all the shares of the company and the remaining shares are available, like those of any other joint stock company, for purchase by the general public.

3 Public sector administrative organisations

(a) Central government departments

These are organisations set up by the government to run their administration. Examples are the Inland Revenue and the Department of Industry.

(b) Local government departments

Local government runs a wide variety of services, e.g. a refuse collection, leisure centres, education, etc. and sets up organisations to run the services on its behalf.

The size of organisations

Figure 1.1 shows the relationship between the number of establishments and the number of their employees for the engineering industry in Britain in 1983. As will be apparent, the greater number of establishments are small, over 80 per cent having less than 100 employees. However, because the large organisations, though far fewer than the small ones, are very large, most of those who work in the engineering industry are employed by large organisations.

The growth of such large organisations has been a feature of the last few decades. The major reason behind the growth of large companies has been the increase in profits that can arise from larger organisations. The term *horizontal integration* is used to describe the expansion of an organisation when it increases the scale of its operations while continuing to specialise in the same range of products. The increase in output of the same products is expected to give a less than proportionate increase in costs, i.e. as output is increased there is a reduction in unit costs. The organisation is said to be benefiting from economies of scale.

Economies of scale can arise from:

1 The larger volume output allowing a greater division of labour, i.e. employees can become more specialist and concerned with a narrower range of skills and hence more proficient in the narrower range. This specialisation may mean that unskilled labour can be used for some jobs whereas previously a skilled person had to be used because of the range of skills required. Hence the labour costs per unit can be reduced.

2 The larger volume output can lead to a greater mechanisation of the

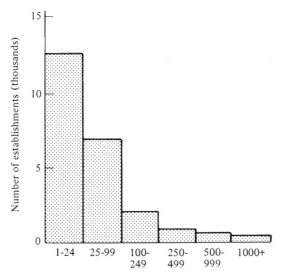

Number of employees per establishment

Figure 1.1 *The relationship between the number of establishments and the number of employees in the engineering industry*
By permission of the EITB from the Engineering Industry: its manpower and training, *RP-1-84*

production process as it becomes more economic to use machines if they are used a lot.

3 There can be economies in purchasing materials and items because larger quantities are required.

4 There can be economies in marketing, e.g. distribution costs per unit can decrease because the distribution costs may not rise in proportion to quantity.

5 Finance may be more easy to raise and on better terms.

However, the larger the organisation the greater the management problem. The rise in administration costs might at some point outweigh the advantages gained by economies of scale. There is also the point that increased division of labour can lead to employees performing such narrow tasks at such a frequent rate that a deterioration in labour relations may occur.

Organisations can also grow by what is called *vertical integration*. Vertical integration is where an organisation involves itself in additional stages of production or distribution. Thus, for instance, a retail organisation concerned with, say, selling clothes might expand into the making of the clothes. This may lead to economies through giving greater efficiency and also increases the power of the organisation over the market.

Organisations might also grow by *lateral integration*. This involves an organisation diversifying its activities, i.e. increasing its range of products. There might be another range of products which an organisation can produce with very little adjustment, there might also be the possibility of utilising a by-product. Such diversification can reduce reliance upon a single product and so reduce the risk factor.

International expansion of an organisation can enable it to be less dependent on the political or economic situation in any one country. It can also enable it to make use of the particular advantages which occur in certain countries, e.g. cheap labour or proximity to the raw materials. It can also increase the size of the market open to the organisation.

Revision questions

1   What are the two primary objectives by which organisations can be classified?

2   State the differences involved in relationship to capital provision and risk for (a) a sole trader, (b) a partnership and (c) a private joint stock company.

3   How does a private joint stock company differ from a public joint stock company?

4   What is meant by *limited liability*?

5   Explain what is meant by *economies of scale* and give three examples of such economies.

6   Explain what is meant by *division of labour*.

7   Explain and distinguish between *horizontal integration, vertical integration* and *lateral integration*.

Assignments and further questions

1   Consider a local large company and classify it by the type of ownership involved. Is the company large by virtue of horizontal, vertical or lateral integration? Substantiate your answer by quoting the evidence.

2   Establish by either visiting your local retail co-operative society or using the resources of a library the form of organisation adopted by that society. Your answer should include details of membership, management, the rights of shareholders and the use made of the Co-operative Wholesale Society.

3   From the financial press find an example of a public company's

prospectus. Write a brief report indicating the product(s) of the company, the form of ownership involved, the nature of the directors, the financial position and the reason for the publication of the prospectus.

4   A small company, with a workforce of twenty-five, is operated by the owner as a sole trader. The company is profitable. Put reasoned arguments for and against the company expanding, outlining the ways by which it could expand and obtain the increased capital required.

5   The following extracts are taken from the 'Offer for sale' prospectus of Wardle Storeys PLC, November 1984.

Introduction

Wardle Storeys is a specialist manufacturer of plastic sheet which it sells to a wide range of customers in the industrial, commercial and automotive fields. The Directors believe that the Group is a leader in the United Kingdom in many of its markets. Its products are used in stationery goods, prams and other nursery products, interior trim for cars and aircraft, sound and vibration insulation, leisure goods, blinds and awnings, furniture, medical products and protective clothing, and have many other uses. The Group has five factories in the United Kingdom.

The Company was established in order to acquire Bernard Wardle from NCC. The acquisition was led by Brian Taylor, Managing Director of Bernard Wardle, and was implemented by him and two senior managers in October 1982 with the financial support of a group of institutions comprising Citicorp Development Capital, British Railways Pension Funds, Electra Investment Trust PLC and Hill Samuel as manager and trustee of Fountain Development Capital Fund.

In February 1983 the Company purchased SIP from Turner & Newall. The two businesses were successfully integrated with the result that Wardle Storeys has been developed into a profitable operation by the present management team. The Group is now cash generative and showing a substantial return on net assets.

The Directors consider that the time is now appropriate to obtain a listing for the Company's shares which, they believe, will enable it better to pursue opportunities for making acquisitions and give greater flexibility in future capital raising; will provide its senior executives and employees with the opportunity to participate in its long-term success through share option schemes; and will enhance the Group's status with its customers and suppliers.

History

The original business of silk, wool and linen fabric printing was established by Mr. Bernard Wardle during the last century, was incorporated as a company in

1923 and became a public company in 1946. It was one of the pioneer manufacturers of plastic coated fabrics. Selling under the brand names of Everflex and Cirrus, the business expanded at the Caernarfon factory supplying the automotive and other industries. In an active diversification programme the following companies were acquired:-

1963   Hispeed (Plastic Welding) Limited (Bangor) – Finished trim parts for the automotive industry

1968   Duraplex Industries Limited (Edinburgh) – Calendered sheet made from PVC

1973   Hardura Limited (two factories in Blackburn) – Noise and vibration insulation products

1978   Armoride Limited (Earby) – Calendered sheet and plastic coated fabrics

In 1980, in common with much of the rest of manufacturing industry, Bernard Wardle experienced a substantial decline in demand, particularly in the automotive market on which at that time it was heavily dependent. The then management had also embarked upon a policy of further expansion and diversification, which involved a substantial increase in overhead and capital expenditure largely financed by increased borrowings. As a result of the combination of these factors Bernard Wardle was incurring substantial and continuing losses.

Bernard Wardle was acquired by Ferguson Investments Limited in March 1980 and by NCC in November 1980.

Brian Taylor joined Bernard Wardle in May 1980 and initiated a programme to ensure the survival of the business and to return it to profitability. The ensuing survival phase, which involved the closure of the factory at Caernarfon and one of the factories at Blackburn and other substantial overhead reductions, took approximately 18 months. By 1982 Bernard Wardle was trading profitably, but overall results were affected by substantial interest charges which remained high because NCC was not in a position to inject new capital. A consortium of investors comprising institutional shareholders and a team of Bernard Wardle's senior managers was formed to purchase Bernard Wardle and to inject new money into the business and the acquisition was completed by the Company in October 1982.

In February 1983 the Company acquired SIP, which comprised the business of the Storeys Industrial Products Division of Turner & Newall, and which operated a factory at Lancaster and another at Brantham. (Details of the acquisition are set out in paragraph 2(2) of 'Statutory and General Information'.) At that time SIP was making substantial losses. The Lancaster factory premises were not acquired and production there ceased, some of the plant and most of the product lines being transferred to the Brantham factory and the Group's existing factory at Earby. On the basis of a five day working week, this increased the utilisation of the Earby calenders from 92 per cent to 100 per cent and of the Brantham calenders from 66 per cent to 90 per cent. Group manufacturing capacity for calendered sheet increased by 93 per cent. The acquisition of SIP also brought additional products to the Group's range and lessened its dependence on the automotive industry by giving it a wider spread of markets. The integration was completed rapidly and successfully, leading to a significant increase in turnover, profit, cash generation and productivity.

Definitions of some of the terms used in the above extract:

Wardle Storeys – the company and its subsidiaries
Bernard Wardle – Bernard Wardle Group Limited, a subsidiary of the company
NCC – NCC Energy Limited
Turner & Newall – Turner and Newall PLC
SIP – Storeys Industrial Products Limited, a subsidiary of the company, acquired from Turner & Newall in 1983

(a) Explain how the original company has grown.
(b) What were the benefits of the company acquiring SIP?
(c) Why is the company now wishing to sell shares?

2 The structure of organisations

Why have a structure?

A small company, perhaps a small shop operated by a sole trader, might have a staff of just a small number of people. They can all operate directly under the instructions of the owner. In such a situation the organisational structure is very simple. Figure 2.1 shows this in terms of what is called an *organisation chart*. The lines joining the employees to the owner represent a direct formal relationship between them. The fact that all the lines emanate from the owner means that he or she alone has responsibility over the others. Thus any query that an employee might have must be raised directly with the owner.

In a large organisation a situation similar to that given in Figure 2.1 for the sole trader would rapidly lead to chaos. Just imagine the situation if all the employees in, say, an organisation of 2000 had to direct all their queries straight to one person. Thus large organisations have a structure so that all decisions do not have to be made by one person and there is a clear breakdown of the decision making process, with different types and levels of decisions being taken by different employees.

Authority

Authority is the right to make decisions, give orders and direct the work of others. In an organisation, unless it is very small like the sole trader example described by Figure 2.1, there will be some delegation of authority. This means that if a supervisor delegates some authority to, say, a foreman then he will be able to make some decisions and direct work. Delegation involves the subordinate being accountable to the superior for the performance of the tasks assigned to him or her. The subordinates can only however be assigned some degree of responsibility, the ultimate responsibility still resides with the superior. Thus while authority can be delegated, responsibility cannot be entirely delegated.

The production manager may give orders to the supervisor. The supervisor may give orders to the foremen. The foremen may give orders to the workers. This sequence of authority delegation is called a *chain of*

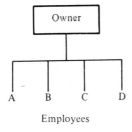

Employees

Figure 2.1　*Sole trader organisation chart*

<u>authority</u>, see Figure 2.2 showing how such a chain is represented on an organisation chart. A person is said to have *line authority* if he or she appears within such a chain, i.e. he or she receives orders from above but has delegated authority in order to be able to give orders to those below him or her in that particular chain. Thus the supervisor shown in the organisation chart of Figure 2.2 has line authority.

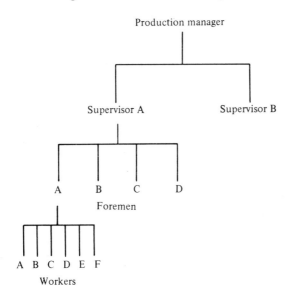

Figure 2.2　*Part of an organisation chart showing a chain of authority from the production manager to worker A*

A person is said to have *staff authority* if he or she is not in the chain of authority but is in the organisation in an advisory capacity. A personnel manager can be considered to have staff authority in relation to the production manager, in that he or she can only advise the production manager. The personnel officer is however likely to have some line authority in relation to his or her own staff.

The term *functional authority* is used when a person is empowered to give orders with respect to just some particular function. Thus the press officer of an organisation might have functional authority with regard to all dealings with the mass media, no other person being allowed to deal with them without the authority of the press officer.

Most organisations are a mixture of both line and staff authority with invariably some people also having functional authority. Figure 2.3 is an example of an organisation chart showing such an organisation.

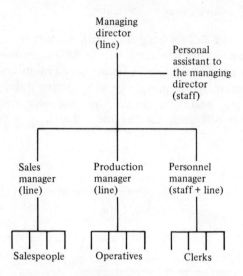

Figure 2.3   *Staff and line authority*

Constraints relating to organisational structure

The basic reason for structuring an organisation is so that it can be effectively co-ordinated and directed towards the achievement of the aims and objectives of the organisation. This is generally done by putting employees in groups.

1   Groups should be organised in such a way as to give the best chance of meeting the aims and objectives of the organisation.

2   No work group should be too large for one person to manage.

3   No work group should be too small, otherwise the manager or supervisor of that group would have insufficient work to do and might be better employed doing the jobs of those under him or her, as well as supervising.

4   The fewer the levels of management the better.

The above are some of the constraints involved in the structuring of an organisation. One common way of structuring is by departments.

Departments

There are a number of ways in which an organisation can be departmentalised. The following are three ways, though in some organisations some parts of the organisation may use one method and other parts a different one.

1 By business function

The employees are grouped according to the business function they are involved with. Thus all employees concerned with marketing may be grouped together in a marketing department, all employees concerned with production in a production department. Thus such an organisaion is likely to have, as well as a managing director, managers for production, finance, marketing, personnel, etc.

2 By product

With this type of structure the employees are grouped according to the type of product they are producing. Thus such as organisation might have a sports car division, a saloon car division and a lorry division. Within each division there will probably be a number of departments, structured according to business function. Thus each division may have a production department, a finance department, a marketing department, etc.

3 By territory

The employees, with this structure, are grouped according to the particular territory in which customers are located. Thus there might be a division for the north of England and one for the south of England. Each division is likely also to be subdivided into departments grouped according to business function.

Grouping by business function has the advantage of groups built around the basic functions of a business and allows employees with similar skills and interests to work together. Departmental managers can be specialists. However, it has the disadvantage of reducing attention to specific products, there being no manager having an overall view of all aspects of a product. Grouping by product overcomes this problem but does lead to a duplications of some services. Grouping by territory has the advantage that all a customer's requirements are handled by one division or department, thus ensuring greater co-ordination at the point of sale. It more easily allows for a better service to the customer. However, it also has the disadvantage of duplicating some services.

Functions of some departments

The following are some of the main functions of departments where the grouping is according to business function.

1   Production department

(a) Liaising with the product designers to ensure that the product can be efficiently and profitably made.
(b) Planning the production process.
(c) Liaising with the marketing department with regard to production schedules, quantities required.
(d) Controlling the production, e.g. control of progress, quality control.
(e) Maintaining the production plant.

2   Marketing department

(a) Establishing what the customers require.
(b) Keeping in contact with market trends and the activities of competitors.
(c) Promoting the product, e.g. advertising.
(d) Forecasting sales.
(e) Sales and the management of salesmen and women.

3   Finance department

(a) Maintaining the organisation's accounts.
(b) Costing services and products.
(c) Providing management with financial forecasts.
(d) Providing management with financial statements.
(e) Payment of wages to employees.

4   Personnel department

(a) At the request of other departments, advertising for and assisting in the interviewing and selection of staff.
(b) Familiarising new staff with the conditions of service.
(c) Developing training programmes for staff.
(d) Ensuring that working conditions meet those laid down in regulations.
(e) Being concerned with industrial relations and the machinery for consultations with employees and unions.
(f) Dealing with dismissal and the redundancy of staff.
(g) Maintaining staff records.

Woodward and organisational structures

The following extracts are taken from J. Woodward, *Management and Technology* (HMSO 1958) and are the results of a survey, carried out between 1953 and 1957 by the Human Relations Research Unit of the South-East Essex Technical College, of manufacturing firms in south Essex, England.

The 100 firms in the survey were organised and run in widely different ways. In only about half did the principles and concepts of management theory appear to have had much influence on organisational development.

In thirty-five firms there was an essentially 'line' or 'military' type of organisation; two firms were organised functionally, almost exactly as recommended by Taylor fifty years ago [see Chapter 4 in this book]. The rest followed in varying degrees a line-staff pattern of organisation; that is, they employed a number of functional specialists as 'staff' to advise those in the direct line of authority.

The number of distinct levels of management between board and operators varied from two to twelve; while the span of control of the chief executive ranged from two to nineteen, and that of the first line supervisor from seven to ninety. (An individual's span of control is the number of people directly responsible to him.)

The firms interviewed can be grouped according to the technical methods they used in their manufacturing. They fall essentially into three groups: those concerned with small batch and unit production, those with large batch and mass production and those with process production. Firms in the same group were found to have similar organisational structures.

The following are some of the research findings related to the technical complexity of the manufacturing process used, process production being more technically complex than mass production and this in turn being more complex than small batch or unit production.

The number of levels of authority in the management hierarchy increased with technical complexity [Figure 2.4].

The span of control of the first-line supervisor on the other hand reached its peak in mass production and then decreased [Figure 2.5].

The following organisational characteristics formed the pattern shown in Figure 2.5. The production groups at the extremes of the technical scale resembled each other, but both differed considerably from the groups in the middle.

1   Organisation was more flexible at both ends of the scale, duties and responsibilities being less clearly defined.
2   The amount of written, as opposed to verbal, communication increased up to the stage of assembly-line production. In process-production firms, however, most of the communications were again verbal.
3   Specialisation between the functions of management was found more frequently in large batch and mass production than in unit or process production. In most unit-production firms there were few specialists, managers responsible for production were expected to have technical skills, although these were more often based on length of experience and on 'know-how' than on scientific knowledge. When unit production was based on mass-produced components more specialists were employed, however. Large and mass-production firms generally conformed to the traditional line-and-staff pattern, the managerial

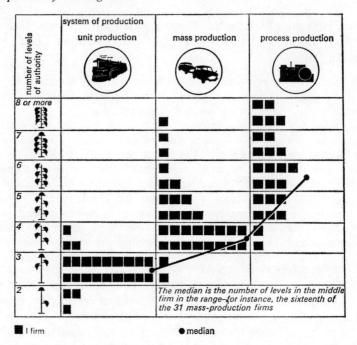

Figure 2.4   *Levels of authority*
By permission of the Controller of HMSO from Management and Technology *by J. Woodward (HMSO 1958)*

and supervisory group breaking down into two sub-groups with separate, and sometimes conflicting, ideas and objectives. In process-production firms the line-and-staff pattern broke down in practice, though it sometimes existed on paper. Firms tended either to move towards functional organisation of the kind advocated by Taylor or to do without specialists and incorporate scientific and technical knowledge in the direct executive hierarchy. As a result, technical competence in line supervision was again important, although now the demand was for scientific knowledge rather than technical 'know-how'.

4   Although production control became increasingly important as technology advanced, the administration of production – what Taylor called 'brainwork of production' – was most widely separated from the actual supervision of production operations in large-batch and mass-production firms, where the newer techniques of production planning and control, methods engineering and work study were most developed. The two functions became increasingly reintegrated beyond this point.

Burns and Stalker and contingency theory

T. Burns and G. M. Stalker in the early 1960s carried out an investigation of twenty industrial companies in the UK. The investigation was to find out

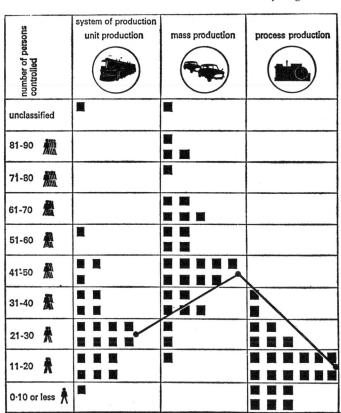

● median   ■1 firm

Figure 2.5 *Supervisor's span of control*
By permission of the Controller of HMSO from Management and Technology *by J. Woodward (HMSO 1958)*

how the nature of the environment affected the type of organisation within the company. They looked at what they termed *stable environments* and *innovative environments*.

A stable environment has the following characteristics:

1 The demand for the product or the service supplied by the organisation is stable and can easily be predicted.
2 The competitors for the same market are unchanging and stable.
3 Technological innovation and the development of new products is gradual and the changes can be predicted well in advance.
4 The policies of the government concerning the regulation of the industry and taxation are stable and change little with time.

An innovative environment has the following characteristics:

1   The demand for the product or service supplied by the organisation can change rapidly.
2   The competitors for the same market can change rapidly.
3   Technological innovation and the development of new products occur at a rapid rate.
4   The policies of the government concerning the regulation of the industry and taxation change rapidly.

In their survey Burns and Stalker found that a rayon mill was operating in a stable environment, the type of organisational structure being referred to as *mechanistic*. Mechanistic organisations have the following characteristics:

1   Highly specialised jobs.
2   Functional division of work.
3   Close adherence to a rigid chain of command.
4   Centralisation of decision making.
5   Small span of control of individual managers.
6   Close supervision of the workers.
7   Functional types of department prevail.

Electronics firms were, however, found to be operating in an innovative environment, the type of organisational structure being found to differ from that of organisations in a stable environment and being termed *organic*. An organic organisation has the following characteristics:

1   The jobs are not clearly defined and the workers have to be adaptable.
2   Division of the work is not by function but by task.
3   Little attention is paid to a rigid chain of command.
4   Few decisions are centralised.
5   Workers exercise self-control and there is no close supervision.
6   There is an emphasis on consultation rather than command.
7   Product types of departments prevail rather than functional types.

In the late 1960s P. R. Lawrence and J. W. Lorch carried out an investigation in large, multi-department organisations. They concluded that different parts of an organisation may be operating in different environments. Perhaps the production department is operating in a stable environment while the sales department is in an innovative environment. Thus the production department could be most effectively organised in a mechanistic way while the sales department would require an organic organisation.

The outcome of this type of research is what is called *contingency theory*. Contingency theory is concerned with obtaining the most effective organisational structure and essentially is postulating that the classic, scientific form of management might be the most appropriate in some organisations while in others a behavioural form would be more appropriate. Neither management theory is right, neither is wrong – it is just a question of choosing the most appropriate form.

Revision questions

1 Explain what is meant by *delegation of authority* and why although authority can be delegated, responsibility cannot be entirely delegated.

2 Explain the terms *staff, line* and *functional authority*.

3 Give an outline organisation chart and identify those having line and those having staff authority.

4 Why do organisations have a structure and what are the constraints on the devising of a structure?

5 Explain how an organisation can be departmentalised by (a) business function, (b) product, (c) territory, and outline the relative advantages and disadvantages of each.

6 Describe how, according to the work of Woodward, the organisational structure of companies was found to depend on the type of production they were engaged in.

7 Woodward in her publications uses the phrase 'in thirty-five firms there was an essentially "line" or "military" type of organisation'. What do you think she meant?

8 Explain the distinction between (a) stable and innovative environments, and (b) mechanistic and organic organisations.

9 Explain what is meant by *contingency theory* when applied to organisational structure.

Assignments and further questions

1 Devise an organisation chart for your own organisation. Identify clearly the chains of authority and whether line, staff or functional authority is exercised.

2 Organisation X has the following structure, devise an appropriate organisation chart.
   The managing director reports to the Board of Directors. Under the managing director are seven managers who report to him. These managers are research and development manager, production manager, distribution manager, commercial manager, finance manager, personnel manager and the plant and services manager. Each of these

managers has a number of departments, each with a manager who reports to him. For example, the research and development manager has three departments: research, product development and design. The commercial manager has five departments: purchasing, marketing, sales, contracts and public relations. The personnel manager has four departments: manpower planning, industrial relations, training and welfare.

3 Consider a company and its organisational structure and classify it in the type of terms used by Woodward.

4 Consider a particular company and argue the case for the type of environment it is operating in and the type of organisational structure it should thus have. Then compare your answer with the type of structure it actually has and try to account for any differences.

5 The following details, taken from the share prospectus, refer to the company Alexandra Workwear plc.

The business was founded in the 1850s by the great-grandfather of the present chairman as a drapery company in Bristol. In the late 1950s the business began to specialise in the supply of workwear, initially by establishing a retail shop and a mail order department in Bristol. The success of this strategy led to a rapid expansion of the mail order business, and to the development of a range of workwear for specialist market sectors.

In the late 1960s the group began to experience difficulty in obtaining workwear of a consistently high quality in the quantities it required, and in 1969 (assisted by finance from Midland Bank Equity Limited) it started production of workwear at Coatbridge in Scotland, establishing a second factory nearby in 1974. The group manufactures over 95 per cent of the garments it sells.

In 1979 the warehouse and despatch facilities moved to premises at the present site at Patchway, near Bristol, which affords easy access to the national motorway network. The sales and administrative functions were relocated to premises on the same site in 1981.

By successfully identifying and leading changes in the UK workwear market, the group has achieved significant growth over the last decade, as reflected in the increase in turnover from £3.6m in the year ended January 1975 to £16.8m in the year ended January 1984. In the same period, the number of garment styles has been increased from some 140 to some 300, enabling the group to meet the requirements of a wider and more diverse customer base.

(a) What changes would you envisage have taken place in the organisational chart of the company since its start in the 1850s?

(b) No single market sector of the company accounts for more than 14 per cent of the group sales. It has fourteen shops in the United Kingdom, warehouse stocking and despatch facilities near Bristol, sales and administrative offices near Bristol, two factories for production of the garments in Scotland and a sales office and warehouse in Holland. The total number of employees is 920, the following list showing the distribution:

	Sales	Warehouse and despatch	Managerial and administrative	Production and quality control	Total
Bristol	50	75	70	2	197
Scotland	2	10	10	636	658
Shops	61	–	–	–	61
Holland	2	1	1	–	4
	115	86	81	638	920

Suggest and justify an organisational plan for the company.

3   Managers and supervisors

The management task

The term manager can be used to describe anyone who is in charge of an organisation or a sub-unit or section of an organisation. The following can be considered to be the basic tasks of any manager.

1 *Planning*

A manager has to set objectives and targets, make predictions and in general make plans.

2 *Organising*

A manager has to decide what activities subordinate departments or employees should undertake and organise their activities. This can involve delegating authority, co-ordinating the work of others, and establishing channels of communication and authority.

3 *Leading*

A manager must provide the necessary leadership for the subordinate workforce.

4 *Controlling*

A manager has to control activities, comparing performance with that planned.

5 *Motivating*

A manage has to motivate subordinates.

In all the above tasks there is one overriding principle – managers make decisions. Chapter 5 expands on this.

An alternative view of what managers do has been given by H. Mintzberg and is derived from a review and synthesis of research on how managers spend their time. This describes the manager's job in terms of various roles, three such roles deriving from the formal authority and status given to the manager by the organisation. These are as follows.

1   Interpersonal roles

This includes the figurehead role, by virtue of the manager's position as head person, the leader role and the liaison role. This last role is where the manager makes contacts with people in the organisation outside his of her own vertical chain of command.

2   Informational roles

The manager has to monitor the environment, contacts and subordinates for information. The manager also has the role of disseminating information to subordinates. He or she also has the spokesperson role, being the source of information about his or her part of the organisation for the rest of the organisation.

3   Decisional roles

The decision-making role can be subdivided into entrepreneur, disturbance handler, resource allocator and negotiator. As entrepreneur the manager seeks to improve his or her part of the organisation.

Managerial effectiveness

The following checklist is taken from the book *Appraising Managers as Managers* (McGraw-Hill, 1971) by H. Koontz and is intended as a check list against which to assess managerial effectiveness. It says a lot about the characteristics required of managers.

Setting his unit short-term and long-term goals in verifiable terms, that are related positively to the goals of the superior and the firm. Making sure the goals are understood by the people reporting to him.

Assisting his people to set their own verifiable and realistic goals for themselves following the accepted company policies and practices when planning for the future.

Understanding the company policies himself and making sure that his people also understand them.

Solving his subordinates' problems by helping them find their own solutions rather then issuing rules or doing it himself.

Helping his subordinates get information they need.

Seeking for a range of possible answers before making a decision.

Recognising the critical requirements and the limiting factors in coming to a decision.

Recognising the size of the commitments his decisions involve.

Checking and following through the plans he makes.

Making decisions that allow for flexibility of time if necessary.

Considering the long-term and the short-term implications of his decisions.

Putting up proposed solutions whenever he has put up a problem to his superiors.

Organising the management structure underneath him so as to reflect the major result areas.

Delegating sufficient authority to match the responsibility he has delegated.
Making his delegation clearly.
Formalizing in writing his subordinates' goals, job descriptions, and extent of authority delegated to them.
Clarifying responsibility for the contributions he expects from his subordinates.
Maintaining adequate control when delegating his authority.
Delegating responsibility as well as authority.
Making sure that once he has delegated authority to a subordinate he does not 'claw back' the decisions for himself.
Making sure that his subordinates properly delegate their authority when necessary.
Maintaining unity of command.
Using staff advice when necessary, recognising that it is only advice.
Teaching his subordinates the difference between line and staff relationships.
Making clear the scope of delegation of functional authority.
Using service departments only when necessary to control efficiency or service.
Not creating excessive levels of organisation.
Not using committees for decisions that should be taken by individuals.
Making sure that committees have proper agendas and that they are served in time with appropriate information.
Distinguishing between lines of authority and lines of information.
Developing people to meet known future requirements.
Taking full responsibility for staffing his department, even when he uses assistance from the personnel department.
Making it clear that promotion is based solely on merit.
Making sure his subordinates have adequate training.
Making sure he coaches subordinates himself.
Not keeping subordinates whose ability is questionable.
Hiring people who are adequately skilled (in other words, not hiring dull people against whom he will shine by comparison).
Appraising his subordinates regularly against appropriate goals.
Recommending people for promotion on the basis of accurate judgement of their potential.
Taking such steps as he can to make sure his subordinates are well motivated.
Guiding his subordinates to get their acceptance of company goals and policies.
Using effective and efficient communication downwards.
Engaging in appropriate amounts of face to face contact.
Creating an environment where people are encouraged to suggest innovations.
Being receptive to innovative ideas, no matter where they originate.
Expecting and welcoming suggestions and objections to policies his subordinates regard as wrong.
Being readily available to his subordinates for discussions.
Helping his subordinates understand company policies and objectives.
Balancing correctly the demands for participative leadership on the one hand and authoritative direction on the other.
Being effective as a leader.
Tailoring his control techniques to his plans.
Using control techniques to spot deviations from plan well in advance.

Developing reliable and effective communication systems.
Developing controls that point out exceptions and critical points.
Developing control techniques that are understood by the people who must take action.
Taking prompt action when deviations occur.
Helping subordinates to take action when deviations from their plans occur.
Operating effectively within budget.
Using devices of control other than budgetary devices.
Understanding the need for network analysis of his control systems.
Utilising newer techniques of planning and control.
Helping his subordinates use effective control techniques and develop new ones where appropriate.
Keeping his superiors informed of significant problems and errors in his operation, together with reporting his actions to correct them.

The role of the supervisor

The term supervisor is generally used to describe the first line of authority that spends the majority of his or her time on supervisory duties. The term first-line manager could be appropriate. Figure 3.1 shows the position of the supervisor in the chain of authority.

Figure 3.1 *Position of the supervisor in the chain of authority*

One way of considering the role of the supervisor is as the link man or woman between the work force and the management, however this to some extent implies that the supervisor is not a manager and he or she certainly has many of the functions of a manager.

The following can thus be considered to be the basic roles of supervisors, almost regardless of the type of industry involved.

1   A first-line manager

As such he or she would carry out the functions of a manager, i.e. planning, organising, leading, controlling, staffing.

2   A link between the work force and more senior management

This involves more than just being a passive link in a chain and passing on down the line decisions of higher management. The supervisor has a vital role in relation to human relations involving the subordinate work force, colleagues and the immediate superiors.

The changing role of the supervisor

The Employment Relations Resource Centre in their September 1982 issue of the journal *Topics* make the point that the role of the supervisor is changing, having been influenced by some fairly fundamental changes over the last twenty to thirty years. These changes have brought problems, for example:

1   Authority

People will no longer accept authoritarian treatment and thus supervisors have to take a more complex approach to leading and motivating them.

2   Law

Employment legislation has meant that hiring and firing workers has become complex and thus many organisations no longer give supervisors the power to do this.

3   Technology

Supervisors who were promoted to that level because of their superior technological knowledge can nowadays find that technology is changing so rapidly that their superiority may vanish virtually overnight.

4   Trade unionism

There has been a large growth in trade unionism among white collar workers. Many of the members of these unions are supervisors. Thus not only is there the fact of belonging to a union but also to a union which is likely to be different to that of the subordinates, both these factors complicating the supervisor's role.

The supervisor in the manufacturing industry

Manufacturing industry can be classified according to the degree of repetitiveness that is possible in the production process. The following is such a classification:

1 Job or unique–product production

This involves the production of unique items, generally to a customer's order and specification. These might be prototypes, 'one-offs', special modifications, special repairs, or work requiring high craftsmanship or special production methods.

2 Small–batch production

This differs little from unique–product production in that only a small batch, rather than just a single product, is required.

3 Large–batch production

This involves the production of large numbers of standard products with the terms mass production or flowline production often being used to describe the process. The products are very often made to stock against future customer's order. With mass production a large number of identical products are required and tools can be dedicated to a single task, as also can workers. Hence the assembly line is possible. Car production for the mass market is an example of mass production.

4 Process production

This term is used to describe the virtually continuous processes used in the manufacture of chemicals or products which essentially involve chemical processes, e.g. brewing. There can be a continuous mixing of the various ingredients, continuous chemical reactions and a continuous production of the finished product.

The research carried out by J. Woodward on companies in Essex, England (see the previous chapter) found that the ratio of supervisory staff to total personnel was affected by the type of production process involved. The following table shows how the ratios depend on whether the type of production involved is job or small batch, large batch or process, also how the ratio depends on the size of the company. The pattern is reasonably clear, whatever the size of the company: the more technically advanced the production method the smaller the span of control of supervisors. Thus the span of control of a supervisor in a company using a process form of production is smaller than the supervisor in a company involved in job or small – batch production.

Table 3.1

Type of production	Employees – to – supervisor ratio for companies by size		
	400–500 employees	850–1000 employees	3000–4500 employees
Job or small batch	22 to 1	36 to 1	26 to 1
Large batch	15 to 1	16 to 1	19 to 1
Process	8 to 1	7 to 1	7 to 1

The reasons for the above lie in the different types of jobs that supervisors have in the different types of organisations. With job or small–batch production there has to be a skilled and versatile workforce, with versatile tools, since neither workers or tools can be dedicated to one particular type of job. Because the workforce is skilled the supervisor needs to be essentially an adviser, though also possessing technical skills often based on experience rather than scientific knowledge. With large–batch production the workforce is less skilled and there are likely to be a number of specialists, or specialist departments, within the organisation. The supervisor thus needs to be able to spot trouble and call in the appropriate specialists. The supervisor must be able to schedule work and deploy the workforce to the best advantage. With the process type of production the work force is likely to be low skilled. The supervisor needs to have an in-depth knowledge of the process concerned since he or she must be able to monitor both the workforce and the equipment, reacting quickly to faults and either rectifying them or calling in specialist help. The important point with the process type of production is that the process should be continuous and not interrupted.

Figure 3.2 summarises, in very general terms, the relative importance of various activities in the job of supervisor in different types of production industry. Thus, as Figure 3.2(a) suggests, planning is required more of the supervisor in unique product, job or small–batch, production than in process production. Similarly such a supervisor is more concerned, as Figure 3.2(b) suggests, with quantity and quality control. The issuing of work instructions is however greatest for the supervisor in mass or large–batch production than in either unique–product or process production. With process production the issuing of work instruction is lower than in any other type of production. Human relations tend to be of greater concern to supervisors in process production than in unique–product production. The smallness of the group of individuals supervised in process control makes for the operation of the group more as a close-knit team than is possible generally with unique–product or mass production.

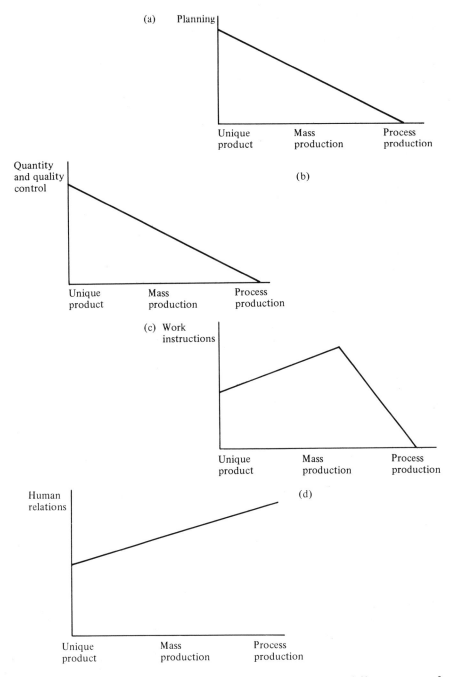

Figure 3.2 *Importance of various supervisory activities in different types of production*

Revision questions

1 Outline the basic tasks of a manager.

2 Define the terms *manager* and *supervisor*.

3 What is meant by the term *span of control* when applied to supervisors or managers?

4 How did the span of control for supervisors in the various forms of production industry vary, according to the research carried out by Woodward?

5 Explain what is meant by *unique–product production, small–batch production, large–batch production, mass production* and *process production* and describe how the role of the supervisor differs in the different forms of production industry.

Assignments and further questions

1 Describe the various tasks carried out by either a particular manager or a particular supervisor during an average week.

2 On the basis of the material in this chapter and in other books produce a critical discussion paper on the role of the supervisor.

3 In their book *Managerial behaviour, Performance and Effectiveness* (McGraw-Hill 1970) J. P. Campbell, M. D. Dunnette, E. E. Lawler and K. E. Weick give a list of opinions of what managers have to do to be effective. Successful managers are said to show the following characteristics:

They manage work instead of people
They plan and organise effectively
They set goals realistically
They derive decisions by group consensus but accept responsibility for them
They delegate frequently and effectively
They rely on others for help in solving problems
They communicate effectively
They are a stimulus to action
They co-ordinate effectively
They co-operate with others
They show consistent and dependable behaviour
They win gracefully
They express hostility tactfully

(a) Carry out a survey among your colleagues of what characteristics constitute a successful manager/supervisor.

    (b) Compare your results, the results quoted above, and the traditional view of the activities of managers.

4   The following extract is taken from the book *People and Performance: The Best of Peter Drucker on Management* (W. Heinemann 1977).

The rise, decline and rebirth of Ford

    The story of Henry Ford, his rise and decline, and of the revival of his company under his grandson, Henry Ford II, has been told so many times that it has passed into folklore. The story is

* That Henry Ford, starting with nothing in 1905, had built fifteen years later the world's largest and most profitable manufacturing enterprise;

* That the Ford Motor Company, in the early twenties, dominated and almost monopolised the American automobile market and held a leadership position in most of the other important automobile markets of the world;

* That, in addition, it had amassed, out of profits, cash reserves of a billion dollars or so;

* That, only a few years later, by 1927, this seemingly impregnable business empire was in shambles. Having lost its leadership position and barely able to stay a poor third in the market, it lost money almost every year for twenty years or so, and remained unable to compete vigorously right through World War II; and

* That in 1944 the founder's grandson, Henry Ford II, then only twenty-six years old and without training or experience, took over, ousted his grandfather's cronies in a palace coup, brought in a totally new management team and saved the company.

    But it is not commonly realised that this dramatic story is far more than a story of personal success and failure. It is, above all, what one might call a controlled experiment in mismanagement.

    The first Ford failed because of his firm conviction that a business did not need managers and management. All it needed, he believed, was the owner with his 'helpers'.

    (a) What are the differences between the functions of managers and 'helpers'?

    (b) The Ford Motor Company grew from a small one-man shop. How would the role of the owner have to differ from the one-man shop concern to that of a large company? Why?

    (c) Give examples of the types of organisation chart that might be appropriate for a small company, run by the owner, and a large company.

4 Management theories

Introduction

This chapter outlines some of the major contributions to management theory that have occurred over the years. The ones chosen are those that have had a significant impact on subsequent management thinking. They should thus not be regarded as defining current management theories or practice.

There can be considered to have been two main forms of management theory: that based on *scientific management* principles and that based on *human relations* or behavioural principles. Scientific management involves an emphasis not on employees as individuals but in essentially the same way as tools – the question then being how best the tools, and employees, can be 'designed' to fit the needs of the organisation. The part of this chapter concerned with the theories of Fayol and Taylor represents the scientific management view.

The investigations of E. Mayo at the Hawthorne plant can be regarded as one of the factors which 'knocked' scientific management theory and advanced the cause of human relations theories. Mayo found that employees often behaved as humans and improved performance was obtained not by scientific design but by motivating them. The issue then became: how to motivate employees? The classic work on motivation was that of A. H. Maslow and while there have been many changes in motivation theory since, that work can be regarded as an important milestone. The extracts from the paper by D. M. McGregor show how a 'human relations' management theory evolved from the work of Maslow. The extracts from a paper by C. Argyris show another way of looking at human relations within an organisation.

Chapter 5 takes a closer look at the functions of management, drawing on the theoretical background given in this chapter and outlining some of the later developments in theories.

Fayol's principles of management

The term *classical theory* is often used for a theory where the emphasis is not on the employees as individuals but where they are effectively 'dcsigncd' to fit thc organisation. Thc theory proposed by H. Fayol in 1916 is an example of such a classical theory.

Fayol set out fourteen principles of management which he had applied most frequently in his capacity as a manager of an organisation. These principles can be summarised as:

1   *Division of work*

Each employee should be highly specialised, concentrating on just a very limited range of activity. The aim of this division of work is to produce more and better work with the same effort, in that the employee acquires a higher skill and so a higher output when only concerned with a limited range of activity.

2   *Authority*

Fayol considers authority as being the right to give orders and the power to exact obedience. He draws the distinction between official authority, derived from the office or rank held by a person, and personal authority, derived from the intelligence, experience, leadership qualities, etc. of the person. A good manager is considered to need personal authority in addition to official authority.

3   *Discipline*

Discipline is seen as being in essence obedience, application, energy, behaviour and outwards marks of respect observed in accordance with both written and implicit agreements between the employees and the company. Fayol considers that discipline is essential for the smooth and efficient running of the company. The fault of a breakdown in discipline is attributed often to the lack of clear and fair agreements between employees and the company. Thus, good superiors and sanctions judiciously applied when discipline breaks down, are seen as the best means of ensuring discipline.

4   *Unity of command*

This is considered to be an important principle: for any action an employee should receive orders from one superior only. If this principle is violated Fayol considers that authority is undermined and discipline is in jeopardy. Examples of situations in which this occurs are when there is imperfect demarcation of departments leading to two superiors issuing orders in a sphere which each thinks his or her own; a superior giving orders to an employee several ranks down without going through the intermediate superiors, i.e. bypassing the chain of authority; when a business organisation has two superiors on equal footing without clearly differentiated duties and authority.

5   Unity of direction

Fayol expresses this principle as: one head and one plan for a group of activities having the same objective. Thus all activities with a common objective should be the responsibility of one person. This leads to the idea of departments determined by their business function. Thus there would be one head for all production activities rather than a head for each type of product. The other aspect is that there should be only one plan for the achievement of the objective.

6   Subordination of individual interest to general interest

The interest of one employee or group of employees should not prevail over the interest of the organisation. The interest of the organisation must come before that of the individual.

7   Remuneration of personnel

The remuneration of personnel is the price of the services rendered and should be fair and as far as possible afford satisfaction to both the employee and the employer. Fayol considered there to be three modes of payment in use with employees:

(a) Time rates, the employee selling the employer a day's work under specified conditions for a predetermined sum. This system was considered to have the disadvantage of being conducive to negligence and demanding constant supervision.

(b) Job rates, the payment to an employee in this case being made on the completion of a specified job and maybe independent of the length of the job.

(c) Piece rates, the payment being related to the work done. This method can be criticised as emphasing quantity at the expense of quality.

   In addition Fayol considers the place of bonuses, profit sharing and fringe benefits, believing all to have a possible role.

8   Centralisation

The term centralisation is used to describe the excercising of control of an organisation from a single central point. Fayol considers that the question of centralisation or decentralisation is simply a matter of finding the optimum degree, the optimum balance, for a particular organisation. In small organisations the manager's orders may go direct to each subordinate and thus there is absolute centralisation. In a larger organisation there will be a chain of authority between the manager and the lower grades and the issue is then the degree of authority that is delegated. The greater the decentralisation the greater the participation in decision making at lower grades and the taking of local decisions on the spot, however the greater the problem of co-ordination.

9 Scalar chain

The term *scalar chain* is used by Fayol to describe the chain of superiors ranging from the head of the organisation to the lowest grades. It is the chain of authority. The need to maintain unity of command means that all communications should start at the top of the chain and proceed, via every link, down the chain. This is not always the swiftest way and thus where there is a need for swift action the respect for the chain of authority may have to be reconciled with this need. Fayol thus sees the need for lateral communications between two subordinates without them having to go through the chain sequence. Figure 4.1 illustrates this with what Fayol terms his *gangplank*. Thus employee D has C as superior while G has F as superior. Following the chain of authority, if D needed to reach a decision with G then he, or she, would have to communicate through the sequence D to C to B to A to E to F to G. However, if C and F authorise their subordinates D and G to deal directly and report back to them on the outcomes then lateral communication becomes possible.

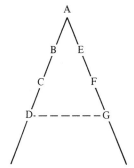

Figure 4.1 *Fayol's gangplank*

10 Order

A place for everything, and everything in its place in the case of material things and a place for everyone and everyone in his or her place for people, sums up Fayol's approach.

11 Equity

For the employees to carry out their tasks with devotion and loyalty Fayol considers that the management must show kindliness and justice.

12 Stability of tenure of personnel

Because time is required for an employee to get used to new work and become adept at it, a stable work force is to be desired if the organisation is to operate efficiently. Instability of tenure is likely to be at one and the same time cause and effect of bad running of an organisation.

13 Initiative

Initiative is the power of thinking out and executing a plan of action. An essential task of an organisation is the encouragement and harnessing of such initiative, within the limits imposed by respect for authority and discipline.

14 Esprit de corps

A strong organisation is one that has a unity of purpose among the employees. Harmony and union among the employees should thus be a concern of management.

To give an example of the 'flavour' of Fayol's writings, the following is an extract from the English translation of *General Industrial Management* (Pitman, 1949).

Authority is the right to give orders and the power to exact obedience. Distinction must be made between a manager's official authority deriving from office and personal authority, compounded of intelligence, experience, moral worth, ability to lead, past services, etc. In the make up of a good head personal authority is the indispensable complement of official authority. Authority is not to be conceived of apart from responsibility, that is apart from sanction – reward or penalty – which goes with the exercise of power. Responsibility is a corollary of authority, it is its natural consequence and essential counterpart, and wheresoever authority is exercised responsibility arises.

F. W. Taylor and scientific management

The term *scientific management* is used to describe an approach to management similar to that which a scientist might use in his or her approach to a scientific problem, namely observation in order to obtain data, analysis of the data and deduction of the solution to the problem. The early pioneer of scientific management was F. W. Taylor. The following extract from his writings outlines his approach to management problems. (F. W. Taylor in *Scientific Management* Harper, 1947).

Under the old type of management, success depends almost entirely upon getting the 'initiative' of the workmen, and it is indeed a rare case in which this initiative is really attained. Under scientific management the 'initiative' of the workmen (that is, their hard work, their goodwill and their ingenuity) is obtained with absolute uniformity and to a greater extent than is possible under the old system; and in addition to this improvement on the part of the men the managers assume new burdens, new duties and responsibilities never dreamed of in the past. The managers assume, for instance, the burden of gathering together all of the traditional knowledge which in the past has been possessed by the workmen and then of classifying, tabulating and reducing this knowledge to rules, laws and formulae which are immensely helpful to the workmen in doing their daily work. In addition to developing a science in this way, the management take on three other types of duties which involve new and heavy burdens for themselves.

These new duties are grouped under four heads:

1 They develop a science for each element of a man's work, which replaces the old rule-of-thumb method.

2 They scientifically select and then train, teach and develop the workman, whereas in the past he chose his own work and trained himself as best he could.

3 They heartily cooperate with the men so as to insure all of the work being done in accordance with the principles of the science which has been developed.

4 There is an almost equal division of the work and the responsibility between the management and the workmen. The management take over all the work for which they are better fitted than the workmen, while in the past almost all the work and the greater part of the responsibility were thrown upon the men....

Perhaps the most prominent single element in modern scientific management is the task idea. The work of every workman is fully planned out by the management at least one day in advance, and each man receives in most cases complete written instructions describing in detail the task which he is to accomplish, as well as the means to be used in doing the work. And the work planned in advance in this way constitutes a task which is to be solved, as explained above, not by the workman alone, but in almost all cases by the joint effort of the workman and the management. This task specifies not only what is to be done but how it is to be done and the exact time allowed for doing it. And whenever the workman succeeds in doing his task right, and within the time limit specified, he receives an addition of from 30 per cent to 100 per cent to his ordinary wages....

In most trades, the science is developed through a comparatively simple analysis and time study of the movements required by the workmen to do some small part of his work, and this study is usually made by a man equipped merely with a stop-watch and a properly ruled notebook.... The general steps to be taken in developing a simple law of this class are as follows:

1 Find, say, ten to fifteen different men (preferably in as many separate establishments and different parts of the country) who are especially skilful in doing the particular job to be analysed.

2 Study the exact series of elementary operations or motions which each of these men uses in doing the work which is being investigated, as well as the implements each man uses.

3 Study with a stop-watch the time required to make each of these elementary movements and then select the quickest way of doing each element of the work.

4 Eliminate all false movements, slow movements and useless movements.

5 After doing away with all unnecessary movements, collect into one series the quickest and best movements as well as the best implements.

This one new method, involving that series of motions which can be made quickest and best, is then substituted in place of the ten or fifteen inferior series which were formerly in use. This best method becomes standard, and remains standard, to be taught first to the teachers (or functional foremen) and by them to every workman in the establishment until it is superseded by a quicker and better series of movements. In this simple way one element after another of the science is developed.

In the same way each type of implement used in a trade is studied. Under the philosophy of the management of 'initiative and incentive' each workman is called upon to use his own best judgement, so as to do the work in the quickest time, and from this results in all cases a large variety in the shapes and types of implements which are used for any specific purpose. Scientific management requires, first, a careful investigation of each of the many modifications of the same implement, developed under rule of thumb; and second, after a time study has been made of the speed attainable with each of these implements, that the good points of several of them shall be united in a single standard implement, which will enable the workman to work faster and with greater ease than he could before. This one implement, then, is adopted as standard for all workmen to use until superseded by an implement which has been shown, through motion and time study, to be still better.

Taylor's approach to management problems can be summarised as:

1 Observation of the problem in order to compile information.
2 Analysis of the results of the observations in order that the best method can be deduced.
3 Selection of the personnel so that they can carry out, after suitable training, the job in accord with the deduced best method.
4 Design of a suitable payment method for the personnel to motivate them.
5 Selection of the best implements for the job.

A significant aspect of this approach to management is that essentially the job is being defined and the workers then made to fit the job, just in the same way as the implements are made to fit the job. The workers are essentially being considered as implements. The aim is to get the operations carried out in the 'best' way, the term best being defined as the most cost–effective way.

Taylor's work has been strongly criticised for this apparent consideration of people as though they were implements and his view of a suitable payment as being the motivator for work.

E. Mayo and the Hawthorne investigation

In 1927 a series of investigations was started, under the direction of E. Mayo, at the Hawthorne plant of Western Electric Company. The findings of that research were to have a very significant effect on management theories, being essentially the beginnings of the human relations approach to management theory. With scientific management workers were regarded as essentially just implements chosen for the job. Each worker was thought of as being in isolation from other workers in that each worker could be regarded individually without any need to consider interaction with other workers. Mayo found however that workers could operate as a group. With scientific management, training and sufficient monetary inducement were considered all that was necessary to motivate workers; Mayo however found that there was a factor called *job satisfaction*.

The first of the investigations was into the effect of the level of illumination on the output of workers, the aim being to find the level which resulted in the best output. The researchers divided a group of workers into two separate groups, the test group and the control group. Lighting conditions were kept constant for the control group but varied for the test group, the outputs of the two groups being compared. The results were perplexing. When the level of illumination for the test group was increased their output increased, but so also did the output of the control group and no changes had been made to their level of illumination. When the level of illumination of the test group was decreased back to its initial value, the output did not decrease but kept on increasing. In fact, whatever was done to the level of illumination the output increased.

The illumination investigation was an investigation along the lines advocated by Taylor, a scientific investigation of the effect of changing one variable in a situation in order to establish the optimum condition of that variable. Changing the level of illumination would seem to be a simple one – variable experiment which should yield a simple answer – a particular level of illumination was the optimum one for production. But it didn't. Why didn't it?

There then followed a series of three investigations extending over a number of years. They were:

1 A small group of women engaged in assembling telephone relays in the assembly test room were segregated from the other workers and a variety of different work conditions tried, the effects on morale and work output being monitored.
2 A factory–wide programme of unstructured interviews with the workers.
3 Observation of a group of men in the Bank Wiring Observation room to observe how a group operates.

The following is the sequence of events in the early part of the assembly test room investigation.

The co-operation of the workers was sought, no changes then being made to working conditions without prior discussion with them.

Period 1   Observation of the regular department, a 48 – hour week being worked.

Period 2   Observation of the group in the test room, a 48 – hour week still being worked.

Period 3   A special group payment rate was introduced.

Period 4   Two five – minute rest periods introduced, total hours per week then becoming 47.05.

Period 5   Two 10 – minute rest periods introduced, total hours per week then becoming 46.10.

Period 6   Six five – minute rest periods introduced, total hours per week then becoming 45.15.

Period 7   A 15 – minute morning break, a 10 – minute afternoon break and lunch provided, total weekly hours then becoming 45.40.

Period 8   As in period 7 but stop work at 4.30 p.m., weekly hours then becoming 43.10.

Period 9   As in period 7 but stop work at 4.00 p.m., weekly hours then becoming 40.40.

Period 10   As period 7.

Period 11   As period 7 but with Saturday morning off, a 41.40 hour working week.

Period 12   As period 3, the working week then becoming the original 48 hours.

Period 13   As period 7 but the workers provide their own lunch and the company provide refreshments, a working week of 45.40 hours.

Output rose almost irrespective of the changes in the conditions. The average weekly output for each worker was:

Period 7   – 2500 units
Period 10 – 2800 units
Period 13 – 3000 units

Thus even when the conditions were the same, periods 7 and 10, the output was higher in the later period. Period 13 gave slightly worse conditions than periods 7 or 10 but the output was higher. Why?

The following extract is taken from E. Mayo, Hawthorn and the Western Electric Company, in *The Social Problems of an Industrial Civilisation* (Routledge, 1949).

This interesting, and indeed amusing, result has been so often discussed that I need make no mystery of it now. I have often heard my colleague Roethlisberger declare that the major experimental change was introduced when those in charge sought to hold the situation humanly steady (in the interest of critical changes to be introduced) by getting the cooperation of the workers. What actually happened was that the six individuals became a team and the team gave itself wholeheartedly and spontaneously to cooperation in the experiment. The consequence was that they felt themselves to be participating freely and without afterthought, and were happy in the knowledge that they were working without coercion from above or limitation from below. They were themselves astonished at the consequence, for they felt that they were working under less pressure than ever before.

The factors which were later considered to account for the changes in performance are:

1   The workers had become a group, a cohesive group, rather than just being a set of individuals.
2   Because of the control they exercised over their work they enjoyed an increase in work satisfaction.
3   The group were flattered by the attentions of the researchers and responded to the feeling that they were something special.
4   The workers changed their attitude to the work.

The assembly test room investigation led to the second phase, a factory – wide programme of unstructured interviews with the workers. This study was designed to find out the various factors involved in the attitudes of the workers to their jobs, the working conditions, the supervision and the general morale. A factor that emerged from this investigation was that a working group collectively determined the output of individual workers by reference to what they considered to be a fair day's work and this was not generally the standard set by work study specialists or the management.

This led to the third investigation in which a group of men in the Bank Wiring Observation room were observed. The intention was to try and establish what constituted normal group working. They found that to an individual the relations with fellow workers were very important in motivation, output of a group being dictated not by the ability of individuals but by group solidarity. Individuals did not 'step out of line' with the others in the same group. Belonging to the group was more important than the earnings an individual might obtain as a result of working harder.

A. H. Maslow and a theory of human motivation

According to Maslow a person has five basic needs, these needs being hierarchial. The needs are, lowest first:

1 Physiological needs

These are the basic needs for food, rest, exercise, shelter, etc. They are the needs which have to be satisfied for the survival of the individual.

2 Safety needs

These are the needs for protection against danger, threats and deprivation, the need for a secure job, etc.

3 Social needs

These are the needs for friends, acceptance by your fellows, e.g. your work group, etc.

4 Ego needs

These are the needs for self confidence, achievement, status, recognition, appreciation, respect of one's fellows, etc. There are essentially two facets to these needs, the need for self esteem and the need for group esteem.

5 Self-fulfillment needs

These are the highest needs and are the needs to realise one's own potential, to be creative, to become the person you know you are capable of being.

While the needs are hierarchial it is not always necessary that a lower need be completely fulfilled before the next need becomes a motivating factor, indeed in the case of some individuals the hierarchy can be inverted in some instances.

A satisfied need is not a motivator. Thus someone who has the basic physiological and safety needs adequately met will not be motivated by being offered, for instance, greater safety in the job. Motivation will be, for that individual, largely determined by the next highest need, i.e. social needs.

D. M. McGregor and theories X and Y

The following extracts are taken from the book *Leadership and Motivation: The Essays of Douglas McGregor*, edited by W. G. Bennis and E. H. Schein (M.I.T. Press, Cambridge, Massachusetts 1966). In the extracts McGregor sets out in theory X what he believes are the conventional views of the workers attitudes to work; in theory Y he states what he feels is a more realistic explanation of the attitudes of workers.

Management's tasks: Conventional view
The conventional conception of management's tasks in harnessing human energy to organisational requirements can be stated broadly in terms of three propositions. In

order to avoid the complicaions introduced by a label, I shall call this set of propositions, 'Theory X':

1 Management is responsible for organising the elements of productive enterprise – money, materials, equipment, people – in the interest of economic ends.
2 With respect to people, this is a process of directing their efforts, motivating them, controlling their actions, modifying their behaviour to fit the needs of the organisation.
3 Without this active intervention by management, people would be passive – even resistant – to organisational needs. They must therefore be persuaded, rewarded, punished, controlled – their activities must be directed. This is management's tasks – in managing subordinate managers of workers. We often sum it up by saying that management consists of getting things done through other people.
4 The average man is by nature indolent – he works as little as possible.
5 He lacks ambition, dislikes responsibility, prefers to be led.
6 He is inherently self-centred, indifferent to organisational needs.
7 He is by nature resistant to change.
8 He is gullible, not very bright, the ready dupe of the charlatan and the demagogue.

The human side of economic enterprise today is fashioned from propositions and beliefs such as these. Conventional organisational structures, managerial policies, practices and programmes, reflect these assumptions.

Is the conventional view correct?
The findings which are beginning to emerge from the social sciences challenge this whole set of beliefs about man and human nature and about the task of management. The evidence is far from conclusive certainly, but it is suggestive. It comes from the laboratory, the clinic, the schoolroom, the home and even to a limited extent from industry itself.

The social scientist does not deny that human behaviour in industrial organisation today is approximately what management perceives it to be. He has, in fact, observed it and studied it fairly extensively. But he is pretty sure that this behaviour is not a consequence of man's inherent nature. It is a consequence rather of the nature of industrial organisations, of management philosophy, policy and practice. The convetioanl approach of Theory X is based on mistaken notions of what is cause and what is effect.

The dynamics of motivation
Perhaps the best way to indicate why the conventional approach of management is inadequate is to consider the subject of motivation. In discussing this subject I will draw heavily on the work of my colleague, Abraham Maslow of Bradeis University. His is the most fruitful approach I know. Naturally, what I have to say will be over-generalised and will ignore important qualifications. In the time at our disposal, this is inevitable.

Physiological and safety needs

Man is a wanting animal – as soon as one of his needs is satisfied, another appears in its place. This process is unending. It continues from birth to death.

Man's needs are organised in a series of levels – a hierarchy of importance. At the lowest level, but pre-eminent in importance when they are thwarted, are his physiological needs. Man lives by bread alone, when there is no bread. Unless the circumstances are unusual, his needs for love, for status, for recognition are inoperative when his stomach has been empty for a while. But when he eats regularly and adequately, hunger ceases to be an important need. The sated man has hunger only in the sense that a full bottle has emptiness. The same is true of the other physiological needs of man – for rest, exercise, shelter, protection from the elements.

A satisfied need is not a motivator of behaviour! This is a fact of profound significance. It is a fact which is regularly ignored in the conventional approach to the management of people. I shall return to it later. For the moment, one example will make my point. Consider your own need for air. Except as you are deprived of it, it has no appreciable motivating effect upon your behaviour.

When the physiological needs are reasonably satisfied, needs at the next higher level begin to dominate man's behaviour – to motivate him. These are called safety needs. They are the needs for protection against danger, threat, deprivation. Some people mistakenly refer to these as needs for security. However, unless man is in a dependent relationship where he fears arbitary deprivation, he does not demand security. The need is for the 'fairest possible break'. When he is confident of this, he is more than willing to take risks. But when he feels threatened or dependent, his greatest need is for guarantees, for protection, for security.

The fact needs little emphasis that since every industrial employee is in a dependent relationship, safety needs may assume considerable importance. Arbitary management actions, behaviour which arouses uncertainty with respect to continued employment or which reflects favouritism or discrimination, unpredictable administration of policy – these can be powerful motivators of the safety needs in the employment relationship at every level from worker to vice-president.

Social needs

When man's physiological needs are satisfied and he is no longer fearful about his physical welfare, his social needs become important motivators of his behaviour – for belonging, for association, for acceptance by his fellows, for giving and receiving friendship and love.

Management knows today of the existence of these needs, but it often assumes quite wrongly that they represent a threat to the organisation. Many studies have demonstrated that the tightly knit, cohesive work group may, under proper conditions, be far more effective than an equal number of separate individuals is achieving organisational goals.

Yet management, fearing group hostility to its own objectives, often goes to considerable lengths to control and direct human effort in ways that are inimical to the natural 'groupiness' of human beings. When man's social needs – and perhaps his safety needs, too – are thus thwarted, he behaves in ways which tend to defeat organisational objectives. He becomes resistant, antagonistic, uncooperative. But his behaviour is a consequence, not a cause.

Ego needs

Above the social needs – in the sense that they do not become motivators until lower needs are reasonably satisfied – are the needs of greatest significance to management and to man himself. They are the egoistic needs, and they are of two kinds:

1 Those needs that relate to one's self-esteem – needs for self-confidence, for independence, for achievement, for competence, for knowledge.
2 Those needs that relate to one's reputation – needs for status, for recognition, for appreciation, for the deserved respect of one's fellows.

Unlike the lower needs, these are rarely satisfied; man seeks indefinitely for more satisfaction of these needs once they have become important to him. But they do not appear in any significant way until physiological, safety and social needs are all reasonably satisfied.

The typical industrial organisation offers few opportunities for the satisfaction of these egoistic needs to people at lower levels in the hierarchy. The conventional methods of organising work, particularly in mass-production industries, gives little heed to these aspects of human motivation. If the practices of scientific management were deliberately calculated to thwart these needs – which, of course, they are not – they could hardly accomplish this purpose better than they do.
Self-fulfillment needs

Finally – a capstone, as it were, on the hierarchy of man's heeds – there are what we may call the needs of self-fulfillment. These are the needs for realising one's own potentialities, for continued self-development, for being creative in the broadest sense of that term.

It is clear that the conditions of modern life give only limited opportunities for these relatively weak needs to obtain expression. The deprivation most people experience with respect to other lower-level needs diverts their energies into the struggle to satisfy those needs, and the needs for self-fulfillment remain dormant.

Problems and opportunities facing management

Now briefly, a few general comments about motivation:

We recognise readily enough that a man suffering from a severe dietary deficiency is sick. The deprivation of physiological needs has behavioural consequences. The same is true – although less well recognised – of deprivation of higher-level needs. The man whose needs for safety, association, independence, or status are thwarted is sick just as surely as is he who has rickets. And his sickness will have behavioural consequences. We will be mistaken if we attribute his resultant passivity, his hostility, his refusal to accept responsibility to his inherent 'human nature'. These forms of behaviour are symptoms of illness – of deprivation of his social and egoistic needs.

The man whose lower-level needs are satisfied is not motivated to satisfy those needs any longer. For practical purposes they exist no longer. (Remember my point about your need for air.) Management often asks, 'Why aren't people more productive? We pay good wages, provide good working conditions, have excellent fringe benefits and steady employment. Yet people do not seem to be willing to put forth more than minimum effort.'

The fact that management has provided for these physiological and safety needs has shifted the motivational emphasis to the egoistic needs. Unless there are opportunities at work to satisfy these higher-level needs, people will be deprived; and their behaviour will reflect this deprivation. Under such conditions, if management continues to focus its attention on physiological needs, its efforts are bound to be ineffective.

People will make insistent demands for more money under these conditions. It becomes more important than ever to buy the material goods and services which can provide limited satisfaction of the thwarted needs. Although money has only limited value in satisfing many higher-level needs, it can become the focus of interest if it is the only means available.

A new perspective

For these and many other reasons, we require a different theory of the task of managing people based on more adequate assumptions about human nature and human motivation. I am going to be so bold as to suggest the broad dimensions of such a theory. Call it 'Theory Y', if you will.

1 Management is responsible for organising the elements of productive enterprise – money, materials, equipment, people – in the interests of economic ends.
2 People are not by nature passive or resistant to organisational needs. They have become so as a result of experience in organisations.
3 The motivation, the potential for development, the capacity for assuming responsibility, the readiness to direct behaviour toward organisational goals are all present in people. Management does not put them there. It is a responsibility of management to make it possible for people to recognise and develop these human characteristics for themselves.
4 The essential task of management is to arrange organisational conditions and methods of operation so that people can achieve their own goals best by directing their own efforts towards organisational objectives.

This is a process primarily of creating opportunities, releasing potential, removing obstacles, encouraging growth, providing guidance.

C. Argyris and the mature individual

Argyris has taken a look at the impact of the organisation upon the individual. In order to do this he considered the way in which people develop in our Western culture from child to mature individual and then considered whether the organisation is treating the individual as a mature individual. The following extracts are taken from *Understanding Organisational Behaviour* (Tavistock, 1960) by C. Argyris.

The development of the individual in our culture

The development of the human personality can be hypothesised to follow the directions and dimensions outlined in the following model.

It is hypothesised that human beings in our culture:

1 Tend to develop from a state of passivity as infants to a state of increasing activity as adults. . . .
2 Tend to develop from a state of dependence upon others as infants to a state of relative independence as adults. Relative independence is the ability to 'stand on one's own two feet' and simultaneously to acknowledge healthy dependencies. . . .
3 Tend to develop from being capable of behaving only in a few ways as an infant to being capable of behaving in many different ways as an adult.

4 Tend to develop from having erratic, casual, shallow, quickly dropped interests as an infant to having deeper interests as an adult. The mature state is characterised by an endless series of challenges, where the reward comes from doing something for its own sake. The tendency is to analyse and study phenomena in their full-blown wholeness, complexity and depth.

5 Tend to develop from having a short time perspective (i.e. the present largely determines behaviour) as an infant to a much longer time perspective as an adult (i.e. where the behaviour is more affected by the past and the future). . . .

6 Tend to develop from being in a subordinate position in the family and society as an infant to aspiring to occupy an equal and/or subordinate position relative to their peers.

7 Tend to develop from a lack of awareness of self as an infant to an awareness of and control over self as an adult. . . .

Some basic principles of formal organisations

Along with the emphasis upon rationality is the specialisation of tasks, the emphasis upon power, conformity to and loyalty for company objectives. These emphases are embodied in four principles (more accurately assumptions) of scientific management theories.

Briefly these principles may be stated as:

1 Task (work) specialisation. If concentrating effort on a limited field of endeavour increases the quality and quantity of output, organisational and administrative efficiency is increased by specialisation of tasks assigned to the participants of the organisation.

2 Chain of command. The principle of task specialisation creates a plurality of parts, each performing a highly specialised task. However, a plurality of parts busily performing their particular objective does not form an organisation. A pattern of parts must be formed so that the inter-relationships among the parts create the organisation. Following the logic of specialisation the planners create a new function (leadership) whose primary responsibility shall be the control, direction and co-ordination of the inter-relationships of the parts and to make certain that each part performs its objectives adequately. Thus the assumption is made that administrative and organisational efficiency is increased by arranging the parts in a determinate hierarchy of authority where the part on top can direct and control the part on the bottom.

   If the parts being considered are individuals, then they must be motivated to accept direction, control and coordination of their behaviour. The leader is therefore assigned formal power to hire, discharge, reward and penalise the individuals in order that their behaviour be moulded towards the organisations's objectives.

3 Unity of direction. If the tasks of every person in a unit are specialised, the objective or purpose of the unit must be specialised. The principle of unity of direction states that administrative and organisational efficiency increases if each unity has a single activity (or homogeneous set of activities) that is planned and directed by the leader.

4 Span of control. The principle of control states that administrative efficiency is increased by limiting the span of control of a leader to no more than five or six subordinates whose work interlocks.

The impact of the formal organisation upon the individual

What is the impact of the formal organisation upon the individual? Clearly, the answer is that it depends upon the individual, the organisation and the context in which these are studied. Thus, as in our discussion of the human personality, we cannot state a priori what will happen in an individual case.

However, some position must be taken if generalisations are to be evolved. We must state the generalisations in such a way that when it comes time to use them in a particular organisation, the uniqueness of the particular case will not be violated.

In developing our generalisations, therefore, we must assume a certain individual and a certain organisation. For the sake of illustration only we will take as our example the case of a relatively mature individual and a formal organisation that maximises the principles of scientific management (e.g. an organisation with an assembly line)....

The impact of the above principles is to place employees in work situations where (1) they are provided with minimal control over their workaday world, (2) they are expected to be passive, dependent and subordinate, (3) they are expected to have the frequent use of skin-surface shallow abilities, and (4) they are expected to produce under conditions leading to psychological failure.

All these characteristics are incongruent to the ones that relatively mature human beings in our culture are postulated to desire. They are much more congruent with the needs of infants in our culture. In effect, therefore, organisations adopt an initial stategy where they are willing to pay wages and provide adequate seniority if mature adults will, for eight hours a day, behave in a less than mature manner.

To put it bluntly – the main snag that Argyris sees to the formal type of organisation is that it has to deal with individual mature human beings. In the organisation endeavouring to mould the human beings to its requirements there is a reaction. The employees, in endeavouring to be mature, will experience frustation, failure, adopt only short time perspectives and there will be conflict. They tend then to react to the formal organisation by creating informal activities, e.g. daydreaming, aggression, apathy, evolving groups which set their own norms, etc.

A total organisation therefore is more than the formal organisation. Conceptualising it as a behavioural system we may conclude that an organisation is a composite of four different but interrelated subsystems resulting in the following kinds of behaviour:
(a) The behaviour that results from the formal organisational demands.
(b) The behaviour that results from the demands of the informal activities.
(c) The behaviour that results from each individual's attempt to fulfill his idiosyncratic needs.
(d) The behaviour that is a resultant of the unique patterning for each organisation of the three levels above.

Revision questions

1   What is meant by *scientific management*?

2 What is meant by the *human relations* approach to management?

3 Give a brief outline of the management principles of Fayol.

4 What was the crucial finding of the Hawthorne investigations?

5 How do theories X and Y differ?

6 Outline Maslow's theory of motivation.

7 What are the basic differences between a child and a mature individual according to Argyris and why does he consider these differences relevant to the demand made on an individual by industry?

Assignments and further questions

1 Compare and contrast the basic approaches to management of the scientific management and the human relations methods.

2 In chapter 3 the terms *organic* and *mechanistic* are used to describe different types of organisational structure, or even different types of departmental structure. Compare and contrast the two types of structure and relate them to scientific management and human relations principles.

3 The following are a number of brief quotations from *People and Performance, The Best of Peter Drucker on Management* (Heinemann, 1977), by Peter Drucker. Critically discuss the quotations.
   (a) 'Scientific management focusses on the work.'
   (b) '[Human relations] rests on a profound insight – the insight summarised when we say that one cannot hire a hand; the whole person always comes with it.'
   (c) 'Its [human relations] favourite saying, that "the happy worker is an efficient and a productive worker," though a neat epigram, is at best a half truth. It is not the business of the enterprise to create happiness but to sell and make shoes.'
   (d) 'Scientific Management purports to organise human work. But it assumes – without any attempt to test or to verify the assumption – that the human being is a machine tool (though a poorly designed one).'
   (e) On Scientific Management: 'it is simply not true that the closer the work comes to confining itself to the individual motion or operation, the better the human being will perform it. This is not even true of a machine tool; to assert it of human beings is nonsense.'

4 Discuss the following statement: Theory X will not work in a developed country because workers do not have needs based on hunger and safety.

5   Discuss the following statement: Theory Y assumes that organisations are staffed by mature adults.

6   It is claimed that changes in job design can produce better employee job performance by virtue of an improvement in employee motivation.
   (a) The terms job enlargement and job rotation are often used when referring to job design. Explain what they mean.
   (b) Why should it be expected that changes in job design could affect job performance?

7   Discuss the significance of the informal group in organisations and how in some situations, e.g. the Hawthorne relay-assembly test room investigation, it can lead to increased productivity while in other situations it can restrict productivity.

5 Functions of management

Introduction

This chapter can be considered to be an extension of Chapter 3 where the tasks of management were considered. These tasks or functions are generally considered to be:

1 Planning.
2 Organising.
3 Leading.
4 Controlling.
5 Motivating.

In all the above functions there is one common function: managers make decisions. This chapter involves a closer look at each of these functions.

Planning

Planning is one of the basic functions of managers and supervisors. Plans are methods that have been worked out beforehand for achieving something. Thus there might be plan for a company to introduce a new model.

Plans always have to answer one or more of the following questions:

1 What should we do?
2 How should we do it?
3 When should we do it?
4 Who should do it?
5 How much should we do?
6 Why should we do it?

The consequence of the plan, giving answers to such questions, is that it then gives a pre-determined course of action which:

1 Provides purpose and direction within the organisation.
2 Provides a unifying framework for decision making in the organisation.
3 Facilitates control, in that control means ensuring that activities conform to plan.

Essentially there are two basic levels of plans, the terms *stategic* and *tactical* or action being used to describe them. Stategic planning involves developing the organisation's major long-term plans, and in doing so specifies the major objectives of the organisation and the policies that will be used to achieve them. Tactical or action planning is much shorter term than the strategic planning and involves, often, the development of departmental objectives, within the overall constraints of the strategic plan.

The planning process

The planning process can be considered to consist, generally, of a number of steps. While many authors have written about what these steps are, and have often defined them in different ways, the sum total of the steps tends to remain the same.

1   Ascertain the basic facts of the situation.
2   Define specific objectives (i.e. where do we want to go, what are the targets).
3   Analyse the objectives and on the basis of assumptions make forecasts.
4   Develop several alternative plans, i.e. ways of achieving the specific objectives (there is generally no unique answer).
5   Decide on a plan and implement it.
6   Review and modify the plan in the light of experience.

Objectives are goals, a statement of where we want to go, what our targets are. Thus an objective in a stategic plan might be to achieve 20 per cent of the total market for a product within ten years. An objective in a departmental plan might be to achieve a 5 per cent reduction in costs within six months.

The criteria for useful objectives can be stated as follows, these criteria being based on those given by P. Drucker in *People and Performance, The Best of Peter Drucker on Management* (Heinemann, 1977):

1   Objectives must be derived from 'what our business is, what it will be, and what it should be'.
2   Objectives must be operational, i.e. capable of being converted into specific targets and assignments.
3   Objectives must make possible concentration of resources and effort, i.e. they should be specific rather than global.
4   Objectives are needed in all aspects of a business, not being restricted to any one type of activity. Drucker identifies eight key areas in which objectives need to be set, these being: marketing, innovation, human organisation, financial resources, physical resources, productivity, social responsibility and profit requirements.

Forecasting

Forecasting is the predicting of some future event or condition, having the business purpose of helping management to make plans to cope with future events or conditions. Forecasting, however, can only indicate probable events or conditions, not certainties.

An important type of forecast for any organisation is an economic forecast. Such a forecast is a projection of the level of economic activity over a period of time. Thus a company concerned with selling machines, or perhaps some particular service, needs to make plans for the future based on an economic forecast of the level of economic activity – will the economy be low and so the demand for machines or the service low or will the economy be in boom and there be a high demand for the machines or service?

There are two basic approaches to economic forecasting. One relies on the use of indicators and the other is based on the construction of mathematical models, the term *econometric forecasting* being used for this approach. There are a wide variety of indicators available to managers, e.g. lay-off of labour in the industry, manufacturers' new orders, raw materials costs, etc. The econometric approach involves the construction of a mathematical model in which the relationships between the various variables are developed and then, when current data is fed into the model, predictions are made about the future.

Some of the factors affecting forecasts are:

1   Population trends.
2   Employment trends.
3   Political stability.
4   Government policy.
5   Technological changes.

Economic forecasts of the business outlook can be found in the financial press. The important point that still needs consideration by a manager is the relationship between the economic forecast and potential sales of his, or her, product.

Organising

Whatever the level of the manager within the organisation there are a number of basic aspects that will come within the task of organising. These are:

1   Determining what tasks have to be done.
2   Allocating the tasks to subordinates.
3   Delegating authority to subordinates.
4   Co-ordinating the work.

Thus a supervisor might have the task of ensuring that the company cars are properly maintained. That is the task. However it can be broken down into a number of smaller tasks and subordinates given various aspects of the task. Thus one group of subordinates might be concerned with daily and weekly routine maintenance, e.g. tyre pressures, oil and water levels, etc., while another group is concerned with servicing the cars every 3000 miles. Within each group the supervisor is likely to give some delegated authority to one individual, perhaps the term foreman might be appropriate for that individual. Delegation can be defined as the moving to a subordinate by a superior of some aspects of authority. It is essentially a balance between the two factors trust and control; the more the supervisor trusts the foreman the less the control he or she has over the actions of the subordinates.

The following can be considered to be some of the barriers to successful delegation by a superior to a subordinate:

1 The superior does not allow the subordinate to do anything of consequence.
2 The superior lacks confidence in the subordinate.
3 The superior is not prepared to take a chance and allow the subordinate to make any decisions.
4 The superior feels the subordinate might be a threat to his or her job.
5 The superior and the subordinate do not trust each other.
6 The subordinate does not want to accept the responsibility.
7 The subordinate does not consider the rewards worth the effort of making decisions.

Co-ordination is necessary if effective organisation is to occur. While co-ordination can be considered in relation to the management controlling the company as a whole, it is also just as necessary for the supervisor of a small group of employees. Co-ordination is the process of achieving unity of action among a group of interdependent activities. The following are some of the methods that can be used for co-ordination:

1   By rules or procedures

Each of the employees is expected to conform to set rules or procedures, i.e. a scientific management approach.

2   By targets

Each of the departments or employees is set targets, then if each attains their targets the result should be an overall plan being attained and hence co-ordination. Thus, for instance, the production department may be set the target of producing 100 items; the sales department the target of selling 100 items.

3 By chain of command

Decisions are all referred up the line and so essentially all decisions are taken by the person at the top.

4 By departmentalisation or grouping

Some forms of departmentalisation can assist coordination. Thus the co-ordination of all the activities associated with a particular product can be enhanced if all the activities fall within one department rather than be scattered over a number of departments. Thus departmentalisation by product rather than by business function can assist co-ordination. At a lower level a supervisor might group subordinates by the product they are working on rather than by their particular type of job.

5 By liaison people or groups

Special liaison people or groups can be used, with the job of ensuring co-ordination.

6 By committees

Interdepartmental committees or special task committees can be set up.

A vital factor in the co-ordination of a group by a supervisor is the span of control (see Chapter 2 for the work by Woodward). While there is no agreement regarding the best span of control there are limits as to the number of subordinates that can report direct to a supervisor if adequate control is to be exercised, numbers of the order of 5 to 12 are often quoted.

Leading

Leadership can be defined as the influencing of one person by another so that they work to some predetermined goal. Leadership can be formal in that the leader has delegated authority, or informal when the leader is selected by general consensus within a group. There are essentially two ways of looking at leadership, one is in terms of the functions carried out by leaders and their styles, the other in terms of the personal characteristics of leaders.

There are many functions carried out by leaders, for example:

1 The translation of directives from higher levels in the organisation into goals for subordinates.
2 Setting and announcing goals.
3 Directing or influencing others to do tasks.
4 Rewarding and punishing.
5 Planning, controlling and monitoring.
6 Making decisions.

7   Setting an example.
8   Organising resources.

There are more functions that can be added to the above list, but it is probably the first one in the list that uniquely describes a formal leader in an organisation.

Leadership styles can be grouped into essentially just two categories, task and people orientation. In a *task–orientated* style the focus is on getting the job done, in a *people–orientated* style the focus is on building and maintaining good interpersonal relationships between the members of the group. While different writers on leadership may use different terms to describe the two basic styles, they are essentially just task and people orientation.

For example, R. Likert at the University of Michigan uses the terms employee–centred supervisors and production–centred supervisors. Employee–centred supervisors regard employees, subordinates, as being individuals, each having personal needs. Production–centred supervisors regard production and its technical aspects as being of prime importance. The two styles are seen as being the extreme ends of a scale with many intermediate points.

Studies at the Ohio University led to the description of leadership styles in terms of two factors: consideration and initiating structure. Consideration is the extent to which the leader shows consideration of subordinates' feelings, trusts and respects their ideas and develops personal relationships with them. Initiating structure is the degree to which the leader defines and organises the work to be done, determines who does what and how, and the channels of communication. These two factors are not seen as being the opposite ends of a scale but two independent factors with the possibility, for instance, of a leader having both high consideration and high initiating structure. A leader with high consideration and low initiating structure can be considered to have a people–orientated style and one with low consideration and high initiating structure a task–orientated style.

The obvious question is: which style of leadership is best, people orientated or task orientated? There is no evidence to suggest that in general one is better than another, rather that in some situations one may be better than the other but it depends on what the situation is as to which one is the best. This approach to leadership is termed the contingency theory.

Fiedler, in work on contingency theory since the 1950s, has evolved a theory on the matching of different styles of leadership to different situations in organisations. He considered three situational factors: leader–member relationships, task structure and position power. The leader–member relationship describes how the leader gets on with the group members and the extent to which he or she is accepted by the group. The task structure refers to the extent to which the group's work tasks are routine and predictable with clear cut goals and procedures. The position power refers to the extent to which the organisation provides the leader with the power to reward and punish, to hire and fire. Figure 5.1 summarises Fiedler's findings. Thus for a situation where the leader–member relationships are good, the task structure is routine and the position power is strong then the most effective leadership style is task orientated. If, however, the leader–member relationship is poor, the task structure is routine and the position power is strong then a people – orientated leadership style would be most effective.

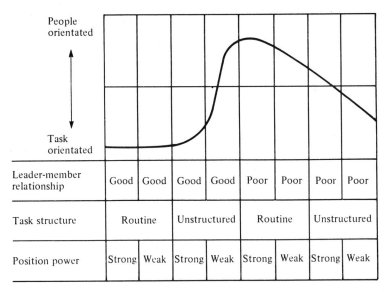

Figure 5.1 *Fiedler's findings on people-orientated and task-orientated management styles*

An implication of considering that leadership style has to match the situation in an organisation is that leadership is an organisational function rather than a personal quality.

The other approach to considering leadership is in terms of the personal characteristics of leaders. Researchers have considered the personal characteristics of large numbers of effective leaders and looked for common characteristics. Stoghill, in an article in *Journal of Psychology* (vol. 25, p. 31) in 1948 listed a large number of personal characteristics associated with leadership. In general, with regard to leaders:

1 Most were older than subordinates but some were younger.
2 Most were taller and heavier than subordinates.

3   Most had greater physical prowess, athletic ability than subordinates.
4   Leaders presented a better appearance than subordinates.
5   They were more fluent, confident and brighter than subordinates.
6   Leaders had better scholastic records than subordinates.
7   Leaders generally had specialised knowledge and an ability to apply it, an ability to make sound judgements, to make quick, accurate decisions, were alert and able to evaluate situations.
8   Leaders tended to have high originality.
9   They were more likely to recognise change and take action in anticipation of the changes than subordinates.
10   More leaders were extroverted than introverted.
11   Leaders were more likely to show initiative, persistence and ambition.
12   Leaders were more likely to show self-confidence.
13   Most leaders were more stable and emotionally controlled.
14   Leaders generally came from higher socio-economic backgrounds, though there were exceptions.
15   Leaders were usually lively, active, restless, daring and adventurous.
16   Leaders were more popular and admired, more likely to be sociable and diplomatic.

Later studies, by R. D. Mann in 1959, showed a high degree of correlation between leadership and the personal characteristics of intelligence, ability to make adjustments, extraversion and to a lesser extent dominance, masculinity and interpersonal sensitivity.

Leadership styles

The previous section of this chapter introduced the idea of leadership styles and their categorisation under the broad headings of task orientated and people orientated. Some of the other terms used by writers were also referred to; this section takes a look at some of the other descriptors that have been used.

Early research on styles of leadership was carried out by Lewins, Lippitt and White in about 1939. They identified three basic styles:

1   The autocratic leader

(a) The leader alone sets the goals, determines the policy and makes the plans.
(b) Plans are only unfolded a small step at a time so that subordinates cannot see how their work fits within the overall plan. Because of this they do not know what their next task will be and so the future is uncertain for them.
(c) The leader determines how the work should be done, the work method to be used and who does what.

(d) The leader keeps himself, or herself, aloof from the work group and behaves in an impersonal way.

2 The democratic leader

(a) Goal setting, policy making and plans are a matter for group discussion and decision with the leader encouraging and assisting the group.
(b) The steps in the plan are discussed by all members of the group so that each member sees how their work fits within the overall plan and hence they know what the future holds for them.
(c) The group organises their own methods and arrangements.
(d) The leader behaves as a member of the group and attempts to encourage the full development of each member.

3 The laissez-faire leader

(a) There is complete freedom within the group and little dependence by them on the leader.
(b) The members of the group sort out their roles in relation to the plan themselves.
(c) Each member sorts out their own work.
(d) The leader does not participate in, or interfere with, the group.

Some of the consequences of the different leadership styles are as follows:

1 Consequences of autocratic leadership

(a) The group becomes highly dependent on the leader and cannot effectively function without him or her.
(b) There is little cohesion witthin the group.
(c) Because the group members do not contribute to the decision making they do not regard the decisions as 'theirs'.
(d) Though there is close supervision of the group the high output may not be associated with high quality.
(e) The group members are liable to be dissatisfied.

2 Consequences of the democratic leader

(a) The group is not dependent on the presence of the leader and can function effectively in his or her absence.
(b) The group can develop a high cohesion.
(c) Group members contribute to the decision making and so regard the decisions as 'theirs'.
(d) There may be a lower output than with the autocratic leader, however the quality may be higher.
(e) The group members are likely to be more satisfied with their work.

3   Consequences of the laissez-faire leader

(a) The group does not depend on or need the leader.
(b) The group has poor cohesion.
(c) Though group members make decisions they do not do it in a co-ordinated way.
(d) Both the output and quality can be variable.
(e) The group members are generally dissatisfied with their work.

This type of designation of leadership style has evolved over the years. A more recent example is that given by Tannenbaum and Schmidt in 1973. The leadership is seen as being a continuum from boss-centred leadership at one extreme to subordinate-centred leadership at the other. The various descriptors of leadership style along that continuum are:

1   Leader makes the decision and announces it.
2   Leader 'sells' the decision.
3   Leader presents ideas and invites questions.
4   Leader presents a tentative decision subject to change.
5   Leader presents the problem, gets suggestions and then makes the decision.
6   Leader defines the limits and asks the group to make the decision.
7   Leader permits the subordinates to function within the limits defined.

Essentially the above progression can be described as leader control, shared control and group control.

Hersey and Blanchard in 1977 have used the descriptors:

1   Telling

The leader tells the group the decision, what the jobs are and how they are to be carried out.

2   Selling

The leader makes the decision and sells the idea to the group, persuading them to accept the decision – possibly by means of an inducement.

3   Participating

Here the group participate in the decision making and how the jobs are to be tackled.

4   Delegating

The leader delegates the decision making to the group, also how the jobs are to be tackled.

Controlling

Controlling is the activity of ensuring that what was planned to happen does happen and the desired result is obtained. Control involves:

1 Setting targets/standards
2 Measuring performance towards those targets/standards
3 Comparing the actual performance with that required to meet the targets/standards
4 Taking corrective action to bring the actual performance closer to that required.

Controlling and planning are closely linked in that planning leads to controlling, i.e. checking that the plan is being achieved, which then leads back via a feedback loop to planning in order to modify plans in the light of the experience gained in operating the plans.

To illustrate the control activity, consider the situation where a production supervisor, in order to meet a production plan, sets the target of no more than ten reject products per day. The measurement activity then consists of determining the number of rejects per day. If the number is less than ten then no corrective action is required , if more than ten then corrective action is required. The corrective action might be the adjustment of a machine. If persistently the number of rejects creeps above the ten then there might be a need to reconsider the plan and modify it in some way, perhaps using a different production process.

Principles of effective control

Effective control can be considered to be control which allows management to see where problems lie and to be able to take remedial action without too significant a time lag. Control should pinpoint problems before they have got out of control. Effective control must also be accepted by the workers, otherwise there could be problems due to evasion by them of controls.

Effective controls can be considered to be based on a number of principles. These are:

1 The standards set must be seen to be fair.
2 The standards set must be observable and measurable.
3 The standards must be specific.
4 The standards set must be seen as being relevant.
5 The standards set must be communicated to the employees concerned and understood.
6 The standards set must be complete, covering all the required aspects.
7 There should be fast feedback of performance to employees.
8 The controls used should fit the task concerned.

9   The control system used should be economical, not costing more than it is worth.

10   The control system used should be capable of yielding information to management in such a way that they can understand it and also of pointing the way to the remedial action.

Motivating

A large part of any manager's job is getting people to do things, i.e. motivating them. But what motivates people? There are many theories of motivation.

One approach is that of Maslow (1943) who identified a hierarchy of needs: physiological, safety, social, ego and finally self-fulfillment needs (Chapter 4 includes a lengthy discussion of these). The theory assumes that the needs follow in sequence and that when one need is satisfied the next one up the list becomes the motivator, a satisfied need not being a motivator. However, the evidence of the hierarchical sequence of the needs is weak.

Another approach is that of Herzberg (1966) with his motivator–hygiene theory. This theory is based on investigations of workers in organisations when they were asked what they felt was good about their jobs and what they felt was bad about them. From this work Herzberg developed two groups of factors involved in job satisfaction. One group he called *motivators* and these are strongly concerned with satisfaction. These factors represent the needs for which people will strive, they contribute little to job dissatisfaction. The other group he called *hygiene factors* and these are strongly concerned with dissatisfaction. They contribute little to job satisfaction.

Motivator factors are achievement, recognition, the work itself, responsibility and advancement. Hygiene factors are company policy and administration, supervision, salary, interpersonal relations and working conditions. Essentially motivators spring from the intrinsic content of the job and hygiene factors from the extrinsic job context.

To get rid of employee dissatisfaction the hygiene factors have to be right. However even if these factors are right there can be no motivation unless the motivator factors are right.

To motivate workers the motivator factors have to be right. It is however also necessary to get the hygiene factors right if the motivators are to work; a dissatisfied worker cannot become a motivated worker.

Another approach is called *expectancy theory*. This postulates that for motivation to occur the value of the particular outcome, or reward for doing a task, must be high enough, and the employee concerned must feel that he, or she, has a reasonable chance of accomplishing the task and obtaining the outcome. Outcomes that are highly valued and have high expectation of being achieved will be good motivators. If either the value of the outcome or the expectation is low then there is no motivation. Thus the outcome for doing a task might be a bonus, and if the employee considers the size of the bonus is great enough and he, or she, has a reasonable chance of obtaining that bonus then motivation can occur. Expectancy theory has evolved through the work of a number of researchers, for example the work of Vroom in 1964 and Lawler in 1967.

Another approach to motivation is called the *equity theory*, formulated by J. Stacy Adams in about 1965. According to this theory, workers will try to achieve equity between their inputs and the outcomes, the rewards. If a worker perceives an inequity then he or she will be motivated to reduce or eliminate the perceived inequity. Thus if a worker considers he or she is paid too little for what they do then there will be demands for higher payments or a reduction in their output to a level which they consider matches their pay. Overpayment can also lead to problems, but an individual's tolerance of overpayment inequities is much greater than of underpayment inequities.

As an example of the application of equity theory consider workers paid on a piece – rate basis. If they think they are underpaid then to reduce the inequity they will produce more but the quality is likely to decrease. If however they think they are overpaid then the quantity will not increase, because this would increase the inequity on a piece-rate basis, but the quality is likely to increase as a means of reducing the inequity. If however a worker is paid a salary then a perceived underpayment is likely to result in a decrease in quantity and quality. If however they think they are overpaid then either the quality or quantity is likely to increase.

Job satisfaction

What makes a worker satisfied with his or her job? Herzberg in his hygiene–motivator theory of motivation considered that job satisfaction stemmed from an entirely separate set of factors to those resulting in job dissatisfaction. Factors which he considered could result in satisfaction, i.e. the motivator factors, were achievement, recognition, the work itself, responsibility and advancement – all factors concerned with the intrinsic content of the job. Herzberg used the term *job enrichment* to describe the process of increasing the motivator factors.

The following are seven guiding principles suggested by Herzberg for enriching jobs:

1 Remove some of the controls on the work task while still retaining accountability.
2 Increase the accountability of the worker for his or her own work.
3 Give workers complete tasks rather than parts of tasks.

4   Give additional authority to the worker in his or her job.
5   Give periodic reports on the work directly to the worker rather than via the supervisor.
6   Introduce new and more difficult tasks for the worker, not the old routine tasks.
7   Assign specific types of tasks to individuals so that they can become experts.

Later workers have however cast doubts on the Herzberg two-factor approach and it is now proposed that both motivator and hygiene factors can contribute to job satisfaction, though motivator factors seem to contribute more than the hygiene factors do.

Hackman and Lawler (1971), and later Hackman and Oldham (1975, 1979), on the basis of an analysis of a large number of jobs, have identified a number of core job dimensions (characteristics) which affect the states of employees. The core job descriptors are:

1   Skill variety

This is the degree to which the job requires employees to perform activities that challenge a variety of skills and abilities.

2   Task identity

This is the degree to which the job requires completion of a whole and identifiable piece of work.

3   Task significance

This is the degree to which the job has a substantial and perceivable impact on the lives of people, either within the immediate organisation or outside.

4   Autonomy

This is the degree to which the job gives the employee freedom to schedule his or her work and determine the procedures to be used to carry it out.

5   Feedback

This is the degree to which the employee gets direct and clear information about the effectiveness of his or her performance.

The above descriptors affect the psychological states of the employees, three such states being affected. These states are:

1   The work is experienced as being meaningful. The dimensions of skill variety, task identity and task significance contribute to this state.
2   The worker experiences responsibility for job outcomes. This is determined by the dimension of autonomy.
3   The worker knows the actual results of work activities.

This is determined by the dimension of feedback.

The personal and work outcomes of such psychological states can be:

1 High internal work motivation.
2 High quality work performance.
3 High satisfaction with work.
4 Low absenteeism and turnover.

However, the degree to which the relationship between the core job dimensions, the psychological states and the outcomes will be true is considered to be moderated by three additional factors. These are:

1 The degree to which the worker has the necessary skills for the job.
2 The degree to which the worker is motivated by the need to 'grow' and sees the work as producing growth.
3 The degree to which the worker is satisfied with the context in which he or she carries out the job, e.g. social and work conditions, pay.

On the basis of this theory, if job enrichment is required then there is a need to look at the core job dimensions. Thus a possible solution might be to create work groups which tackle entire jobs, rather than for a supervisor to delegate small aspects of the job to individual workers. The group could also be given more say in the planning, production and control of their work, with care being taken to ensure that adequate feedback from the job occurs.

Decision making

Managers have to make decisions. Some decisions may be fairly routine ones where definite procedures can be worked out before the event. Thus the decision as to the reordering of materials for the store can be made routine, perhaps along the lines: for material X – when the stock drops to 200 reorder 300. However not all decisions that a manager will need to make are routine ones which can be worked out in advance, some will be decisions in new situations.

However diverse the problem requiring a decision, it is possible to conceive of four basic steps that should be taken in the making of the decision. These are:

1 Defining the problem for which the decision is required.
2 Developing alternative solutions to the problem.
3 Analysing and comparing the alternatives.
4 Making the decision as to the optimum solution to the problem.

The first step is an important part of the decision process – defining the problem. What is the real problem? Suppose a decision is required on a course of action to be taken because of a drop in sales of product X. Before solutions can be proposed the real problem has to be identified, not the drop in sales because this is the consequence of the problem. The problem might be that the product is overpriced. Then solutions have to be evolved to the problem of the overpricing. The problem might be however that product X is out-of-date. This is a different problem and different solutions will need to be evolved.

There is almost invariably no unique solution to business problems and thus alternative solutions should be developed so that the optimum one can be ascertained. Thus suppose we have the problem that the quality of the goods produced by machine operator Y is persistently below acceptable levels. Possible solutions might be:

1   Dismiss the operator.
2   Train the operator.
3   Relocate the operator.
4   Redesign the operation.
5   Lower the required standards.

Having obtained a number of possible solutions to the problem the next step is to compare them and hence decide on the optimum solution. However, on what basis should they be compared? Is the optimum solution the lowest cost solution? But lowest cost over what period of time? There might be solutions which have high initial costs but low running costs and others with low initial costs and high running costs. For example, in considering solutions to a manufacturing problem there might be a choice between sand casting or die casting. Sand casting has the same cost per item produced regardless of how many are produced. Die casting has a high setting up cost and then low costs per item produced. Thus for a small quantity of a product send casting will be cheaper than die casting but if a very large number are required then die casting will be cheaper per item produced.

Three basic criteria are involved in comparing alternative solutions, these being:

1   The financial cost

How much money will the solution cost?

2   The real cost

What is the real cost to the organisation of the solution? What will the organisation have to forego if that solution is adopted?

3   The social cost

What is the cost to society of that solution, e.g. pollution, unemployment, poor working conditions, etc.?

Revision questions

1   For managers explain what is meant by (a) planning, (b) organising, (c) leading, (d) controlling and (e) motivating.

2   Why should a manager make plans?

3   Outline the basic steps involved in a planning process.

4   What is meant by the term objectives and what are the criteria for useful objectives?

5   What is meant by (a) *economic forecasting*, and (b) *econometric forecasting*?

6   Explain what is meant by delegating and outline some of the barriers to successful delegation.

7   What is meant by co-ordination and how might it be achieved in organisations?

8   State the main functions carried out by a leader.

9   What is meant by *task-orientated* and *people-orientated* leadership styles?

10   Describe in outline Fiedler's *contingency theory* as applied to leadership.

11   What are the common personal characteristics likely to be found in leaders?

12   Explain the differences in style between (a) the autocratic leader, (b) the democratic leader, and (c) the laissez-faire leader, and their consequences on subordinate group behaviour.

13   Explain the descriptors of management style used by Hersey and Blanchard, i.e. telling, selling, participating and delegating.

14   State the principles of effective control.

15   Describe Herzberg's *motivator-hygiene theory*.

16   Explain the *equity theory* of motivation and give an example of its application.

17   What is meant by *job enrichment?*

18   Explain the Hackman and co-workers' *theory of job satisfaction*.

19   What are the basic steps involved in decision making?

Assignments and further questions

1 Consider a particular product and outline the plans that would be required from the first conception of the possible product to the product being on sale to the public.

2 The class of students is considering producing and selling summary lecture note books of key aspects of the course. Make plans for this activity.

3 Write notes which could be given to other students on your course on the topic of management by objectives.

4 Look though the financial press and obtain an economic forecast from which you can argue a case for potential sales of some product.

5 Suppose you are a supervisor and have twelve subordinates. You have the option of having all twelve reporting direct to you or making two of them as your deputies with each then having responsibility for five people. Present the cases for both possibilities.

6 Suppose you are the manager of a company having 200 employees. Propose a plan by which you can co-ordinate the work of all the staff.

7 Suppose you have been proposed as the team leader for the development of a new product. You envisage that the development will involve a number of activities, e.g. research, development of production techniques, market research, etc. Propose a plan for the organisation and co-ordination of the work.

8 Some managers delegate too much and some too little. Discuss this statement.

9 Write a critical analysis of a range of different theories on leadership.

10 Consider a particular organisation and present arguments as to the styles of leadership that could be most appropriate in the different parts of that organisation.

11 Leaders are born not made. Discuss this statement.

12 Discuss the traits possessed by a number of successful leaders, e.g. political leaders.

13 Present arguments on the most appropriate leadership style for leaders in the following situations, (a) leader of a research team, (b) supervisor of an assembly line, (c) leader of a political party.

14 Think of a job that you personally felt highly motivated about doing. What made you feel so motivated?

15 Consider a particular situation in an organisation and then present an argument for a job enrichment programme for those concerned.

16 Describe the control procedures by which a lecturer controls a class and what consitutes effective control.

17 As a supervisor you have to work out a payment scheme for your subordinates. Write notes on the arguments for and against (a) a piece-work per individual scheme, (b) a group piece-work scheme, (c) a salary with no rewards directly linked to output. You may like to consider a particular aspect of an organisation, e.g. the supervisor of a sales force, in your answer.

18 Your managing director states that one of his main objectives is to make the workforce happy. A fellow manager states that such an aim is the last thing he wants if he is to maintain output levels: the workers would be happy doing nothing all day long. Present a reasoned argument to your fellow manager defending the managing director's statement.

19 Michael Argyle in his book *The Social Psychology of Work* (Penguin, 1972) suggests that the supervisor is the 'man in the middle' in an organisation and is under pressure from those above to concentrate on initiating structure and those below on consideration. Discuss this suggestion.

Part Two   Industrial relations

This part of the book consists of four chapters on the various aspects of industrial relations.

Chapter 6 Trade unions.   This chapter traces the growth of trade unions, the way their powers have changed and the way they currently operate.

Chapter 7 Labour laws and the individual.   This considers the aspects of legislation that affect the individual at work, in particular, contracts of employment, discrimination in all its forms, dismissal, redundancy and the role of industrial tribunals.

Chapter 8 Collective bargaining. The structure of the collective bargaining process is considered, along with various facets such as negotiations, industrial action, the closed shop, ACAS and the Employment Act, 1982.

Chapter 9 Health and Safety at Work. This chapter considers the development of safety legislation leading to the Health and Safety at Work Act, 1974 and the main aspects of that Act. Reference is also made to The Safety Representatives and Safety Committees Regulations, 1977 and to the Factories Act, 1961.

6   Trade unions

The growth of trade unionism

Trade unions were a development from the Industrial Revolution in Britain. The Industrial Revolution started late in the eighteenth century and was a change from a society based on agriculture and crafts where workers operated individually or in small groups, to one based on industry where workers were brought together into large groups. This operation as an industry evolved from such inventions as the steam engine, which was able to supply larger amounts of power than was either available from individuals or usable by them, and from new machines which enabled traditional craft occupations to be mechanised, e.g. the mechanisation of spinning by the invention of the water-frame by Richard Arkwright.

In the early days of the Industrial Revolution small local trade clubs evolved. These contained workmen in a particular occupation in that locality and ran such activities as sickness and burial funds for their members. With time their activities increased, as they grew in size and became less a purely local club. They began to become involved in wage negotiations. However in the early nineteenth century these trade clubs were still very weak, only a small fraction of workers belonging to such a club. The clubs were isolated from each other; remember that the railway network in Britain did not come about until almost the mid-nineteenth century, as also the telegraph system and the present form of postal system. Also, the clubs were essentially illegal. In 1799 a Combination Act had been passed by Parliament which forbade the establishment of any combination of workmen to try to decrease hours of work or increase wages.

The Combinations Acts were repealed in 1824. This and the development of effective communication systems in the country, i.e. a railway system and cheap postage, were to lead to the development of the trade clubs in regional and then national trade unions. A turning point in the development of trade unions was the establishment in 1851 of the Amalgamated Society of Engineers. This union had a national membership of skilled men, the engineers who were the key agents in the development of the new industrial age. There was a regular subscription from the members, sickness and unemployment benefits, formal rule books and a full-time officer, in fact aspects characteristic of modern trade unions. During the 1850s and 1860s many such unions developed for the skilled trades.

The conditions for the birth and development of national trade unions can thus be considered to be:

1 Industrial developments which resulted in the concentration of manpower under fewer employers.
2 The concentration of similar types of industry into regions where coal or raw materials were located.
3 Improvements in communications.

Significant events in the growth of trade unions

The following are just some of the significant events in the early development of trade unions, events which can be considered to have had some effect on the development and operation of modern trade unions.

1 *The Grand National Consolidated Trades Union*

This was founded in 1833 with the aim of covering all the trades in the country. Within a year its membership had reached over half a million. However employers resisted the growth of the union, for instance they compelled employees to sign a statement that they were not members of the union and sacked those who refused. Just as rapidly as the union had grown, it collapsed.

2 *The Tolpuddle martyrs*

In 1834 six agricultural labourers were arrested and charged with taking an illegal oath. They were members of the Friendly Society of Agricultural Labourers and were trying to resist a cut in wages. They were charged under the Mutiny Act of 1797. This Act laid down that it was unlawful to take oaths of allegiance to anyone other than the King. The six, who have become known as the Tolpuddle martyrs, were convicted and sentenced to transportation to Australia for seven years. Following a public outcry they were pardoned in 1836.

3 *The Trade Union Act, 1871*

A Royal Commission on the Organisation and Rules of Trade Unions and other Associations was set up in 1867. Following an investigation they gave an essentially favourable report which led to the Trade Union Act of 1871. This Act gave legal status to trade unions and in doing so opened the way for the growth of trade unionism.

The main effects of the Act were:

(a) Trade unions were not illegal.
(b) While trade union agreements in restraint of trade could not be legally enforced, they were not illegal.
(c) Provision was made for the voluntary registration of unions with the Chief Inspector of Friendly Societies, such registration giving them legal protection for their properties and funds.

4 The Criminal Law Amendment Act, 1871

While the Trade Union Act in 1871 was popular with the trade unionist, the Criminal Law Amendment Act passed in the same year was not. This law forbade picketing, imposing heavy penalties on such 'obstruction', as well as on threats and intimidation.

5 The Conspiracy and Protection of Property Act, 1875

In 1875 the Criminal Law Amendment Act of 1871 was repealed and replaced by the Conspiracy and Protection of Property Act. This Act legalised peaceful picketing, provided that the pickets did not forcibly try to prevent employees from going to work and that they were there solely in order to obtain or to communicate information.

6 The Trades Union Congress

In 1868 the Trades Union Congress (TUC) was founded. This was, and is, an organisation to which indidual unions are affiliated, with a prime aim of considering policies and issues of general relevance to unions.

7 The Great Dock Strike of 1889

In the summer of 1889 the London dockers came out on strike for a minimum wage of sixpence an hour, an increase of one penny. For nearly a month they closed the port of London. Support for the dockers came from a wide range of people and eventually the dock owners gave way. It was a significant point in trade union history for it led towards an increasing awareness of the effectiveness of unions and so to a growth of unionism. Prior to this time the unions had grown among skilled workers; now the growth involved unskilled workers, i.e. the worst paid workers.

8 The Taff Vale judgement of 1901

Following a strike on the Taff Vale Railway in South Wales the railway company had lost money and sued the Amalgamated Society of Railway Servants for damages. It won the case and was awarded £23,000. The judgement was thus that a trade union could be held liable for damage suffered by employers. Thus even if the union won a strike the cost to the union might be ruinous.

The judgement led to a strong outcry from union members that the law should be changed and led to the unions setting up a political fund to pay

Labour Members of Parliament. In the election of 1906 an appreciable number of Labour Members were elected and new legislation was passed, the Trades Dispute Act of 1906. This Act reversed the Taff Vale judgement and made the unions not liable for actions for damages for civil actions (i.e. non-criminal actions).

9 The Osborne case of 1909

The political fund to support Labour MPs was obtained from a political levy on all trade union members. One railway worker, called Osborne, objected to paying such a levy. The courts ruled in favour of Osborne and this was confirmed by the House of Lords in 1909 It was thus illegal for unions to collect money for political ends. This ruling threatened the existence of the Labour party and its Members in Parliament.

In 1911 Parliament decided that all Members of Parliament should receive a salary, up to that time there had been no such salary. This aided in particular the Labour Members of Parliament who no longer received money from the unions. The political levy was however made legal in the Trade Union Act of 1913, provided that it was approved by the majority of the members in a union. Individual members of a union could however 'contract out' of the levy, i.e. declare they did not wish to pay it.

10 Union amalgamations in the 1920s

Through a series of amalgamations and mergers large and powerful unions emerged in the 1920s, e.g. the Transport and General Workers' Union and the National Union of General and Municipal Workers.

11 The General Strike

The General Strike arose from a decision by the TUC to support the miners who had been out on strike against the mine owners who were proposing longer hours and lower wages. At midnight on May 3, 1926 the strike began. Though there was widespread union support for the strike the non-union public did not support it and volunteers manned buses, trains, etc. and assisted in keeping the country running. After nine days the TUC called off the strike, the miners however stayed out for another six months before they gave in and accepted the longer hours and lower wages. The effect of the General Strike was a sharp drop in union numbers, over half a million workers leaving unions.

A consequence of the strike was the Trades Disputes and Trade Union Act of 1927. This made general strikes illegal, forbade civil service unions from belonging to the TUC and required that political levies should only be by 'contracting in', i.e. members had to state if they wanted to pay the levy. This Act was not repealed until 1946.

12 Rookes v Barnard case, 1964

In 1963 a case occurred in which an employee claimed that his employer had dismissed him as a result of intimidation in the form of a union threat to strike. The House of Lords, in 1964, ruled in favour of the employee. The employee had been dismissed by the employer for not joining a union, under the threat to the employer of industrial action if the employee was not dismissed. This ruling exposed to the unions to civil actions.

The Trade Disputes Act 1965 restored to the unions immunity against civil actions on these grounds.

13 Trade union legislation since 1971

In 1971 the Conservative government passed the Industrial Relations Act, 1971. This Act was subject to much opposition, both before and after it became law, by trade unionists. It included the right of an individual not to belong to a union. The Labour government of 1974 however repealed the Act and replaced it with the Trade Union and Labour Relations Act, 1974 and an amendement to the Act in 1976. This established that employees could be dismissed for refusing to join a union where the group of workers were covered by a closed shop agreement. However this position was then reversed by the Employment Acts of 1980 and 1982.

The 1971 Act effectively removed trade union immunities to civil actions, however the 1974 Act restored that immunity to the situation that had prevailed under the 1906 Act. The Act states that acts in contemplation or furtherance of a trade union dispute shall not be actionable in civil proceedings for damages. The 1982 Act however repealed this and made acts in contemplation or furtherance of a trade dispute liable to civil proceedings for damages if they are not between the workers and their employer, e.g. disputes between workers and another employer do not have immunity.

The 1980 and 1982 Acts also included legislation on picketing. For instance, picketing is confined to those employees directly involved in the dispute and to their own place of work or a clearly connected establishment. Secondary picketing is not protected by the law.

The Trade Unions Act, 1984 made it necessary for trade unions to ballot their members if they legally wish to have political funds. Such political funds are widely used to support the Labour Party. The Act also lays down the need for a ballot of members before industrial action can legally be taken.

Types of unions

Trade unions can be classified into four types:

1   *Craft unions*

These are concerned only with workers having specific trade skills, irrespective of the industry in which they work.

2   *Industrial unions*

These are concerned only with workers in a single industry, irrespective of their trade or occupation.

3   *General unions*

These have no industrial or occupational limits on their recruitment, mainly being concerned with semiskilled and unskilled workers.

4   *White-collar unions*

These are concerned only with white-collar workers, though they may restrict their membership to narrow occupational categories, to broad occupational groups or an industry, or may be more broadly based. Thus white-collar unions can be essentially considered to exist in each of the three types of category specified above.

Trade union membership

Table 6.1 illustrates how the membership of trade unions has changed over recent years. It also shows how the union density and number have changed. The union density is the proportion of employees, both employed and unemployed, who are in a trade union.

Table 6.1

Year	Membership (millions)	Union density (%)	Number of unions
1945	7.88	38.6	781
1955	9.74	44.5	688
1965	10.32	44.2	591
1975	12.03	51.0	501
1979	13.45	55.4	456
1980	12.95	53.6	438
1981	12.18	51.0	421

From 1845 to 1979 there was an increase in the membership of trade unions and the percentage of employees in unions. Since that time however there has been both a decrease in the membership and a decrease in the percentage of employees in unions. This recent change correlates with the rise in unemployment. The other factor shown by the table is the rapidly diminishing number of trade unions, as a result of amalgamations and mergers. In 1945 the average size of a union was about 10,000 members, by 1981 this had become almost 30,000. In 1981 the largest union was the Transport and General Workers' Union with 1,695,800 members, with the Amalgamated Union of Engineering Workers with 1,099,900.

An interesting facet of the growth of union membership over the years has been the growth of unionisation among white-collar workers. In 1945 some 14 per cent of the total union membership was due to white-collar workers; by 1980 this had risen to about 40 per cent. Bain, in *The Growth of white collar Unionism* (OUP, 1970) has suggested that the main reasons for the growth of white-collar unionism are:

1 There is a high degree of employment concentration, i.e. large numbers of white-collar workers in one place.
2 Employers are willing to recognise white-collar unions.
3 Recognition is encouraged by the government.

Trade union officers

The development of the early local trade unions into national unions led to the need for full-time salaried officers. While such officers could more efficiently run large national organisations, they also had the advantage in wage negotiations of not being vulnerable in the way an employee presenting a claim to his or her own employer would be.

The full time union officers generally fit the following organisational pattern:

1 The general secretary. This is an elected post and is the top post in the organisational structure among the full time officers.
2 National officers. These are officers who operate from the union's headquarters.
3 Regional officers. These are officers who operate at regional or district level.
4 Local officers. These are the first-line officers who operate within the local branch of the union. They are directly concerned with the union members in their locality. By far the greater number of full-time union officers are local officers.

Full-time officers are generally elected or appointed from members within the union who have been active as voluntary officers. The main activities of the full-time officers are, according to a TUC survey:

1 Routine office work.
2 Negotiations at the workplace.
3 Preparing materials for negotiations.

4 Supervising shop stewards.
5 Attending branch meetings.
6 Recruiting new members.

Shop stewards

The term *shop steward* is used for the unpaid representative of a trade union at the workplace. Other terms are used in some industries, for example the term Father or Mother Of Chapel is used in the printing industry. Shop stewards are elected by union members in a particular company and represent the union, and the members, in that company. Their functions can be considered to be:

1 To act as recruiting officers for the union.
2 To inspect union cards to check that contributions are paid up to date.
3 To represent their members in discussions with management over such matters as hours, meal and rest breaks, discipline, dismissals, etc.
4 To represent their members who have grievances.
5 To see that working agreements between management and the union are carried out.
6 Until the Health and Safety at Work Act, 1974, they were also involved with safety problems, however that Act required the appointment of employees as safety representatives and this removed much of the work from shop stewards.

In large organisations there are frequently many shop stewards. This often leads to a structure amongst them involving senior shop stewards and convenors, such posts being filled by elections amongst the shop stewards. The *convenor* is the shop steward charged with the convening of shop steward meetings, acting as the chairman of such meetings.

In large, multi-union, companies there can be meetings involving shop stewards from all the unions, the term *joint shop stewards' committee* being used to describe such meetings. The chairman of such a committee is often referred to as the *works convenor*.

The structure of a union

The structure of a union can be considered to be:

1 The union members at the workplace.
2 The shop stewards elected by the union members at the workplace. They act, unpaid, as the union's representatives in the company.
3 Union members in an area belong to the area branch. They can attend meetings and each can voice his or her thoughts on the running of the union and its policy. Each branch has an elected secretary, a chairman

and a committee. It sends delegates to the union's national, annual conference. This conference determines union policy.

4 The national executive committee is elected at the national conference by the delegates or by a direct ballot of the union members. This committee acts on behalf of the total membership of the union.

5 Most trade unions are members of the TUC and this enables them to have a voice in national matters affecting trade union members.

Revision questions

1 What was the industrial revolution and when did it occur in Britain?

2 What factors can be considered to have been responsible for the growth of trade unions in the mid-nineteenth century?

3 Explain the significance of the following Acts in the growth of trade unions: (a) The Trade Union Act, 1871, (b) the Conspiracy and Protection of Property Act, 1875.

4 Explain the significance of the Taff Vale judgement of 1901.

5 What is meant by a political levy?

6 What is meant by immunity against civil actions, for trade unions?

7 Explain what is meant by picketing.

8 What is meant by white-collar unions?

9 Describe the role of full-time salaried union officers.

10 Describe the role of shop stewards.

Assignments and further questions

1 Write notes indicating how changes have occurred over the years in:
 (a) the right to join or not to join a trade union
 (b) the right to picket
 (c) the immunity of trade unions to civil actions

2 Describe the role of the TUC in modern-day trade unionism.

3 Since 1979 trade union membership has declined. Discuss possible reasons for this decline.

4 Write a job specification which describes the work of a shop steward in your industry.

5 Describe the functions, membership, and organisational structure of a particular union.

6 Discuss why unions arose in the days of the Industrial Revolution and then consider their position today.

7 The number of unions has declined as a result of amalgamations and mergers. Suggest reasons why this is occurring.

8 Shop stewards can be a blessing or a curse to a manager. Discuss this statement.

7 Labour laws and the individual

Contracts of employment

The term *contract* is used for a legally binding agreement between two or more parties. Such a contract exists from the moment an employee has agreed to work for an employer and that employer has agreed to pay wages for that work. The contract does not have to be in writing for it to be legally binding on both the employee and the employer. From that point both the employee and the employer have certain basic rights and responsibilities.

Most contracts of employment consist of terms that may be written, spoken and implied. Thus if the job advertisement offers, for example, six weeks per year holiday, that can be part of the terms, as also are the letter of appointment and acceptance. Spoken acceptances or offers are also part of the contract. There may also be implied terms, for example the normal customs and practice of that trade or industry.

The first specific Act of Parliament to cover contracts of employment was the Contracts of Employment Act, 1963, this being amended in later Acts. The Employee Protection (Consolidation) Act, 1978 now requires that all employees who work for sixteen or more hours per week be given written particulars of the main terms of their employment within thirteen weeks of being engaged. These particulars must include:

1 The names of the parties involved.
2 The date of commencement of employment.
3 The job title.
4 Details of remuneration and intervals of payment.
5 Terms and conditions relating to hours of work.
6 Terms and conditions relating to holidays and holiday pay.
7 Terms and conditions relating to sick pay and any pension scheme arrangements.
8 The length of notice the employee is required to give and entitled to receive in terminating employment.

The minimum length of notice that must be given by an employer is stipulated in the Act, this depending on the length of service. For continuous service between four weeks and two years the minimum is one week's notice, with a further entitlement of one week for each succeeding year's continuous employment up to 12 years.

Also under the same Act, employers are obliged to give employees itemised pay statements. Such statements should indicate how their gross pay is made up, how it is worked out, the net pay and the frequency of payment and all deductions should be itemised.

Items that may be implied, rather than stated in the contract, are often covered by the common law. Thus employees have a duty:

1   To be ready and willing to work.
2   To offer personal service to their employer, i.e. not to ask or pay someone else to do the work.
3   Not to misconduct themselves, e.g. frequent or long absences from work, insolence, dishonesty.
4   To obey reasonable orders given by the employer or his or her agents.
5   To respect the employer's trade secrets.
6   To show honesty and loyalty to their employer's interests, e.g. not to take bribes.
7   To work for the employer in the employer's time.

In the case of employers, they have a duty:

1   To pay the agreed remuneration.
2   To provide reasonable opportunity to the employee to earn that remuneration (it appears to be uncertain whether an employer is compelled to provide work).
3   To indemnify employees from injury sustained during employment.
4   To indemnify employees against expenses incurred by an employee acting on his or her employer's behalf.

Discrimination

Legislation against discrimination on grounds of race or sex is contained in the Race Relations Act, 1968, amended 1976, the Equal Pay Act, 1970 and the Sex Discrimination Act, 1975.

The Sex Disrimination Act, 1975 makes it unlawful for an employer to discriminate against a woman or a man with regard to recruitment, dismissal or terms of service on the grounds of their sex. Thus, for example, advertisements for jobs must be sexually neutral. There are however exceptions where being of a particular sex is a genuine qualification for the job.

The Race Relations Act, 1976 is similar to the Sex Discrimination Act except that it applies to discrimination on racial grounds. Unlike the Sex Discrimination Act, which only applies to companies with more than five employees, there are no exceptions for this Act and it applies to all companies.

The Equal Pay Act, 1970 seeks to eliminate discrimination between men and women with regard to their pay, aiming to give equal pay for like work. The Act:

1 Establishes the right of an individual to equal treatment with a member of the opposite sex when doing work which is the same, or similar or which has been rated as of equal value by job evaluation.
2 Provides for a Central Arbitration Committee to remove discrimination in collective agreements, statutory wages orders and employers' pay structures.

Complaints about discrimination under the above Acts are made to Industrial Tribunals. Such a tribunal could, for instance, make an order that a complainant be given equal pay and conditions by a company who were judged to be discriminating on the grounds of sex.

Dismissal

The Industrial Relations Act, 1971 first provided for legal redress for what is defined as *unfair dismissal*. Individuals who considered they had been unfairly dismissed could bring their cases before an Industrial Tribunal. This act has since been repealed and the legislation pertaining to individual employee rights in this and in the Employment Protection Act, 1975 has been consolidated in the Employee Protection (Consolidation) Act of 1978.

With regard to unfair dismissal this Act:

1 Covers, with some exceptions, all employees with more than 52 weeks of continuous employment with an employer. They must be working 16 or more hours per week for the employer, or if 8 or more hours per week they must have worked for at least 260 weeks continuously. Excluded from this are self-employed persons, registered dock workers, those over the employer's normal retirement age, members of the armed forces, etc.
2 Permits a dismissed employee, provided he or she, is not excluded as indicated above, to present a case for unfair dismissal before an Industrial Tribunal.

The Act lays down the main grounds on which dismissals can be judged as fair, these being where the dismissal is:

1 Related to the employee's capababilities or qualifications for performing work of the kind which he, or she, was employed to do.
2 Related to the employee's conduct.
3 Because the employee was redundant.
4 Because the employee could not continue to work in the position he or she held without breaking a legal duty or restriction.

Before the Employment Act, 1980 the onus was on the employer to prove that the dismissal had been fair. However since that Act it is now the responsibility of the tribunal to determine whether the dismissal was fair. However, even though the dismissal was determined as being fair it could still be ruled unfair if the employer did not act in a reasonable way in dismissing the employee. The procedures adopted by an employer in dismissing an employee are thus as important as the reason for the dismissal. In 1977 Parliament approved a Code of Practice relating to disciplinary practice and procedures in employment, this having been prepared by the Advisory, Conciliation and Arbitration Service (ACAS). This Code is a guide to establishing and assessing disciplinary practice and procedures within organisations. It should be emphasised that the Code is only a guide and failure to observe it will not necessarily mean that the dismissal will be ruled as being unfair, however there is a greater chance it will be.

The Code advises that:

1   Disciplinary procedures should be in writing.
2   They must specify to whom they apply.
3   They should provide for speedy action.
4   They should indicate the disciplinary actions that can be taken.
5   They should provide for a system of warnings.
6   The employee should have a chance to state his or her case.
7   There should be a reasonable time allowed for the employee to improve his or her behaviour.
8   There should be an appeals procedure against dismissal.
9   Records should be kept of all disciplinary matters.
10 All employees should be made aware of the disciplinary procedures in operation in their organisation and the possible consequences of infringing them.

To give an example of dismissal, consider an employee whom the employer deems to be incompetent. The employee must be warned of his or her incompetence and allowed time to change his or her behaviour before dismissal can occur.

As well as stating the grounds on which dismissal is fair the Act also gives some instances where dismissal will be unfair. Employees cannot be dismissed on the grounds of:

1   Membership of a trade union or for trade union activities.
2   Non-membership of a union, in certain circumstances, where a closed shop exists.
3   Sex or race.
4   Taking part in industrial action, unless the employer dismisses all those taking part in the action.

Dismissal is also unfair if an employer behaves in such a way as to lead the employee to resign or become dismissed. Such enforced dismissals are known as *constructive dismissals*.

Redundancy

The Employment Protection (Consolidation) Act, 1978 defines redundancy as being where an employee is dismissed because:

1 The employer has ceased or intends to cease carrying on the business.
2 The employer has ceased or intends to cease carrying on the business in the place where the employee was employed.
3 The requirements of the business to carry out work for which the employee was contracted have ceased or diminished.

Redundant employees are entitled to compensation, the amount being determined by their age, length of service with the employer and their average earnings. The employer pays the compensation but can receive a 40 per cent rebate from the Redundancy Fund.

However when a redundancy situation occurs an employer can offer such employees suitable alternative employment. If an employee unreasonably declines this new employment for a trial period, not lasting longer than four weeks, then they can be dismissed without compensation. If during this trial period the employee finds the new employment unsuitable then he or she can claim the redundancy payment.

Industrial tribunals

Industrial tribunals were first set up under the Industrial Training Act, 1964 to hear complaints from employers against assessments for training levies. The Act involved the setting up of Industrial Training Boards with the remit of:

1 The provision, or securing of the provision, of sufficient training courses and other facilities for employees in the industrial sector for which a Board had responsibility.
2 Advising on the nature and length of training and appropriate further education.
3 Checking the levels of attainment and awarding suitable certificates.
4 Making grants to firms providing suitable training courses.
5 Imposing a levy on employers in their sector of the industry.

Since 1964 the work of the Industrial Tribunals has increased and they now deal with a variety of claims under a number of Acts. These include cases of discimination, under the Race Relations Act 1968, 1976, the Equal Pay Act, 1970 and the Sex Discrimination Act, 1975. Also dealt with are cases of unfair dismissal under the Industrial Relations Act, 1971 and contractual and redundancy matters under the Employment Protection (Consolidation) Act, 1978.

Each tribunal has a chairman who is legally qualified with at least seven years, legal experience. The chairman is advised by two lay members, each having considerable experience in industrial relations. One adviser is drawn from a panel nominated by the TUC and the other from one nominated by the CBI. The tribunals operate according to the Industrial Tribunals (Rules of Procedure) Regulations, 1980.

These regulations require the following procedures to be adopted:

1   The applicant must make an application to the tribunal using a standard form. This form states the parties concerned and the grounds of the action.

2   The form is sent to the Central Office of Industrial Tribunals where a decision is taken as to whether the case comes within the jurisdiction of an industrial tribunal.

3   The Central Office then forwards the application to the appropriate Regional Office of Industrial Tribunals. They then contact the party against which the complaint is laid and give them fourteen days to decide whether or not to contest the application.

4   The Advisory, Conciliation and Arbitration Service (ACAS) then attempt though a conciliation officer to get the complaint settled by mutual agreement before it is heard by the tribunal.

5   The tribunal may then require written particulars to be made available to it.

6   The tribunal then hear the case and make a decision. The decision may be unanimous or a majority one.

Revision questions

1   What is meant by a *contract of employment*?

2   What must be included in the written particulars supplied to a new employee with reference to the employment?

3   Which legislation must an employer be concerned with to avoid discrimination?

4   Outline the main conditions of the Equal Pay Act, 1970.

5   According to the Employee Protection (Consolidation) Act, 1978 what are the grounds for (a) fair dismissals and (b) unfair dismissals?

6   Outline the main features that ought to be present in the procedures of

an employer with regard to discipline and dismissal.

7 Define redundancy, according to the Employee Protection (Consolidation) Act, 1978.

8 What are the general functions of Industrial Tribunals?

Assignments and further questions

1 Obtain details of the disciplinary and dismissal procedures for a company and discuss them in the light of current legislation.

2 Discuss and critically analyse the information supplied to a new employee, including that which is written, spoken and implied.

3 Discuss and critically comment on the following situations.
   (a) John Smith, a machinist, does work which is consistently of inadequate quality. On the advice of the foreman the Personnel Officer of the company dismisses John.
   (b) Company X has decided not to produce a particular product and so has no need of the staff in the heat treatment section. Rather than declare them redundant the company offers them jobs in the dispatch section.
   (c) Company Y has a strike. Following settlement of the strike the company sacks the shop steward who led the dispute.
   (d) Mary Smith receives an offer of employment from company Z. After accepting it she decides she does not want the job and sends her sister to the company to do the job instead of going herself.
   (e) Jean Smith is convinced that she is doing the same type of work as Bill Smith but is paid less. She complains to the company and to her union but gets nowhere.
   (f) Joan Smith was frequently absent from work because of poor health. Following repeated warnings to her the company sacks her. Joan feels this is wrong and appeals to an Industrial Tribunal.

4 The following extracts are taken from an article by B. Napier 'Equal value in 1985' in *Topics* (January 1985), published by the Employment Relations Resource Centre. It refers to a case involving anti-discrimination law. Discuss the case and the implications for your company.

Julie Hayward was a young cook, employed in the canteen of Cammell Laird Shipbuilders. Her legal victory took the form of a successful application to a Liverpool industrial tribunal, in which she argued that she was entitled to equality of pay with a group of male tradesmen (painter, engineer and joiner) employed at the same establishment. The tribunal found, after considering the report of a job evaluation carried out by an independent expert appointed by the tribunal, that her work was of equal value to that done by the men with whom she sought comparision, and granted her a declaration that her pay was to be brought into line with theirs. Apart from its symbolic importance as the first successful equal value claim, the decision deserves study not so much because of its standing as a legal precedent, but as an illustration of the right (and wrong) ways to go about approaching some of the central issues likely to arise in an equal value claim.

In the Hayward case the expert based his report and his finding in support of the applicant on a job evaluation which was, by his own admission, straightforward and simple. Taking the different jobs under comparison, he analysed them in terms of different demands made on the employee – physical, environmental, planning and decision making, skill and knowledge – and ranked each demand as 'low', 'intermediate' or 'high'. The employer tried to dispute the adequacy of such a simple approach, but was not sympathetically received by the tribunal, which took a very definite non-interventionalist line. Adopting a view which mirrors that of the Employment Appeal Tribunal's most recently expressed attitude to the issue of fairness in unfair dismissal, the tribunal noted the absence of guidance in the statutory provisions themselves, and indicated it would intervene to correct an expert only when he had gone 'badly wrong' – something which it refused to find on the facts of the case before it. By stressing the importance of what it termed 'industrial common sense' in assessing the issue of equal value, the tribunal's decision emphasises what many writers have already noted – the fact that the wide discretion vested in the expert by the legislation and his key role in the proceedings makes it exceedingly difficult to challenge his conclusions on equal value.

8 Collective bargaining

The collective bargaining process

Collective bargaining can be defined as negotiations about working conditions and terms of employment between an employer (or representatives of employers) and one (or more) organisations representing the employees, with a view to obtaining an agreement. Collective bargaining is a method of jointly determining working conditions and terms of employment, rather then unilateral determination by just one side. While collective bargaining can take place with a single employer, a group of employers or an employer organisation, it does require a collective organisation for the employees.

Agreements arrived at as a result of collective bargaining are only a part of the rules governing employment and working conditions. Other sources of such rules are government statutes and regulations, rules determined unilaterally by employers and also by trade unions, arbitration awards and general custom and practice.

Agreements arrived at by collective bargaining can however he considered to have certain advantages over rules determined by other means. These are:

1 Those directly affected by the rules participate, through their representatives, in determining them.
2 Collective agreements can be designed to fit the requirements of particular industries or particular companies.
3 They do not rely for their interpretation and application on the legal system, the spirit of an agreement often being the main emphasis rather than the precise wording.

Collective bargaining does however have some problems. It is considered for example to:

1 Reduce managerial freedom of action.
2 Reduce the effects of market forces and thus, in the opinion of some, act as a cause off inflation.
3 Allow the better organised and more powerful employee groups to gain better rewards at the expense of the less well organised and less powerful groups.

Bargaining structures

It is possible to identify a basic structure or framework in which collective bargaining occurs. Four features have been identified (Department of Employment Manpower Paper No 5, 1971, *The reform of collective bargaining at Plant and Company Level*).

1 Bargaining level

This term refers to the levels at which bargaining occurs within an industry or organisation. Thus bargaining could take place nationally, at the level of a particular company, or at the level of a particular department in a company, etc. There may, for instance, be a national agreement on minimum pay levels and an agreement on a bonus scheme at company level.

2 Bargaining unit

This term refers to the specific group or categories of employees covered by a particular agreement. Bargaining units may be broad, e.g. a single unit covering all the manual workers in a company, or narrow, e.g. just the process workers. The structure of the bargaining units will vary from one bargaining level to another. Also the bargaining unit may depend on the type of agreement concerned. Thus a very broad bargaining unit, e.g. all the employees in a company, might be concerned with an agreement for the length of the working week, but wage rates might be handled with very small bargaining units within that company, particularly if piece rates are involved.

3 Bargaining scope

This term refers to the range of topics regulated by collective bargaining, as opposed to those determined by other means. Thus, for example, the bargaining scope might include issues like wages, hours, the working week, overtime rates, disciplinary procedures, redundancies, etc. but might exclude other issues such as manning levels, training, working methods, etc.

4 Bargaining forms

This term refers to the forms in which agreements are expressed, e.g. written and formally signed, unwritten and informally understood, etc.

To illustate the above consider the electrical supply industry. The bargaining level is national and involves five bargaining units: the national joint industrial council for manual workers, the national joint council for administrative and clerical staff, the national joint board for technical engineering staff, the national joint committee for building and civil engineering workers and the national joint committee for managerial and higher executive grades. The bargaining scope is very wide and the bargaining form, written and formally signed.

The development of collective bargaining

In Britain collective bargaining has been evolving over many years, ever since the early developments of trade unions in the early nineteenth century when the unions were struggling to establish the principle of being able to negotiate on behalf of their members. The second half of the nineteenth century saw the emergence of conciliation boards, i.e. meetings of employers with trade union representatives, to negotiate working conditions and terms of employment. At the beginning of the twentieth century employers' associations emerged as a negotiating factor on an industry basis.

Near the end of the First World War the reports of the Whitley Committee, 1917–1918, advocated the development of joint negotiating committees at industry level, and in next few years many such committees were established. These reports were instrumental in persuading many employers to recognise trade unions and become involved in negotiations with them.

In 1965 a Royal Commission was set up which produced a report in 1968, referred to as the Donovan report. They suggested that in practice there were two systems of industrial relations in Britain, one being the formal system based on industry-wide collective bargaining at national level, and the other the informal system of bargaining between managers, shop stewards and work groups at the place of work. The formal system assumes industry-wide organisations capable of imposing their decisions on their members. According to the Commission these two systems of collective bargaining are in conflict, with the informal system undermining the formal system. Symptoms of this conflict were the failure of national disputes procedures to contain unoffocial strikes at company level, the persistence of restrictive labour practices and low productivity, and the gap between nationally agreed rates and actual earnings at the workplace. To remedy this they proposed a more orderly approach to local collective bargaining over such issues as incentive schemes, hours, the use of job evaluation, work practices, the linking of pay to performance, facilities for shop stewards and disciplinary rules and procedures. They did not consider that such issues could be dealt with effectively by national bargaining but recommended that comprehensive company agreements should be negotiated, with national agreements being only used for those matters which could effectively be nationally determined. Thus a two-tier structure of collective bargaining was advocated.

In 1979 the Labour government published its white paper 'In place of strife'. This took account of the Donovan proposals but included some important differences. The Donovan report relied on voluntary reform and did not advocate legislation. The Labour government proposed 'cooling-off' periods in the case of strikes and strike ballots. Such proposals were however unacceptable to the trade unions. Before the proposals could be considered for legislation there was a change of government. In 1980 the Conservative government introduced more comprehensive legislation in their Industrial Relations Act, 1971. The act however proved unworkable. The Trade Unions Act, 1984 introduced legislation requiring ballots to be held before any industrial action could be taken. In the absence of such a ballot a union would be liable to civil legal actions for damages. All attempts, so far, to legislate on aspects of collective bargaining have run into problems with the unions who are strong advocates of the need for voluntary arrangements.

Negotiations

Trade unions leaders are essentially concerned with establishing or maintaining satisfactory relations with the members and the employers with which they are concerned. Satisfactory relations with members involves them in maintaining or improving an existing relationship between their wages and those paid to other workers, especially other workers which the union members implicity regard as their standard of comparision. Satisfactory relationships with employers are also necessary as each party has to assume that the other is going to be around for some time and there will be further negotiations in the future. The employers in such negotiations might be thought of as trying to find the wage levels which would lead to the greatest profits, however it is more likely that they are merely attempting to find the wages levels which will secure the desired quantity and quality of labour and at the same time not so high a level as would put them at a disadvantage in the market for the products of the company. Thus in negotiations both the trade unions and the employers are looking at what others earn and what others charge, hence an obvious way both parties have in arriving at a wage level is by imitation, i.e. doing what the others do.

In considering negotiation on wages between unions and employers there are probably three main factors involved:

1　Both parties are going to be around for some time and there will be further negotiations between them in the future.
2　A work stoppage is costly to both parties; the anticipated gains from such a stoppage must therefore over a period of time be greater than the losses due to the stoppage.
3　Both parties are looking for a settlement they can live with, in the case of the employer one that will not put him or her at a disadvantage with

regard to his or her competitors and in the case of the union one that compares well with that obtained by other workers.

In wage negotiations both parties will generally make comparisons with other parties, for example:

1 The wage rates in other companies.
2 The traditional relationship between the wages paid by the firm and those paid in other firms.
3 Changes in the cost of living.
4 Worker productivity in comparison with competitors.
5 The effect of wage levels on product prices in relation to those of competitors and the consequential effect of being higher priced than competitors.

Industrial action

The term *industrial action* is used to describe some action taken by a union or its members in furtherance of a trade dispute. Possible forms of such action are:

1 An overtime ban

The members still get their basic wage but by banning overtime may be able to disrupt production schedules and cause problems to the management.

2 Working to rule

Because of the complexity of many organisation rules workers can often very effectively slow down operations in a company by working slavishly to the rules.

3 Go-slow

By slowing down the pace of their work the workers may be able to cause considerable disruption in a company.

4 Strikes

This is the complete withdrawal of labour by the workers. A strike is said to be official if it is called or sanctioned by the union concerned, and unofficial if it has no union backing.

5 Lock out

This is where the employer closes the place of work and in doing so prevents the workers from working and receiving remuneration.

6   *Sit-ins*

This is where the workers move into the company and occupy its premises. In so doing they prevent work being done by any employees whether they are involved in the action or not.

Picketing

The legal right of union members to establish a picket in a strike was established as long ago as 1875. However in the 1970s *picketing* took on a number of new forms, widespread use being made in disputes of flying pickets and both mass and secondary picketing. Flying pickets are where coaches and cars are used to enable large numbers of pickets to descend on a particular place, a noticeable example of this being the 1972 miners' strike when very large numbers of pickets descended on the Saltley gasworks and prevented it operating. The term *mass picketing* is used when very large numbers of pickets are used, often attempting to block all entry to the place being picketed. *Secondary picketing* is when the place being picketed is not directly involved in the dispute. Thus the example quoted of the Saltley gasworks was both mass and secondary picketing. The Saltley gasworks was a long way from any mine. The effect of these forms of picketing was a change in the law relating to picketing in the Employment Act, 1980.

The 1980 Act stated that it was still lawful for strikers and associated trade union officials to picket at their own workplace but it effectively barred secondary picketing. Enforcement of the law was however in the hands of those picketed, not the police. The Act restated the purpose of picketing as being to give and receive information and, peacefully to persuade workers to abstain from working.

In addition to the 1980 Act a Department of Employment Code of Practice was issued which sets out guidelines for picketing. This proposes that there should be no mass picketing, that pickets should not exceed six in number. This is not a legal limit but the police were given discretionary powers to limit the number of pickets. The role of the police was merely to uphold the law and not to take sides, they had however no responsibility for enforcing the civil law. Thus secondary picketing was deemed to be a civil law issue and not a criminal law issue, hence action rests with those wronged and not the police.

There are however some aspects of picketing which can involve the criminal law and so involve prosecution by the police. Obstruction of the highway, being a public nuisance, obstructing the police in their duties and criminal damage are examples of such actions.

To illustrate the above and also to indicate the type of information contained in the Code, the following is an extract from that Code.

The law does not impose a specific limit on the number of people who may picket at any one place; nor does the Code affect in any way the discretion of the police to limit the number of people on a particular picket line. It is for the police to decide, taking into account all the circumstances, whether the number of pickets at any particular place is likely to lead to a breach of the peace. If a picket does not leave the picket line when asked to do so by the police, he is liable to be arrested for obstruction either of the highway or of a police officer in the execution of his duty if the obstruction is such as to cause, or be likely to cause, a breach of the peace.

Closed shop

A *closed shop* is said to exist when there is at a place of work a 100 per cent membership of recognised trade unions (not necessarily all the same union) and there is an agreement between the unions concerned and the employer that this situation should be maintained. The term pre-entry closed shop is used where the company could only employ new workers if they were already members of the appropriate union. The term *post-entry closed shop* is used where a non-union person, or member of a different union, may be appointed but must join the appropriate union within a given time.

There are some people who consider that the closed shop is a violation of the liberty of the individual – in such a situation you can only work if you belong to a union and if that union expels you then you cannot work. On the other hand in collective bargaining all the workers are represented by the union, or unions, and thus there is a strong bargaining unit for the employees.

Prior to 1971 and the Industrial Relations Act there were no laws relating to the closed shop. The 1971 Act declared the closed shop to be, with a few exceptions, illegal and introduced a legal right for an individual not to belong to a union. This act was repealed by the Labour government in 1974 when legal protection was given to the closed shop and dismissal because an individual did not belong to a union in a closed shop situation was regarded as fair. The 1980 Employment Act, by the Conservative government, allowed an individual not to join a union (a) on grounds of conscience or other deeply held conviction and (b) in cases where a new closed shop agreement was introduced after the Act came into effect without that agreement having been approved by at least 80 per cent of those eligible to be covered by it in a secret ballot. The 1982 Act further widened the grounds for lawful objection to an individual joining a union and allowed Industrial Tribunals to make unions pay compensation where an employee was dismissed unfairly by virtue of the action of a trade union.

ACAS

ACAS, the Advisory, Conciliation and Arbitration Service, was set up by the Employment Protection Act of 1975. It was charged with the general duty of promoting the improvement of industrial relations and, in particular, of encouraging the extension of collective bargaining and the development and, where necessary, reform of collective bargaining machinery. Under this remit ACAS provides a wide range of services:

1   They can intervene in industrial disputes at the request of one or more of the parties involved with the aim of bringing about a settlement through collective conciliation between employers and unions.

2   They can offer conciliation in cases between individual employees and their employers (see the previous chapter and discussion of the role of Industrial Tribunals).

3   They can provide facilities for arbitration, mediation and investigation into trade disputes.

4   They can provide advisory work for employers and unions on such matters as disputes and disciplinary procedures, contracts of employment, etc.

5   They issue Codes of Practice containing guidance for promoting improvement in industrial relations. There have been, for instance, codes issued on picketing and the closed shop.

6   They can undertake enquiry work aimed at improving industrial relations in particular industries or companies. Thus, for example, in 1976 they mounted a major inquiry into the industrial relations situation in the newspaper printing industry.

The Employment Act 1982

In order to give an indication of the type of legislation with which unions and employers have to be concerned, the following are some extracts (Crown Copyright and reprinted by permission of the Controller of Her Majesty's Stationary Office) from the Employment Act 1982.

58.–(1) Subject to subsection (3), the dismissal of an employee by an employer shall be regarded for the purposes of this Part as having been unfair if the reason for it (or, if more than one, the principal reason) was that the employee –
(a) was, or proposed to become a member of an independent trade union, or
(b) had taken part, or proposed to take part, in the activities of an independent trade union at an appropriate time, or
(c) was not a member of any trade union, or of a particular trade union, or of one of a number of particular trade unions, or had refused or proposed to refuse to become or remain a member.
(2) In subsection (1) 'an appropriate time', in relation to an employee taking part in the activities of a trade union, means a time which either –
(a) is outside his working hours, or

(b) is a time within his working hours at which, in accordance with arrangements agreed with or consent given by his employer, it is permissible for him to take part in those activities;

and in this subsection 'working hours', in relation to an employee, means any time when, in accordance with his contract of employment, he is required to be at work.

(3) Subject to the following provisions of this section, the dismissal of an employee by an employer shall be regarded for the purposes of this Part as having been fair if –

(a) it is the practice, in accordance with a union membership agreement, for employees of the employer who are of the same class as the dismissed employee to belong to a specified independent trade union, or to one of a number of specified independent trade unions; and

(b) the reason (or, of more than one, the principal reason) for the dismissal was that the employee was not, or had refused or proposed to refuse to become or remain, a member of a union in accordance with the agreement; and

(c) the union membership agreement had been approved in relation to employees of that class in accordance with section 58A through a ballot held within the period of five years ending with the time of dismissal.

(4) Subsection (3) shall not apply if the employee genuinely objects on grounds of conscience or other deeply-held personal conviction to being a member of any trade union whatsoever or of a particular trade union.

(5) Subsection (3) shall not apply if the employee –

(a) has been among those employees of the employer who belong to the class to which the union membership agreement relates since before the agreement had the effect of requiring them to be or become members of a trade union, and

(b) has not at any time while the agreement had that effect been a member of a trade union in accordance with the agreement.

(6) Subsection (3) shall not apply if. . . .

58A– (1) Subject to the following provisions of this section, a union membership agreement shall be taken for the purposes of section 58 (3) (c) to have been approved in relation to the employees of any class of an employer if a ballot has been held on the question whether the agreement should apply in relation to them and either –

(a) not less than 80 per cent of those entitled to vote, or

(b) not less than 85 per cent of those who voted,

voted in favour of the agreement's application.

(2) Subsection (1) (b) shall not apply if the agreement –

(a) has not previously been approved in accordance with this section in relation to the employer's employees of the class in question, and

(b) came into force in relation to them after 14 August 1980.

(3) The persons entitled to vote in a ballot under this section, in relation to the application of a union membership agreement to the employees of any class of an employer, shall be all those employees who belong to that class and who –

(a) in the case of a ballot in which votes may only be cast on one day, are in the employment of the employer on that day; or

(b) in any other case, are in that employment on the qualifying day.

(4) 'Qualifying day' means the day specified as such by the person conducting the ballot; but no day shall be specified which –
(a) falls after the last of the days on which votes may be cast in the ballot; or
(b) is so long before that date as to be unreasonable in relation to that ballot.
(5) A ballot under this section shall be so conducted as to secure that, so far as reasonably practicable, all those entitled to vote –
(a) have an opportunity of voting, and of doing so in secret; and
(b) in a case which does not fall within subsection (3) (a), know, before they cast their votes, which day has been specified as the qualifying day.
(6) . . . .

Revision questions

1 Explain what is meant by *collective bargaining*.

2 List some of the advantages and some of the disadvantages of collective bargaining over agreements arrived at by other processes.

3 With reference to bargaining structures explain what is meant by the terms bargaining level, bargaining unit, bargaining scope and bargaining form.

4 What were the main features of the Donovan report?

5 List five forms industrial action may take.

6 What is meant by *flying pickets, mass picketing* and *secondary picketing*?

7 In what way can picketing involve criminal law?

8 What is meant by a *closed shop*?

9 Distinguish between pre-entry and post-entry closed shops.

10 What are the main functions of ACAS?

11 Outline the main effect of the Employment Act 1982 on the closed shop.

Assignments and further questions

1 For a particular company identify the various aspects of the bargaining structure.

2 Write notes on the content and problems arising from (a) the Labour government's white paper in 1979 'In place of strife' and (b) the Conservative government's Industrial Relations Act 1971.

3 Trace the history of a specific example of industrial action, from cause to solution.

4 Discuss these two opposing statements, (a) from a trade union point of

view picketing is essential in promulgating the views of those on strike, (b) from an employer's point of view picketing is just mob rule and should be banned.

5 Present arguments both for and against the closed shop.

6 Obtain a copy of the Employment Act, 1982 and write a precis of its main aspects.

7 Consider yourself to be presenting a case for a wage increase in a particular company. Outline the arguments that would form the basis of your approach.

8 Consider yourself to be an employer, presented with the demand from a trade union for a closed shop. What procedures, according to the Employment Act, 1982, must be followed?

9 The following are extracts taken from the January 1983 journal *Topics*, published by the Employment Relations Resource Centre: they give a government view, and a trade union view of the Employment Act, 1982. Discuss and compare these two views.

A government view

The general approach of the 1982 Act is particularly evident in the changes which it makes to trade union immunities. And one point is worth making straight-away. The legality of by far the most common form of industrial action in this country – that is action by employees against their own employer about their pay or other conditions of employment – is totally unaffected by the Act.

What the Act does is once again to tackle particular abuses. Thus it affects industrial action where an employer has no dispute with his own employees; industrial action taken mainly for political reasons; and industrial action taken in response to certain disputes overseas. All these types of action have one thing in common – they generally involve a dispute which the employer can do little if anything about. And yet he has to pick up the tab along with his customers and suppliers for the disruption caused. That is why the Act provides that there is a lawful trade dispute only if it is between workers and their own employer and is wholly or mainly about matters such as the workers' pay, jobs or conditions.

A trade union view

The Thatcher Government is deeply and fundamentally anti-trade union. Most of her Government's domestic policies are geared to attempting to corral trade unions into manageable pens. This is the purpose of the Employment Acts of 1980 and 1982. This is a major aim of the Government's economic policies.

10 M. Marchington and R. Armstrong in an article in *Topics*, November

1983, (published by the Employment Relations Resource Centre) make the point 'the importance of building strong bargaining relations and the commitment to jointly agreed procedures should outweigh any short-term tactical victories'. Discuss and explain this statement.

9 Health and safety at work

The historical development of safety legislation

Legislation to protect workers dates back more than a century. There was, for example, a Factories Act in 1833. This included a limit on the employment of children in the textile industry of ten hours per day. There was however a problem in implementing such legislation and thus in 1833 a limited form of state factory inspection was established. Over the years a piecemeal approach to safety legislation occurred, with no coherent and consistent policy. By 1970 there were thus some 30 Acts of Parliament, 500 statutory sets of regulations and seven separate inspectorates. The Acts were the means by which Parliament gave ministers powers to issue the statutory regulations.

With the exception of the mining industry the legislation had the following basic characteristics:

1 A basic statutory code, supplemented by regulations relating to technical matters concerned with the physical environment of the workplace.
2 Enforcement by a specialist inspectorate with powers to enter premises, ask questions and prosecute offenders.
3 Reliance on petty criminal financial sanctions for punishment.
4 Legal responsibilities usually imposed upon organisations and not on managers or officials.
5 The imposition of general responsibility upon the employers for what went on within their own premises.

A problem with this type of legislation was that the people who might be directly responsible for contravening the legislation, e.g. the managers and the supervisors, were not liable to prosecution. It was the employers who were prosecuted.

During the 1960s there was increasing concern about Britain's poor record in health and safety at work. There was also concern about the piecemeal approach to legislation that existed at that time. In 1970 Lord Robens was asked by the government to chair a commission to investigate the situation. Its terms of reference were very wide: to review the provisions made for securing health and safety at work, to consider what changes were needed in existing legislation, to examine the nature and extent of voluntary action by management and employees in securing safe working conditions, and to state what steps should be taken to protect the safety of the general public as well as employees.

The Robens' report criticised the existing legislation and proposed:

1 There needed to be a systematic approach to legislation rather than the piecemeal, empirical, approach that was then being used. There was too much specialised legislation and it should be replaced by a single general law.
2 The present legislation was too complex and the mass of detail should be replaced by a few simple precepts.
3 Enforcement procedures were inadequate. The emphasis should be placed on prevention rather on prosecution.
4 Previous legislation had concentrated on the workplace, safety legislation needs also to protect the public in general.
5 Stress should be placed on management's responsibilities for providing and maintaining safe systems of working.
6 The previous system had not involved the workforce in the safety effort; nothing but good could result from their active involvement.

The outcome of the Robens' report was the Health and Safety at Work Act, 1974.

The Health and Safety at Work Act, 1974

The Act consists of four parts, Part I being concerned with health, safety and welfare in connection with work and the control of dangerous substances and certain emissions into the atmosphere; Part II is concerned with the Employment Medical Advisory Service; Part III with the Building Regulations and Amendment of Building (Scotland) Act, 1959 and Part IV with miscellaneous and general matters. The Act did not immediately replace earlier legislation and regulations but allowed them to remain current until revoked and replaced by new regulations or Codes of Practice issued under the Act.

Part I of the Act has four basic objectives:

1 To secure the health, safety and welfare of people at work.
2 To protect persons other than persons at work against risks to health or safety arising out of or in connection with the activities of those at work.
3 To control the keeping and use of explosive or highly flammable or otherwise dangerous substances and generally prevent the unlawful acquisition, possession and use of such substances.

4 To control the emission into the atmosphere of noxious or offensive substances.

As the above indicates, this Act is much broader in scope than previous legislation, covering all people at work rather than just one particular category of people engaged in some specific working activity. It also extends to the covering of the general public.

Part I of the Act establishes the general duties of employers.

2 – (1) It shall be the duty of every employer to ensure, so far as is reasonably practicable, the health, safety and welfare at work of all his employees.

(2) Without prejudice to the generality of an employer's duty under the preceding subsection, the matters to which that duty extends include in particular –

(a) the provision and maintenance of plant and systems of work that are, so far as is reasonably practicable, safe and without risk to health;

(b) arrangements for ensuring, so far as is reasonably practicable, safety and absence of risks to health in connection with the use, handling, storage and transport of articles and substances;

(c) the provision of such information, instruction, training and supervision as is necessary to ensure, so far as is reasonably practicable, the health and safety at work of his employees;

(d) so far as is reasonably practicable as regards any place of work under the employer's control, the maintenance of it in a condition that is safe and without risks to health and the provision and maintenance of means of access and egress from it that are safe and without such risks;

(e) the provision and maintenance of a working environment for his employees that is, so far as is reasonably practicable, safe, without risks to health, and adequate as regards facilities and arrangements for their welfare at work.

In addition the employer must also undertake other duties:

1 Provide a written statement of the organisation's general policy with respect to the health and safety of the employees and how it will be carried out.
2 Safety representatives elected from and by the employees have to be consulted by the employer on safety matters.
3 If the safety representatives so request, a safety committee must be established.

Part I also specifies that employers have general duties to conduct their business in such a way that persons not in their employment are not thereby exposed to risks to their health and safety. In addition, those responsible for places of work have duties with respect to those using the premises who are not their employees, e.g. visiting workers carrying out maintenance or repair.

For the first time a general duty is imposed on those who design, manufacture, import or supply any article for use at work:

(a) to ensure, so far as is reasonably practicable, that the article is so designed and constructed as to be safe and without risks to health when properly used;

(b) to carry out or arrange for the carrying out of such testing and examination as may be necessary for the performance of the duty imposed on him by the preceding paragraph;

(c) to take such steps as are necessary to secure that there will be available in connection with the use of the article at work adequate information about the use for which it is designed and has been tested, and about any conditions necessary to ensure that, when put to that use, it will be safe and without risks to health.

Employees also have duties with respect to health and safety at work.

7 It shall be the duty of every employee while at work –

(a) to take reasonable care for the health and safety of himself and of other persons who may be affected by his acts or omissions at work; and

(b) as regards any duty or requirement imposed on his employer or any other person by or under any of the relevant statutory provisions, to co-operate with him so far as is necessary to enable that duty or requirement to be performed or complied with.

The term employees covers everybody who is employed by an organisation, i.e. managers, supervisors and workers. This section of the Act could thus be invoked in the case of a supervisor who failed to implement some safe system of working or an operative who endangered others by the reckless use of some machine.

Two other general duties are imposed:

8 No person shall intentionally or recklessly interfere with or misuse anything provided in the interests of health, safety or welfare in pursuance of any of the relevant statutory provisions.

9 No employer shall levy or permit to be levied on any employee of his any charge in respect of anything done or provided in pursuance of any specific requirement of the relevant statutory provisions.

Thus, for instance, an employee removing the safety guards from a machine or playing about with a fire extinguisher could be prosecuted under this part of the Act.

Two bodies were set up by the Act: the Health and Safety Commission and the Health and Safety Executive. The Commission consists of a chairman appointed by the Secretary of State, three members resulting from consultations with organisations representing employers, three from consultations with organisations representing employees and up to three other members drawn from other activities. The Executive consists of three people, one appointed by the Commission to be the director of the Executive and the others appointed by the Commission after consulting the director.

The Commission is charged with the task of making arrangements for the carrying out of research, the provision of training and information, advisory services and the development of regulations. The Executive exercises on behalf of the Commission such of its functions as the Commission directs it to exercise e.g. carrying out investigations, and acting as a source of information.

An important aspect of the work of the Commission is the issuing of regulations and codes of practice. Regulations are legally binding; codes of practice are guidance. Failure to observe a code of practice does not render a person liable to criminal or civil proceedings but where that person has broken a general duty in the Act or regulations, the fact that he or she has failed to observe a code of practice is liable to be taken as conclusive evidence that he or she did not do all that was reasonably practicable to ensure the health and safety of those at work.

The task of enforcing the statutory provisions is given to the Executive, in co-operation with local authorities and other enforcement bodies. Every enforcing authority may appoint inspectors, each such inspector being given a written document specifying his or her powers. The powers can vary from inspector to inspector. If so required, in the execution of his or her duties an inspector should produce this document.

20 – (1) Subject to the provisions of section 19 and this section, an inspector may, for the purpose of carrying into effect any of the relevant statutory provisions within the field of responsibility of the enforcing authority which appointed him, exercise the powers set out in subsection (2) below.

(2) The powers of an inspector referred to in the preceding subsection are the following, namely –

(a) at any reasonable time (or, in a situation which in his opinion is or may be dangerous, at any time) to enter any premises which he has reason to believe it is necessary for him to enter for the purpose mentioned in subsection (1) above;

(b) to take with him a constable if he has reasonable cause to apprehend any serious obstruction in the execution of his duty;

(c) without prejudice to the preceding paragraph, on entering any premises by virtue of paragraph (a) above to take with him –

(i) any other person duly authorised by his the inspector's enforcing authority; and

(ii) any equipment or materials required for any purpose for which the power of entry is being exercised;

(d) to make such examination and investigation as may in any circumstances be necessary for the purpose mentioned in subsection (1) above;

(e) as regards any premises which he has the power to enter, to direct that those premises or any part of them, or anything therein, shall be left undisturbed (whether generally or in particular respects) for so long as is reasonably necessary for the purpose of any examination or investigation under paragraph (d) above;

(f) to take such measurements and photographs and make such recordings as he considers necessary for the purpose of any examination or investigation under paragraph (d) above;

(g) to take samples of any articles or substances found in any premises which he has the power to enter, and of the atmosphere in or in the vicinity of any such premises;

(h) in the case of any article or substance found it any premises which he has power to enter, being an article or substance which appears to him to have caused or to be likely to cause danger to health or safety, to cause it to be dismantled or subjected to any process of test (but not so as to damage or destroy it unless this is in circumstances necessary for the purpose mentioned in subsection (1) above);

(i) in the case of any such article or substance as is mentioned in the preceding paragraph, to take possession of it and detain it for so long as is necessary for all or any of the following purposes, namely –

(i) to examine it and do to it anything which he has power to do under that paragraph;

(ii) to ensure that it is not tampered with before his examination of it is completed;

(iii) to ensure that it is available for use as evidence in any proceedings relating to a notice under section 21 or 22;

(j) to require any person whom he has reasonable cause to believe to be able to give any information relevant to any examination or investigation under paragraph (d) above to answer (in the absence of persons other than a person nominated by him to be present and any persons whom the inspector may allow to be present) such questions as the inspector thinks fit to ask and to sign a declaration of truth of his answers;

(k) to require the production of, inspect, and take copies of or of any entry in–

(i) any books or documents which by virtue of any of the relevant statutory provisions are required to be kept; and

(ii) any other books or documents which it is necessary for him to see for the purposes of any examination or investigation under paragraph (d) above;

(l) to require any person to afford him such facilities and assistance with respect to any matter or things within that person's control or in relation to which that person has responsibilities as are necessary to enable the inspector to exercise any of the powers conferred on him by this section;

(m) any other power which is necessary for the purpose mentioned in subsection (1) above.

If as a result of an investigation an inspector considers a situation to be contravening relevant statutory provisions he or she may serve an improvement notice requiring the situation to be remedied. This notice must be acted on within the time specified in it, or else an appeal lodged with an Industrial Tribunal. If at the end of the specified time the notice has not been acted on a criminal offence will have been committed. If the situation involves, in the inspector's opinion, a serious risk of personal injury he or she may issue a prohibition notice. Such a notice requires the activity concerned to cease until the situation has been remedied. Appeals can be lodged against such notices with an Industrial Tribunal.

Failure to comply with notices can result in prosecution and fines and/or imprisonment.

The safety representatives and safety committees regulations, 1977

As part of its work the Health and Safety Commission submitted proposals for the above regulations to the Secretary of State. After some modifications the regulations were accepted by Parliament and came into effect. These are an example of the types of regulations that arise from the Health and Safety at Work Act, 1974.

A recognised trade union may appoint safety representatives from amongst the employees in all cases where one or more employees are employed by an employer. These representatives have the following functions:

(a) To be consulted by the employer with regard to making and maintaining arrangements which will enable the employer and the employees to co-operate effectively in promoting and developing measures to ensure health and safety at work.
(b) To investigate potential hazards and dangerous occurrences at the workplace and to investigate the causes of accidents at the workplace.
(c) To investigate complaints made by any employee he or she represents regarding that employee's health, safety or welfare at work.
(d) To make representations to the employer regarding any issues arising from such investigations and on general matters.
(e) To carry out inspections in accordance with the regulations.
(f) To represent the employees in consultations with inspectors and receive information from those inspectors.
(g) To attend meetings of safety committees.

The regulations require employers to make available to safety representatives the information they need to be able to fulfill their functions. However there are some types of information which an employer need not provide, e.g. information for which the disclosure would be against interests of national security or where it could cause substantial injury to an employer's undertaking.

Employers must give safety representatives time off, with pay, during their normal working hours to the extent necessary for them to carry out their functions and also for them to undergo training.

An employer has to establish a safety committee when at least two safety representatives request it. The functions of such committees are covered by a guidance note issued by the Commission. They might thus include:

(a) The study of accident and disease statistics in the workforce so that reports can be made to management on unsafe and unhealthy conditions and practices, with recommendations for corrective action.
(b) Examination of safety audit reports.
(c) Consideration of the reports and information provided by inspectors.

(d) Consideration of reports from safety representatives.
(e) Assistance with the development of works safety rules and systems of work.
(f) A watch on the effectiveness of the safety content of employee training and on the adequacy of safety and health communications at the workplace.
(g) The provision of a link with the appropriate inspectorates.

The Factories Act, 1961

The Health and Safety at Work Act, 1974 is, as new regulations and codes of practice come into effect, steadily replacing previous legislation. Until all has been replaced the older Acts are still in force. An important Act in this context is the Factories Act, 1961. The following are some of the provisions included within that Act:

1   An abstract of the Act and certain prescribed information must be kept posted at the principal entrance of a factory.
2   Every factory must be kept clean and free from drain smells; dirt and refuse to be removed daily and workroom floors cleaned weekly.
3   Each worker should have a minimum space of 400 cubic feet, no space higher than 14 feet above the floor being counted. This rule is to avoid overcrowding.
4   After the first hour a temperature of 60°F (15.5°C) is to be maintained where work people are sitting down most of the time. This has later been amended to include an upper limit of 66.2°F or 19°C.
5   Adequate ventilation and suitable lighting must be provided.
6   There must be sufficient and suitable conveniences provided.
7   Adequate drinking water must be provided with facilities for washing.
8   Accommodation for clothing not worn during working hours must be made available.
9   First aid equipment must be provided and maintained.
10   All stairs, passages and gangways are to be kept free from obstruction.
11   Safe means of access must be provided to every workplace.
12   Also included were provisions regarding the safe use of machinery e.g. all dangerous parts of machinery should be securely fenced.

Revision questions

1   What were the basic characteristics of the legislation concerning safety prior to the Health and Safety at Work Act, 1974?
2   How in essence did the Health and Safety at Work Act, 1974 differ from previous legislation concerning health and safety at work?

3 What were the basic objectives of Part I of the Health and Safety at Work Act, 1974?

4 What were the general duties imposed by the Health and Safety at Work Act, 1974 on (a) the employers and (b) the employees?

5 What are the functions of (a) the Health and Safety Commission and (b) the Health and Safety Executive?

6 What are the duties of inspectors appointed according to the Health and Safety at Work Act, 1974?

7 Explain the functions of (a) improvement notices and (b) prohibition notices.

8 What are the general functions of safety representatives?

Assignments and further questions

1 Obtain from a company its policy documents for safety and critically discuss them in the light of the Health and Safety at Work Act, 1974.

2 Obtain an accident report form from a company and critically discuss its format.

3 Obtain a code of practice and discuss the implications of the application of the code for both employers and employees.

4 Determine how a safety committee actually functions in a company.

5 Carry out an analysis of the safety policy in a company, in all its aspects.

6 Discuss the following situations and consider what actions should be taken or what consequences could occur.
   (a) A worker removes the safety guards from a machine because they reduce the number of items he can produce and hence his wages, which are based on piece-rate.
   (b) The frequency of accidents in the machine shop is very high.
   (c) The company is short of storage space for a large consigment of goods that have just arrived and so they temporarily stack them in the passage ways leading to the main exit from the factory floor.
   (d) A worker is just about to become married and in celebration the fellow workers let off the fire extinguishers.
   (e) An inspector wants to go into the tool room but the management tell him that they will not allow it because the work there is commercially highly secret and he might tell their competitors.
   (f) An inspector wants to talk to a worker about his machine but the worker refuses to talk to him.

(g) The trade union representing most of the workers in a company appoints a safety representative. However the management say that they will not allow him to have any time off for safety matters during work hours.

(h) A visitor to the company trips over a box lying in a gangway and sprains his ankle.

(i) People living near a factory complain about the smell coming from the factory.

(j) Business is booming so the management take on extra workers and pack large numbers of them into a small room by reducing the number of gangways. The workers are very unhappy about the conditions resulting from this.

(k) An inspector has put a prohibition notice on a particular machine. The management however consider that they cannot stop using the machine because of the consequential effect on production targets. They therefore continue to use the machine.

Part Three   Communications

This part of the book consists of four chapters on communications in organisations.

Chapter 10 Principles of communication.   This chapter considers the basic principles of communication: the stages involved in communicating, interpersonal communication, transactional analysis, communication in groups, communication chains, the functions of language and non-verbal communication.

Chapter 11 Meetings.   This chapter considers the types of meetings that take place in organisations, committees, the processes that take place in groups, and interview and grievance handling meetings.

Chapter 12 Written and graphical communication.   The basic characteristics of internal and external written communications are considered, in particular report writing and designing forms and letters.

Chapter 13 Management information systems.   This is a brief consideration of management information systems, i.e. a computer-based information system.

10   Principles of communication

Stages in communication

With regard to an organisation, communication can be considered as the means whereby people in an organisation exchange information and transmit meanings regarding the operations of the enterprise. It is important to realise that communication is not just about exchanging information; unless the person receiving the information understands its meaning no effective communication has taken place.

Communication can be considered to be a process involving a number of stages.

1   Conceiving the message, the information, that is to be communicated.
2   Encoding the message into a form that can be transmitted. Forms include the spoken word, the written word, numbers, drawings, symbols, and non-verbal forms such as expressions or gestures.
3   Selecting the communication channel through which the message is to be transmitted, e.g. the postal system, the telephone system, shouting.
4   Receiving and decoding the message. This involves establishing what the message forms used signify.
5   Interpreting the message, i.e. extracting the meaning.
6   Feedback to indicate to the sender that the receiver has received the message, decoded it and interpreted the meaning of it. Also that the receiver is ready for a further transmission.

One aspect that can affect the receiving and decoding of the message and so affect its interpretation is noise during the transmission. Thus if the communication channel used is the spoken word, if there is a lot of background noise due to perhaps machinery then there may be difficulty in decoding the message and so establishing what is being said.

Interpersonal communication

Consider the exchange of information of messages between two people, i.e. *interpersonal communication*. This is a frequent occurrence in an organisation, e.g. a supervisor giving orders to a worker, a worker selling an idea to a superior, etc. For effective communication the following points are worth bearing in mind:

1   Clarify your ideas before you start to communicate.

2   Choose the most appropriate form for transmitting the message. Thus would it be, for example, best to tell *X* or write a memo to *X*? Could you best convey the information about the material required for a product in words or by an annotated drawing?

3   Choose the most appropriate channel of communication. In choosing the most appropriate form for transmitting the message there is often an implied choice of the channel of communication.

4   So that the message can be decoded, make certain you choose a form of language that is fully comprehensible to the receiver

5   So that the message can be correctly interpreted by the receiver, ensure that the language you use avoids ambiguity, vagueness, etc. and precisely conveys the required message.

6   Check the feedback from the receiver. Does the feedback indicate that the message has been understood? The feedback might be non-verbal, e.g. the expression on the receiver's face indicates understanding of the message.

In interpersonal communication the following are some of the difficulties that can occur and act as barriers to effective communication.

1   The language used in the message may be incomprehensible to the receiver, e.g. technical terms may be used which are not known to the receiver.

2   The receiver may be unable to extract the meaning from the message because it is, for instance, all wrapped up in a long, complex, unordered piece of writing.

3   The speed of the transmission of the information may be too fast for the receiver. Time may be needed for assimilation.

4   The physical surroundings may intrude and inhibit effective communications, e.g. excessive noise.

5   Differences in perception of the message may occur between what the receiver thinks was transmitted and what was thought to have been transmitted. People often hear what they expect to hear rather than what was actually said.

6   Non-verbal communication may not be in agreement with the verbal communication. Thus, for instance, if the receiver nods his or her head

signalling agreement but saying no, then there is a conflict between the verbal and non-verbal communication which a receiver will have difficulty in interpreting. In interpersonal communications non-verbal communication plays a very significant part.

Transactional analysis

Transactional analysis is a useful approach to gaining an understanding of interpersonal behaviour, the theory originating in 1961 from the work of E. Berne. According to the theory all people have three *ego states*. They are essentially three types of person rolled into one and at any moment one of the three states can prevail over the other two. The three states are:

1   The parent ego state

When in the parent ego state a person acts and speaks like a parent, i.e. setting standards, controlling, nurturing. The type of language used by a person in this state includes words like 'we've always done it this way', 'why don't you listen', 'let me do that for you', 'don't worry', 'always', 'never', 'I'll tell you'.

2   The adult ego state

When in the adult ego state a person acts and speaks like an adult, i.e. cool, unemotional and independent. Such a person seeks and gives factual information, using logic to reach decisions. The type of language used by a person in this state includes words like 'why', 'where', 'when', 'Have you checked it', 'What can we predict'.

3   The child ego state

When in the child ego state a person acts and speaks like a child, i.e. is impulsive, complies with authority, is intuitive, creative, exhibits awe. The type of language used by a person in this state includes words like 'won't', 'don't blame me', 'it's all your fault', 'help me', 'terrific', 'not again'.

In all three ego states there are also different non-verbal behaviours. Thus in the parent ego state the tone of voice might be harsh or patronising, while in the adult ego state the tone is likely to be clear and calm and in the child ego state it can be rebellious or whining.

Any interaction between two people can be considered in terms of a transaction between their ego states. All such transactions can be then classified as either complementary, crossed or ulterior. Figure 10.1 shows examples of these three types.

With *complementary transactions* the ego state that is doing the sending is the same one as is being addressed by the other person. Thus, for example, the sender might be a manager in the parent ego state, perhaps stating that reports should be handed in on time, while the receiver is a

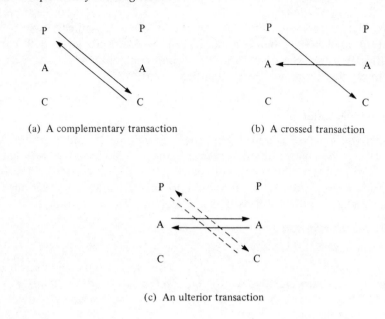

(a) A complementary transaction   (b) A crossed transaction

(c) An ulterior transaction

Figure 10.1   *The three types of transaction between ego states*

subordinate in the child ego state who might reply 'Yes, sir'. When both the participants in the communication are happy to act and react from the ego states that each perceives the other to be in then no problems occur.

With *crossed transactions* this is not the case. Communications between the two people do not have common origination and termination ego states in each person. Thus the sender might be a manager in the parent ego state and addressing a subordinate whom he wishes to be in the child state. However the subordinate reacts in the adult state, perhaps saying 'I'm not sure this can be done with the pressure of work'. He thus sends back a communication as if between two adults. The result of such crossed transactions is that the communication is hard to continue. Such transactions tend to be short lived and the two people either break off the transaction or revert to a complementary form.

With *ulterior transaction* more than one type of transaction may be going on at the same time. Thus though the words used might indicate a transaction between, say, two adult ego states there are hidden meanings and they involve perhaps a parent-to-child transaction.

Ulterior transactions are the basis of what Berne calls games. Games are recurring sets of transactions involving a complementary transaction, an ulterior transaction and a payoff. Thus for example, there is the game involving a manager and subordinates where the manager asks them for suggestions, apparently an adult-to-adult transaction. However each suggestion is met by a 'Yes, but' from the manager who argues that the suggestion is unacceptable. In the end the subordinates run out of ideas and the manager thus wins the game by having maintained power, as parent ego, over the subordinates.

Communication in groups

Consider a group situation, perhaps a supervisor speaking to a group of workers. Because of the size of the group not everybody may be able to see the non-verbal communication signals of the supervisor and also the supervisor may have difficulty in receiving feedback signals from all members of the group, so he or she might have difficulty in knowing whether everybody in the group has received and understood the message. There is also the problem that the same language or method of presenting the message may not be appropriate for every member of the group. Thus, for instance, showing them a technical drawing may be alright for those members who can read such drawings but may present great problems for those who have difficulty interpreting such drawings. Thus there are extra problems in communicating with groups when compared with interpersonal communication. These can be summarised as:

1 Non-verbal communication becomes difficult.
2 Feedback becomes difficult.
3 The group may not be homogeneous, hence a difficulty in determining the language level to be used.
4 Is the message for all members of the group or is it directed at some more than others?

Communication chains

One method of analysing communication in groups and organisations is in terms of *communication chains* or nets. Thus if we take a group of people – A, B, C, D, E – who communicates with whom in that group? We might have the situation that *A* is the group leader and all communications effectively flow to or from *A*. This situation can be described by Figure 10.2(a). We could have a group situation where everybody communicates equally with everybody else and there is no dominant communication path, Figure 10.2(b) illustrating that situation. Another possibility is that *A* communicates with *B* who then communicates with *C* who then communicates with *D* who then communicates with *E*, Figure 10.2(c) illustrating this. This last situation is common in organisations where a manager communicates to a deputy manager who communicates to a supervisor who then communicates to a worker.

Different forms of communication chains or nets have different characteristics. Thus, for instance, the arrangement described in Figure 10.2(a)

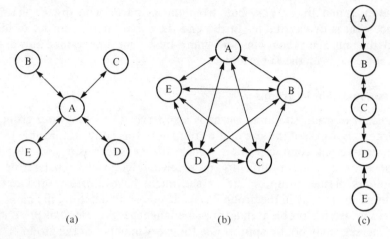

Figure 10.2

(a)   *A dominates communications*
(b)   *No dominant person*
(c)   *A linear chain of communication*

where all communications flow through one person (A) has the advantage of being a quick and accurate way of communicating, with A being the dominant person. This might describe communications between a managing director and four senior managers. With the system described by Figure 10.2(b) there is a completely decentralised structure with everybody contributing equally. This form of communication implies no leader. It is an effective method of communication where a problem has to be solved and all minds bear on the problem. The communication chain described by Figure 10.2(c) is a slow method of communicating information and can also be poor. It is slow since the information has to pass though many people, and as some misinterpretation might occur at any stage it can also be a poor method since the final communication arriving at the end of the chain might have become distorted.

Within any organisation there are likely to be a number of different types of communication nets in different parts of the organisation. The pattern will obviously depend on the degree of centralisation adopted by an organisation, the communication paths often, though not always, following the lines of authority.

The term *vertical communication* is used to describe the communication in an organisation that occurs from the top decision makers down to the employees at a lower level who have to implement the decisions and also the communication that occurs from the employees up to the decision makers. The term *horizontal communication* is used to describe the communication that occurs between employees who operate at the same or similar levels in the organisation.

Vertical communication in an organisation is a planned matter which is linked to the structure of the organisation. Horizontal communication might not always be planned but it invariably occurs. Unplanned horizontal communication might be called the grapevine and it is by such means that rumours spread rapidly. Such horizontal communication might be considerably faster than the vertical communication, since the horizontal communication net might be like Figure 10.2(b) while the vertical one is like Figure 10.2(c).

There are barriers which can restrict or distort communication in an organisation, for example:

1 Distortion occuring at each link in a linear chain so that the final message received is significantly different from the one that started.
2 Jumping links in a communication chain so that somebody or group affected by a decision is not consulted or communicated with.
3 Geographic distance, e.g. from one plant to another in a different locality, can mean that unless careful planning occurs proper communication does not always occur at all levels.
4 Task specialisation in a group may make it difficult for that group to communicate effectively to others.
5 Status differences may lead to someone not accepting communications from another person, or mistrusting the communication.
6 Competition between groups, e.g. for status, may lead to a lack of communication between them.

Formal and informal communications

Communications in organisations can be considered to be both formal and informal. *Formal communications* are those that can be considered official by the organisation. Such communications involve orders given by superiors to subordinates; inter-departmental communications concerning, for example, budget statements or work-in-hand statements; and communications received from outside the organisation which require processing, for example orders for products. *Informal communications* are not formally sanctioned but many of them are necessary for the effective running of the organisation. They are, for example, the informal day-to-day communications between people in different departments or within departments. There are however informal communications which are often not so desirable, these being the spreading of rumours, i.e. the grapevine.

The functions of language

Language can be considered to have two basic functions: the denotative and the connotative functions. The *denotative function* is where the meaning of a word is precisely what is indicated by the word. Science, for example, uses words in a precise manner, often defining the meanings of words so that there is no doubt about their meaning. The *connotative function* is where words have associated with them general ideas or feelings. Everyday language often uses words in this way. Words thus can have more than their literal meaning. Hence to interpret a communication involving words you need to establish whether they are being used in a denotative or connotative function and if connotative what the 'hidden' meanings are.

Language can be used in more specific functions. It can be used in an expressive function, the language then serving often not only to communicate information but also to express feelings. Swearing is an obvious example where the literal meaning of the words is generally irrelevant but the expression of feeling is not. Language can be used in a *directive function*, the language then being used to make something happen. In such cases there may be a mixture of connotative and denotative functions in the words used. Language can also be used in a *social function*, i.e. small talk. This can be used to establish social cohesion between people but also to establish social positions within a group. Language can also have a *ritual function*, words then being uttered because the situation requires those particular ones to be used. The origins of the ritual language may have become lost and the exact words irrelevant nowadays but ritual may demand that they still be used.

Language thus serves multiple functions and to understand a communication you need to establish what functions are being served by the language used.

Misuses of language

Language can be misused and thus lead to misunderstanding. The following are some examples:

1   Report, inference or judgement

When a statement is made there may be doubt as to whether it is a factual report, an inference or a judgement. Thus, for example, a statement – the components are faulty – might be a statement of fact because I have personally inspected them and found them to be faulty, or it might be an inference (because some machine is not working I deduce that the components must be faulty), or it could be my opinion that the components are likely to be faulty.

2   Words have different meanings

The same word can mean different things to different people, or perhaps different people will use different words for the same thing. Thus a correct understanding of the meaning of words can mean that a knowledge of the person using the words is required.

3 Generalising

Statements can often be generalisations about a situation based on just a knowledge of a few facts rather than all the facts. Thus the statement – all the components are faulty – might be a correct statement because all the components were inspected or it might be a generalisation based on a sample of the components being inspected.

4 Polarisation

Polarisation is when someone speaks about a situation as though it consisted of two extremes rather than as one containing graded variations.

5 Undelayed reaction

People often respond before they have had time to think through their reply. Thus the language might reflect their unconsidered view rather than their considered view.

Non-verbal communication

The term *non-verbal* is used for communications that involve no words or give added meanings to words. Such communications can be classified in a number of ways.

1 Body language

This includes body posture, gestures, touching, facial expressions, eye contact and gaze.

2 Voice quality

The way something is said, e.g. the pitch of the voice, speech rate.

3 The use and perception of space

For example, the manager who sits behind a big desk and keeps the employees distant is communicating differently to one who sits in close proximity to the employees.

4 Time

The timing of communications can be a non-verbal communication. Thus, for example, the manager who keeps an employee waiting before seeing him is communicating different non-verbal signals to one who sees him instantly.

To illustrate the above consider the following situations and the non-verbal communication element. When the supervisor talks to a subordinate the subordinate nods his head, the supervisor then concludes that the non-verbal communication from the subordinate is indicating agreement. When a supervisor reprimands two workers, worker *A* is seen to be clenching his fists while worker *B* is seen to be tapping his fingers on the desk. The supervisor might then conclude that worker *A* is angry but worker *B* is nervous. A worker goes to the supervisor and in a high pitched voice, speaking rapidly, tells him that the machine is at fault. The supervisor might then conclude that urgent action is needed, while if the words had been uttered in a low pitched voice, at a slow rate, he might have concluded that it was not urgent.

Non-verbal communication can:

1 Significantly affect the type of relationship that forms between people.
2 Express emotions.
3 Significantly affect the meanings of verbal communications.

Non-verbal communication can affect verbal communications in a number of ways. It might be used to accentuate the verbal message, to complement it or perhaps to contradict it. Thus the person who states 'I didn't do it' while looking very guilty by perhaps shifting nervously from one foot to the other is sending signals which might lead the receiver of the message to conclude that he or she did do it.

Revision questions

1 Outline the stages that can be involved in communication.

2 Explain how the stages involved in a communication apply to *interpersonal* communications.

3 List some of the barriers that can occur to effective interpersonal communication.

4 In what way does communication in groups differ from interpersonal communication?

5 What is meant by *communication chains* or nets?

6 Draw a diagram to illustrate the communication chains involved in a supervisor communicating to three foremen who each communicate to five workers.

7 Explain the difference between *vertical* and *horizontal communication* in an organisation.

8 Distinguish between *formal* and *informal communications* in an organisation and give examples of each type.

9 Explain the importance of *ego states* in transactional analysis.

10 Explain what is meant by language having two basic functions, the *denotative* and *connotative functions.*

11 Explain what is meant by *non-verbal communication* and give examples.

Assignments and further questions

1 Draw the communication nets for a part of a particular organisation and discuss the effectiveness of the arrangement.

2 Observe and analyse a discussion between two people, paying particular attention to the non-verbal communication used. Consider the effectiveness of the communication form used and the problem of decoding.

3 Identify a number of groups within an organisation and the ways in which they communicate with each other.

4 Identify the situations under which rumours are likely to occur and spread within an organisation.

5 Use transactional analysis to analyse discussions between two individuals.

6 Analyse a written or spoken communication and consider whether the language used is denotative or connotative.

7 Analyse a discussion between two people and identify the non-verbal parts of the discussion.

8 Write a note explaining to a supervisor the importance of non-verbal communication in dealings with subordinates.

11 Meetings

Formal and informal meetings

In the operation of any organisation there are invariably a large number of meetings in a variety of forms. Meetings can be classified as *formal* or *informal*, though in reality these two terms just represent the opposite ends of a continuous spectrum. With formal meetings there are rules of procedure and the meetings are fully documented; with informal meetings there are no formal rules of procedure and the outcomes of the meeting may not be fully documented.

Some companies are required to hold certain meetings as a result of government legislation, the precise rules of such meetings being specified in the company's articles. The rules will specify how the notice of the meeting should be given, the minimum number of members who must attend if business is to be conducted, the sort of business the meeting should conduct and when and where it should be held. This is thus an example of a formal meeting.

An example of an informal meeting might be a managerial meeting where a department manager meets with his or her staff to perhaps discuss department plans and progress. No rules are laid down for such meetings and there might be only a brief note of the outcomes as a reminder to those participating in the meeting.

The following are just a few of the possible types of meetings that might take place within an organisation, ranging from the very formal to the very informal.

1 **Company general meeting.**   Rules determined by the company's articles.

2 **Joint consultative committee.**   Negotiation meetings between trade unions and an employer or employers with agreed rules.

3 **Board of directors' meeting.**   Meeting of the directors of a company to agreed rules.

4 **Managerial meetings.**   Probably no formal rules.

5 **Inter-departmental meetings.**   Probably no formal rules.

6   Task forces.   Special groups set up to tackle a problem, likely to be very informal.

7   Brain-storming meetings.   Inevitably very informal.

There are many sorts of committees that can be set up within an organisation. The following are some of the terms used to describe different status among committees.

1   Executive committee.   A committee having power to act on decisions.

2   Standing committee.   One which has an indefinite life.

3   Ad hoc committee.   A committee set up to carry out a specific task.

4   Subcommittee.   A committee which is a sub-section of a larger committee, reporting to it.

5   Consultative committee.   One which is consulted, having no power to make decisions, and thus is advisory.

6   Working party.   This is a group set up to work on some task, reporting possibly to an executive committee. The term party rather than committee implies a lower status.

Committees

The membership of a formally constituted committee is likely to be composed of:

1   A chairman/chairwoman.   The chairman is the 'leader' of the committee and has the principal duty to see that all the business conducted by the committee is conducted both fairly and to the rules. All discussions are expected to take place through him or her. Thus if a committee member wishes to raise a point, perhaps about something said by another member, he or she will address their remarks to the chairman rather than the other member.

2   A vice-chairman/chairwoman.   The vice-chairman is able to deputise for the chairman if he or she is not present at a meeting.

3   A secretary.   The secretary assists the chairman in the planning of the meeting and has the job of ensuring that a record is kept of the proceedings of all meetings.

4   A treasurer.   The treasurer has the role of keeping track of the committee's finances.

5   Committee members.   These are entitled to attend meetings and vote.

6   Co-opted members.   These are members co-opted to a committee for a specific purpose and might not be given the right to vote.

The proceedings of the meeting are planned ahead of the date and circulated to the members in an agenda, with any relevant papers. The agenda is the list of the items planned for discussion in the meeting. An agenda usually includes, in sequence:

1   A heading.

This indicates the name of the committee and the date, time and place of the meeting.

2   Apologies for absence

When this item is reached in the meeting those members who are unable to be present and have notified the secretary are indicated as offering their apologies for absence.

3   Minutes of the previous meeting

The minutes, i.e. the record of the proceedings, of the previous meeting are considered from the point of view of whether they are an accurate record of what took place.

4   Matters arising from the minutes

While some items may be listed on the agenda as items on which further reports are to be made, any item that was on the previous minutes can be raised for further discussion.

5   Specific items of business

Following the matters arising item there are then the specific items of business that are to be brought before the committee.

6   Any other business

This will be the last-but-one item on the agenda and is an opportunity for any member of the committee to raise an item not listed on the agenda.

7   Date of the next meeting

This is the last item on the agenda.

For any business to be conducted and decision made there has to be a *quorum* present at the meeting. A quorum is a certain proportion of the possible number of committee members. Thus there might be a quorum rule that more than one-third of the members should be present.

The term *motion* is used to describe a proposal being discussed in a meeting before it is accepted by the meeting. The procedure adopted is that, following some general discussion, a member of the committee may propose a motion, giving the precise words of the decision being requested from the meeting. Another member has then formally to second the motion, i.e. agree that the motion should be discussed. The motion, in the precise words put forward, is then discussed. A vote may then be taken and if it is in favour the precise words of the motion become the decision of the committee and are then referred to as a *resolution*.

During the discussion of the motion no changes can be accepted to the wording without an *amendment* being formally proposed, seconded and agreed following discussion. Then the amended motion can be voted on.

A decision is said to be *unanimous* if all members present are in favour of it.

Group processes in meetings

What type of processes go on in a meeting, perhaps a committee meeting? There are two types of processes that can be considered: those that take place within a single meeting and those which evolve over a number of meetings. R. Bales (1952) has proposed that within a single meeting there are a number of stages that the members go through as they move through the agenda. These are:

1 Identifying and agreeing the structure of the problem

Members supply and exchange information without selecting the information favourable to a particular view. The problem for the chairman is to direct attention to the relevant information and prevent the discussion going off into irrelevant directions.

2 Members put forward suggestions

This is the second stage and involves members in putting forward suggestions for decisions. Conflict and tension can occur at this stage. There may also be some signs of dominance or deference by some groups of members.

3 Resolution

This is the final stage, when a dominating view is accepted by the committee as a whole. This acceptance can show in the release of tension.

The above stages show how, for a particular item, a meeting can move towards a decision. However changes also occur over a number of meetings. We can use the term the group *matures*. The following are some of the stages that may occur in this process.

1 Forming. The individual members of the group gradually merge their separate identities into a group identity, the word *I* changes to *we*.

2 Setting norms. The group establishes norms or standards of practice.

3 Conflict. Many groups go through a stage where the originally accepted objectives and norms come under strain. This can show itself as the word *we* changing to *I*. Without careful leadership at this stage the group may loose its coherence.

Why groups?

Why are groups used so often for decision making? The following are some of the advantages of groups:

1 Tasks which are too complex for an individual can be tackled.
2 A group can generate ideas or solutions better than an individual when information is initially dispersed among several people and when mutual stimulation is needed to get members to become creative.
3 A group can serve a liaison or co-ordinating function between several individuals or departments.
4 A group can be used to facilitate the implementation of a complex decision.
5 Groups can be more influential than individuals.

Liaison and co-ordination between several individuals, and the facilitating of the implementation of a decision are key factors in the role of many committees. All the members of a committee are involved in the making of the decision and so have both knowledge of it and an involvement, so if the committee is 'mature' the decision is taken in the collective name of the committee and all members identify with it.

There are some disadvantages to groups, the following illustrating some of them:

1 An individual might be more creative than a group.
2 The group is often slower than an individual.
3 Groups may lack flexibility.
4 Individuals are not so easily rewarded for their work, so perhaps work less hard in a group than alone. Groups quite often have 'passengers'.
5 Groups tend to take riskier decisions than individuals. A possible explanation of this is that responsibility for the decision is diffused among the members and no individual is responsible.
6 Groups tend to seek unanimity and those members with deviant views are pressurised to conform, thus leading the group to reflect not an accurate analysis but the dominant opinion.

Interviews

Interviews are meetings of two or more people for a particular purpose. This purpose might be to select someone for a job, promotion, discipline, to enquire into an accident, to obtain information, etc. The special feature of an interview compared with other forms of meeting is that the meeting is conducted by one or more people, the interviewer(s), and that one person, or more, is the subject of the interview, i.e. the interviewee(s).

Before conducting an interview a prime requirement is to define the task. Thus if it is a job interview, precisely what type of job is it. In a job interview the following sequence of steps has been suggested as leading to effective interviewing (Webster in *Decision making in the employment interview*, Industrial Relations Centre, McGill University, 1964):

1 The interview should commence by the interviewee being asked to talk about his or her early life.
2 The interviewee should then bring the story up to date and give the reasons for wanting to change from their present job.
3 The interview should then become more probing.
4 The application form should be reviewed with the interviewee.

The aim of the early part of this technique is to put the interviewee at ease with the request for simple factual information which has the prime use to the interviewer of supplying background. After such an interview the interviewer or interviewers should take time to clarify the impressions gained and formulate a judgement.

The interview method of selecting personnel has been criticised as not always or consistently selecting the best person. Judgements made by a number of interviewers considering the same applicants for the same job can differ. Some problems that might occur during an interview and affect the outcome are:

1 Premature decisions made before or during the early stages of an interview may bias the interviewer against information supplied later in the interview. Thus, for example, a mis-spelt word on the application form might bias an interviewer against the interviewee despite any other information that might be supplied in the interview. Similarly the interviewee's appearance on entering the interview room might lead to a bias.

2 Unfavourable information influences an interviewer more than favourable information. The interview is often a search for negative information and the interviewee with the fewest negative factors gets the job!

3 The interviewer may not clearly know the job, or may perhaps even think they know it when they do not. This might lead to the wrong person being selected for the job.

4 The sequence in which the applicants are interviewed can affect how they are rated. An interviewee being rated after a poor applicant has been interviewed is likely to be rated higher than if he or she has been interviewed after a good applicant.

5 Pressure on the interviewer to appoint someone may mean that an appointment is made when no suitable applicant was interviewed.

Many employers use tests as part of the selection procedure. There are, for instance, standardised tests for achievement and performance in topics such as typing or mathematics; aptitude tests designed to establish an applicant's aptitude or potential for a job; personality tests to measure aspects of an applicant's personality; interest tests to establish an applicant's interests so that comparisions can be made with others working in the same job who have previously taken the test. Careful evaluation of the results of such tests is important. Tests can only measure, at the best, what they were designed to measure and thus, for example, a typing test which determines an applicant's typing speed should only be interpreted as giving that information and not as yielding information that can tell you whether the applicant will slot into the typing pool and work happily with the other typists. Tests should be regarded as a source of information supplementary to the selection process, there invariably being more factors involved than a single test can give answers to.

Grievance handling

A task which falls the way of supervisors and managers is handling grievances from the workforce. The following is the approach to such situations developed by Courage (Central) Ltd, and described in the May 1983 issue of *Topics* (published by the Employment Relations Resource Centre).

The four-step systematic approach

Step 1   Get at the grievance

Find out what the grievance is and why it exists.
- Initial interview. Don't put it off.
- Good questioning.
- Attentive listening.

Step 2   Check it out

Investigate the issues involved.
- Assumptions?
- Conclusions?
- Facts?
- Talk to others concerned.
- Check records.

Step 3   Identify your constraints

Identify what you can and cannot do.
- Are you in procedure?
- Knock-on effects?
- Precedents?
- Company policy?
- Your authority?

Step 4   Resolve the grievance

Work with your subordinates to find a solution.
- Agree the grievance.
- Agree constraints.
- Identify possible solutions.
- Final solution.
- Communicate results.

Revision questions

1 Explain the difference between formal and informal meetings and give an example of each.

2 Explain the function of the following officers of a committee, (a) chairman, (b) secretary, (c) vice chairman.

3 Explain the following terms when used in relation to a committee, (a) agenda, (b) minutes, (c) motion, (d) proposal, (e) quorum, (f) proposer, (g) seconder.

4 List some of the advantages and disadvantages of groups rather than individuals as decision makers.

5 List some of the problems that can occur with the use of an interview for selection for a job.

Assignments and further questions

1 Explain the implications of the following statements, issued in the offer for sale of shares by Wardle Storey plc.

The Articles of Association of the Company contain provisions, inter alia, to the following effect –
(1) Voting rights
On a show of hands every member who (being an individual) is present in person or (being a corporation) is present by a duly authorised representative shall have one vote and, on a poll, every member shall have one vote for every share of which he is the holder, save that a member shall not be entitled to exercise such right to vote if he, or any person appearing to be interested in the shares held by him, has been duly served with a notice under Section 74 of the Companies Act 1981 (requiring disclosure of interests in shares) and has failed to supply the Company with the requisite information within 28 days.
(2) Variation of rights
The rights attached to any class may be varied or abrogated with the consent in writing of holders of three fourths in nominal value of the issued shares of the relevant class or with the sanction of an extraordinary resolution passed at a separate general meeting of the holders of the shares of the class. To every such separate general meeting the provisions of the Articles relating to general

meetings shall apply, but the necessary quorum at any such meeting other than an adjourned meeting shall be two persons together holding or representing by proxy at least one-third in nominal value of the issued shares of the class in question.

2   Obtain the rules of some formal meeting and write a precis of the salient features regarding the holding of a meeting and the quorum so required.

3   Explain the functions of brain-storming meetings and describe the operation of one.

4   Participate in role-playing exercise concerned with a meeting on issues relating to employment relations. Determine who shall be chairman and who the secretary, compile an agenda and papers, conduct the meeting and then the secretary should write the minutes. After the event analyse the performance.

5   Obtain a number of consecutive sets of minutes for some committee. Analyse them in the light of the processes by which groups operate.

6   Participate in a role-playing exercise involving the interviewing of applicants for some job. After the interviews analyse the way the interviews went and consider how effective they were in selecting the 'right' canditate.

7   Use the grievance-handling procedure given in this chapter to carry out a role-playing exercise. You might like to consider an employee having the grievance that (a) he or she should have received a bonus with their last week's pay, or (b) he or she feels that the foreman is always picking on them and they are unfairly treated in comparison with the others in the team.

12 Written and graphical communication

Internal written communications

Within an organisation there are likely to be a significant amount of written communications in the cases of communications occurring downwards from managers to departmental heads to supervisors to workers, upwards as information is fed to the management, and laterally and diagonally between departments. The most frequently used written forms of internal communication are likely to be memoranda (memos), reports and forms. In addition there may be instructions for operating machines, etc., though these might come from outside in many cases rather than being purely internal.

1 The memorandum

The term means a note to help the memory, and as such memos are generally brief and to the point. They have a supportive action in helping personnel to recall, plan or act. Thus there could be memos to remind the sales manager of the date of the next regional sales meeting, or perhaps a change in the rules relating to sick pay, or a request for information about a production breakdown,or an order to a supervisor to carry out some instruction, etc.

2 The report

Reports are used to circulate information and ideas. While a memo is likely to be a single sheet of paper reports are invariably longer. There are many types of report: factual reports giving accounts of accidents or sales or the state of production of some product, and reports with ideas, views, recommendations, etc., as in a research report or a market survey report or a staff appraisal report.

3 Forms

Forms are pre-printed documents designed for the collection of information. A wide variety of forms are used in most organisations, though many forms are being replaced by computer entries into what is essentially forms on a computer instead of on paper. Examples of forms are accident report forms, job sheets, material requisition forms, etc. A well-designed form will be easy and quick to fill in and will yield information to the recipient that can be quickly and unambiguously interpreted.

Reports

Whatever the type of report it is likely to have the following features:

1   A title page

Generally showing the title of the report, the author's name, the date of submission and sometimes the authorisation.

2   A table of contents

This lists every section and subsection of the report, including the contents page and any appendices.

3   An abstract or summary of the report

This summarises the entire report, concentrating on the main issues or recommendations. A function of this is to 'sell' the report, tell people what they will learn if they read it.

4   The main text of the report

A variety of ways can be used to present the main text of the report, the aim being to present a logical, readable account for the readership to which the report is directed. Thus, for instance, technical language can be freely used if the readership can be assumed to be familiar with such langauge but if they are not then the type of writing will need to be different. Reports are often written in sections and subsections, a section being devoted to each of the main aspects of the report and then subdivided into its components. A numbering method is often used to distinguish clearly between sections and subsections, sections being numbered 1, 2, 3, etc. while subsections are numbered 2.1, 2.2, 2.3, etc.

5   Conclusions/recommendations

Conclusions and recommendations should be based on the information presented in the report and be presented in a clear, unambiguous, way.

6   Bibliography

This includes details of any publication used or referred to in the text. For each such publication the author's name, the title, the publisher and the date of publication are given.

7 *Appendices*

This is where information is put which is relevant to the text but too detailed to include in the main text without disrupting its flow.

While the main text of a report can be presented in many ways it will often follow the pattern of:

1   An introduction indicating what the report is aiming to deal with.
2   The terms of reference for the report, or perhaps background history.
3   The method or procedure adopted to obtain the information.
4   The information found.
5   Analysis of the information and the main factors emerging from it.
6   The conclusions or recommendations then round off the report.

Forms

Forms are a simple way of collecting relatively simple information. Thus, for example, a material requisition form might request the following information:

1   Date of origin of the request.
2   The origin of the request, i.e. the department and the signature of an authorised person.
3   The job number against which the materials are to be charged.
4   The material required, with code number and specification information.
5   The quantities required and the form of the materials, i.e. sheet, rod, etc.

There then might be spaces on the form for the following further information to be included by the storekeeper on receipt of the requisition:

1   The actual materials issued by the store.
2   The date of issue.
3   A signature of the storekeeper issuing the materials.

There then might be a further entry, a signature, to be entered on receipt of the materials by the person requesting them.

Such a form is likely to be used with a number of copies. The form might thus consist of a three sheets, perhaps differently coloured, with carbon paper being used to ensure that entries made on the top copy pass through to the others. When the form is first filled in for the materials request the bottom copy is detached and filed for future reference. The top sheet and one copy are then sent to the store, where after making their entries the staff detach the copy for their records and send the top sheet back to the recipient of the materials.

The above illustrates the type of information that might be collected by a form and the way in which it can be used to maintain records of transactions. These are very common uses of forms.

In designing a form there are a number of aspects which need to be considered.

1   The layout of the form should be such that the person filling it in can easily see which parts he or she has to complete, which parts are explanatory notes and which are parts to be filled in by someone else. Thus different typefaces might be used, notes might be on a separate sheet or in a margin, and the parts to be completed by someone else might be in a special box or perhaps not apparent on the top copy to be filled in initially but only visible on the copy sheet.

2   The instructions should be clear and concise, helping the form-filler to correctly fill the form in.

3   The questions on the form should be easily understood and not capable of more than one interpretation. Some forms might not use directly worded questions but might just have headed spaces, e.g. 'quantity', with the implied question of 'what quantity?'

4   The form should be designed so that not only can it be easily completed but also so that the information can be easily read-off it.

5   If spaces are left for answers to questions they must be big enough for the answers to be written in them. Perhaps the answers can be simplified to the point of deleting a word or words, e.g. YES/NO, or ticking a box.

6   The vital fact however in designing a form is for the designer to be perfectly clear as to what information he or she requires and then only to obtain that information, nothing extraneous.

External written communications

Communications to and from external bodies can take place in a variety of ways, e.g.

1   Forms.   These are likely to be used to receive or give orders for materials or products.

2   Letters.   A significant use of letters is to request or give information, to register or rectify a complaint, etc.

3   Advertising materials.   The written word is one of the main methods used by an organisation to receive or give information about products or services.

4 Publications. Articles in journals and the press in general are a significant method of exchanging information on market data and technical information.

Letters

Formal letters, i.e. letters from or to an organisation, conform to certain conventions regarding layout. Thus, for example, there will be:

1 A printed letterhead

This indicates the trading name of the organisation, its status if a limited company, its registered number and its location, e.g. England, the company directors, the address of its registered office, the address of the part of the organisation sending the letter, the telephone number, telex number and other telegraphic information, and the logo of the organisation. Part of the above will be at the head of the sheet of paper and there may be possibly a part at the bottom of the sheet.

2 References

Near the top of the letter sheet will be entries for Your ref: and Our ref:. This if often top left on the letter sheet and is to allow the display of reference codes given by the organisation sending the letter and those given earlier by the correspondent. The codes identify the location of the letter's origin within an organisation. A common system that is used is to give the letter writer's initials, the typist's initials and then the file reference, e.g. WB/SC/A121.

3 The date

This is generally put at the top on the right of the letter sheet.

4 The letter's recipient

The name and address of the person or organisation to whom the letter is addressed is placed at the top left, below the reference information.

5 Salutation

This is placed below the recipient's address, e.g. Dear Sir, Dear Mr. X, etc. The salutation 'Dear Sir' is generally used for situations in which the letter is formal, where the recipient and the writer have not met, or where the recipient is at a higher position than the writer.

6 Subject heading

A heading is often then given above the main body of the letter, the heading being to indicate the main theme.

7   *The body of the letter*

The body of the letter will generally consist of at least three paragraphs. The first paragraph gives the reason for the letter; it puts the message in context. Thus it might acknowledge the receipt of an earlier letter, giving the date and subject of that letter, and might supply the reason for the reply. The middle paragraphs of the letter develop the detail of the

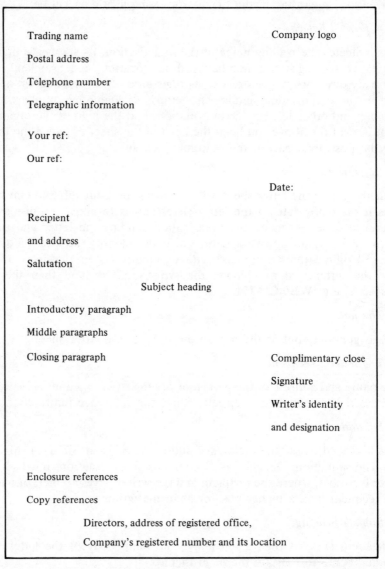

Trading name	Company logo
Postal address	
Telephone number	
Telegraphic information	
Your ref:	
Our ref:	
	Date:
Recipient	
and address	
Salutation	
Subject heading	
Introductory paragraph	
Middle paragraphs	
Closing paragraph	Complimentary close
	Signature
	Writer's identity
	and designation
Enclosure references	
Copy references	
Directors, address of registered office,	
Company's registered number and its location	

Figure 12.1   *Layout of a formal letter*

message. The closing paragraph generally provides a brief resume of the main points and indicates any action planned or required.

8   *Complimentary close*

The style of complimentary close is linked with the style of salutation used. Thus 'Yours faithfully' is used for formal situations, where the recipient and the writer have not met or where the recipient is at a higher position than the writer. The 'Yours sincerely' form of close is considered more friendly and is likely to be used where the salutation involves the name of the person concerned.

9   *Signature and writer's identity and designation*

Following the complimentary close will be the writer's signature and typed name and job designation, e.g. Managing Director.

10   *Enclosure references*

Below the signature and designation, are given the references to any material enclosed with the letter.

11   *Copy references*

With the enclosure references are also copy references. These indicate who else is to receive a copy of the letter.

Figure 12.1 summarises the above in one possible verion of a letter layout.

Technical communications

Within, for instance, a manufacturing organisation there will be technical communications between employees in order that the manufacturing process can happen in a planned manner. There will thus be engineering drawings, showing perhaps various views of a component in sufficient detail to enable the item to be manufactured. In the training manuals for workers there might be illustrated instruction sequences on how to carry out particular manufacturing operations.

Illustrated instruction sequences might also be used in leaflets supplied to customers of the company when they buy its products. Thus, for instance, a company manufacturing electric mains plugs might supply a card with the plug on how to wire it up.

The above are all examples of what can be termed *technical communications*. Such communications when written are essentially one-way process communications in that the reader has generally to act on the written material without being able to receive immediate feedback on whether the communication is being correctly interpreted. Thus such communications must be clear, precise and without ambiguity. Errors can cost money, and perhaps be dangerous. Thus, for instance, an error in a drawing might mean the production of a large quantity of products which then become rejects or require costly further processing to bring them up to the right quality. In the case of the leaflet or card supplied with the mains plug, an error can be dangerous if the customer wires up the plug incorrectly.

Flow charts

A type of chart that is widely used by management as a way of specifying plans, and as the basis of translating processes into a form that can be handled by computers, is the *flow chart*. A flow chart shows the breakdown of some problem into a number of simple steps.

Thus, to take a trivial problem as an example, consider the problem of finding the answer to three multiplied by five. This can be broken down into a number of simple steps:

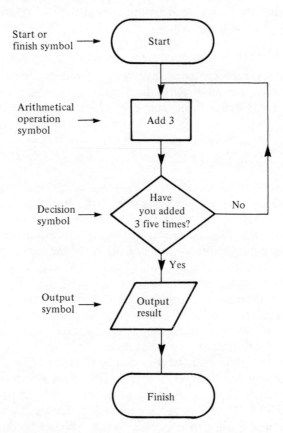

Figure 12.2   *Simple flowchart*

1 Start.
2 Add three.
3 Have you added three five times? If not, repeat step 2. If yes, go to the next step.
4 Output the result.
5 Finish.

The above can be represented diagramatically, using symbols to represent when decisions are required, when there is an input, when an output, when to start, when to stop and arithmetical operations. Figure 12.2 shows such a diagram.

The above is a trivial example. The merit of using flowcharts does however lie with complex problems in that it clearly enables the various stages involved in solving the problem to be identified and clearly seen. Thus a production process for a product is a very complex operation requiring materials, workers and machines all to be brought together in the right sequence. For example, there could be the situation where for the making of a product steel sheet has to be drawn from the stores, transported to the production line, machined, transported and then formed, transported and then cleaned, then brought together with sub-assemblies from other parts of the production line to be assembled into the product. In drawing a flowchart for a production operation different symbols to those shown in Figure 12.2 are sometimes used, e.g. an arrow shape to represent physical movement of materials or product, an inverted triangle to represent storage, a circle to represent an operation carried out on the material and a square for inspection.

Revision questions

1 What type of information is predominantly communicated within an organisation by memos?

2 Outline the main structure of reports.

3 What are the purposes of appendices to reports?

4 What aspects need to be considered in designing a form?

5 What are the main forms of internal written communication in an organisation?

6 Describe the general layout conventionally adopted for letters.

7 Give an example of a technical communication used within an organisation.

8 What are flow charts?

Assignments and further questions

1   Obtain a sample of different types of internal written communications used within an organisation. Discuss the purpose of each type and critically comment on the effectiveness of the communication.

2   Design a form for some purpose with which you are familiar.

3   Obtain a form used in some organisation and critically analyse its design and effectiveness.

4   Write an outline plan for a report on some aspect with which you are familiar. Be clear as to what you are trying to communicate.

5   Write a letter which might be sent by an organisation following a complaint from a customer concerning one of the company's products, assuming that the customer has a valid complaint.

6   Obtain copies of the logos used by a number of companies on their headed stationary and critically comment on the effectiveness of the logos.

7   Critically analyse the technical instruction leaflet supplied with some product.

8   Write a technical leaflet for use with some product, e.g. a mains plug, considering carefully the audience for which the leaflet is being designed.

9   Write an instruction sequence suitable for a new trainee on how to use some particular machine.

10   Draw a flow chart for some particular production process with which you are familiar.

13 Management information systems

Information systems

Within any organisation there are generally many types of information systems. Thus there is likely to be a financial system involving data on budgets, income, costs and profits. Such a system will involve the collection of data from a number of sources and it all has to be brought together so that management can see how the organisation is operating financially and so make appropriate decisions. There might also be a production system involving data on planned production, actual production, quality, etc. Such information will be needed for production decisions to be made.

Much, if not all, of the data on which such information systems are based might originate in returns on forms. Thus in the case of the production system there might be:

1 A works order giving the information to the production department about an order for goods.
2 An operation sheet which lays out the plan of the processes, materials, etc. required.
3 A job schedule which is a more detailed plan of the way a job is broken down into its constituent tasks.
4 A loading schedule which outlines the tasks to be carried out by a specific operator or machine.
5 An operator's work record which shows the operations completed by that operator.
6 Job cards which specify the jobs to be done for a particular component and which are completed by each operator in turn as they complete their part of the job.
7 Quality control charts which give the results of inspections of the products.

Information systems thus tend to involve large amounts of information, which has all to be processed so that management may have the information it needs for decision making.

Management information systems

The term *management information system* (MIS) is used to describe a system designed to provide instantly the information needed by management for effective decision making. The term is usually used only in connection with computer-based systems, designed to integrate many if not all of the organisation's subsidiary information systems.

The elements of computer systems

The term *hardware* is used to describe the computer equipment. This can be considered to consist of:

1　An input device.　This enables instructions and data to be transferred into the computer, e.g. a keyboard.

2　A central processing unit.　This consists of three elements: a memory to act as a store for numbers and instructions, an arithmetical unit to carry out arithmetical operations and a control unit to cause the computer to perform the required operations in the right sequence.

3　An output device.　This converts the output from the computer into a form which can be read or used in some way, e.g. images on a screen (referred to as a visual display unit or VDU) or printed on a roll of paper.

The term *software* is used to describe the program of instructions that are used to tell the computer what data to work on, what operations to carry out and in what sequence, and what to do with the results.

Compared with using people to process information using computers has the following advantages:

1　They can handle large amounts to information at high speed.
2　They can do complex calculations at high speed.
3　They can be programmed to make decisions.
4　They can transmit information, processing it in one place and making it available to people in other places.

What can the computer do for the business world? That is a question Peter Drucker addresses in his book *People and Performance, The Best of Peter Drucker on Management* (Heinemann 1977) and he comes up with five major tasks:

1　The computer can be used as a mechanical clerk, handling large amounts of repetitive but simple paperwork.
2　The computer can collect, process, store, analyse and present information at high speed.
3　The computer can help design physical structures, such as building a road.

4   The computer has the capacity to control a process, restoring a process to some preset condition. Thus it can be used for stock control.
5   The computer can assist in strategic business decision making. Here the the computer can be set up to work out what might happen if certain things were done under certain assumed conditions. A model of a situation is used and then the computer makes predictions of what will happen for different inputs to that model. The predictions can only be as good as the model used to describe the real world situation.

Designing a management information system

Designing a management information system revolves round the problem of determining what information the managers need, finding that information and then putting it in a form that they can use. The information needs of different managers are very likely to be different. Thus, for example, upper management will probably need information relevant to policy making and strategic planning while lower management will need information concerned with the maintenance and implementation of daily activities, e.g. the personnel manager will want data on staff turnover, wages, training programmes, etc. Thus a comprehensive system needs to be able to supply different employees with different information.

The sequence that is likely to be adopted in designing a management information system is:

1   Determine the information needs of those who will be using the system in the organisation.
2   Determine the information sources.
3   Design a system to collect and present the information in a form appropriate to the needs, i.e. develop computer programs and procedures.
4   Arrange for the information to be transmitted to where it is required and in an appropriate form.
5   The vital final step is that the information is used to enable decisions to be made.

Revision questions

1   What is meant by the term *management information system*?

2   What is meant by the terms *hardware* and *software* when applied to a computer system?

3   What are the advantages of a computer processing information when compared with a person?

4 Give two examples of what a computer can be used to do in the business world.

Assignments and further questions

1 Find out, from a particular company, what use they make of a computer.

2 Peter Drucker in his book *People and Performance, The Best of Peter Drucker on Management* (Heinemann, 1977) makes the following points. Critically discuss them.
   (a) The computer multiplies human capacity.
   (b) It (the computer) can accept only information capable of being quantified and dealt with logically. This is only part of the information necessary in the business world. The information most important to business people is not capable of being quantified. It can only be perceived.

Part Four Economic and financial aspects of supervision

This part of the book consists of two chapters concerned with costing and budgetary control.

Chapter 14 Costing. Both historical and standard costing are considered. Direct labour and materials costs, together with ways of apportioning overheads, are considered for absorption costing for jobs, batches and processes. Marginal costing is also considered. Finally there is a discussion of the technique of break-even analysis.

Chapter 15 Budgetary control. Forms of budgets and their construction are considered, sales and production budgets being considered as examples. There is a brief discussion of the role of the balance sheet. Budgets are considered in relation to their control function within an organisation.

It should be noted that both the above chapters give only an appreciation of costing and budgetary control, more specialist texts should be consulted if you are planning to engage in cost and management accountancy, e.g. *Cost and Management Accountancy for Students*, J. Batty (editor), published by Heinemann in association with the Institute of Cost and Management Accountants.

14 Costing

Cost accounting

The term *cost accounting* can be defined, according to the Institute of Cost and Management Accountants, as – the application of accounting and costing principles, methods and techniques in the ascertainment of costs and the analysis of savings and/or excesses as compared with previous experience or standards.

The term *historical costing* is used where the costs are determined after the production of goods has occurred, the term *standard costing* being used where costs are estimated before the production occurs on the basis of standards that have been predetermined for materials and labour. With historical costing the costs are determined from records taken during the production of the materials, labour and machines used. With standard costing the standards to be adopted for the costs of the various parts of the process are obtained from past experience of manufacturing the same or similar work. Thus standard costing is not the actual cost of the production but an estimate of what the cost will be; historical costing gives the actual cost. The advantage to management of using standard costing is that it enables cost control to be exercised in that there is a cost forecast before production and this can be compared with the actual cost and the factors responsible for any discrepancy in costs identified.

Standard costing is widely used where there is repetitive manufacture, i.e. where the processes and materials used are close enough to past experience to enable standards to be determined. With one-off production or where a new process is being used or a new product being produced it may not be possible to use standard costing as there might be insufficient experience to make standards feasible.

The price of a product

The selling price of a product can be considered to be made up of a number of elements:

1 Prime costs

These are the costs of the material and labour directly involved in the production of the product. They are referred to as *direct costs* when they can be separately identified as relating directly to the product concerned. Hence the direct material cost is the cost of the materials consumed or incorporated in the production of the product, the direct labour cost is the cost of the labour directly involved in the process.

2   Production overheads

These are the costs involved in the production process which cannot be directly attributed to the product concerned, e.g. the cost of the machinery, maintenance, storekeeping, etc. This type of cost is called an *indirect cost*.

Elements 1 and 2 above represent the total production costs for a product. This however is not the selling price in that further costs have to be included as well as a profit element.

3   General administration and selling overheads

These include the costs of distribution and marketing and part of the general administration costs of the organisation.

4   Profit

Elements 1, 2 and 3 above constitute the total product cost. Added to that to give the selling price is the profit element.

Direct labour costs

With historical costing the direct labour costs can be found from the records kept of each person's involvement in the production process and the labour rates. Thus there might be two hours by an operator on machine X at a labour rate of £5 per hour and then one hour by an operator on machine Y at a labour rate of £6 per hour, and finally half-an-hour on machine Z at a labour rate of £4 per hour. The total direct labour cost is, in this example, £10 + £6 + £2 = £18.

With standard costing the direct labour cost is found from a consideration of the standard times specified for each part of the process, adjusted for the target level of operator performance, and the labour rates. The standard time for a job is defined as the time needed for a qualified worker to carry out the job at the defined level of performance. Such times can be determined by work measurement in which investigators observe workers carrying out the process concerned and time the various parts of the job. Effectively this defines a standard worker in that the work measurement investigators adjust the times they determine to take account of the general tempo of the work to give time values corresponding to the standard worker. The operator performance is a measure of how a particular worker compares with the performance expected of this standard worker, an operator rated at 100 being equivalent to the standard worker while one rated at less than 100 performs at a higher rate and one at more than 100 at a slower rate.

Hence the standard cost for a job is given by

Standard cost = standard time × operator rating × labour rate

Thus for a job for which the standard time is 2 hours, the operator rating 110 and the labour rate £6 per hour, the standard cost is

$$\text{Standard cost} = 2 \times (110 \div 100) \times 6$$
$$= £13.20$$

Direct materials costs

Where materials are bought specifically for a particular job then the actual cost can be put against that job. However in many instances the materials used on a particular job are drawn from stocks held by the company. Materials are thus bought for the store and then issued from the store as required. Since the materials drawn from the store for a particular job may use materials bought at different times and at different prices it is not always feasible to use the actual cost of the materials in arriving at the direct materials cost. A number of methods are used to arrive at a cost figure for materials in such cases.

1 Standard cost

The material issued from the store for a job is charged at a standard cost. This is a cost that has been chosen for that particular material and is not necessarily the real price paid for it.

2 First in, first out (FIFO)

The cost of the oldest of that type of material in the store is used, it being assumed that the material that was first in is first used.

3 Last in, first out (LIFO)

The cost of the most recent purchase of the material is used, it being assumed that the material last into the store is the first used.

4 Highest in, first out

The cost is taken as being that of the most highly priced purchase, regardless of the date at which the material was bought.

5 Average cost

The average price of the stock held of a particular material is used as the cost.

6   *Market price*

The cost is taken as the market price of the material on the date the material is taken from the store, regardless of the price actually paid for the material.

7   *Replacement pricing*

The cost is taken as the price that it is anticipated will have to be paid to replace the material drawn from the store.

In general the method most used where standard costing is used for a job is standard cost for the materials, however in other situations the average cost is widely used.

Overhead costs

The term *overheads* is used to describe the costs which cannot be specifically allocated to any particular job or product, i.e. the indirect costs of materials, labour and other expenses. Indirect materials are those materials which are used to further the manufacturing process but which cannot be directly identified in the end product, e.g. cutting oil. Indirect labour consists of all wages and salaries paid to those people not directly concerned with the production of a product, e.g. supervisors, managers, clerks, typists, salespeople, etc. Indirect expenses include all the expenses incurred by the company in carrying out their business activities which are not capable of being directly identified with a specific job or product, e.g. rent, electric power, insurance, depreciation, etc.

The procedure generally used, under what is termed *absorption costings* for recovering the overhead costs is:

1   Divide the company into cost centres.
2   Apportion the overhead costs between these cost centres.
3   The overhead costs within service cost centres are transferred to producing cost centres and then the collective overhead cost is apportioned in some way to the units of product or jobs and so absorbed and passed on to the customer.

The term *cost centre* is used for any section of an organisation for which costs are separately identified. Thus the production department might be a cost centre, or there might be a number of production cost centres according to the different products produced. The justification for a particular cost centre is that financial control is aided by separately identifying such costs.

Two types of cost centres can be identified within a manufacturing company, *service cost centres* and *producing cost centres*. Service cost centres are those which do not actually make products, e.g. personnel, stores, etc. Producing cost centres are those concerned with actually making the products.

Apportioning overhead costs to cost centres

The overhead costs have to be apportioned in some equitable way between the cost centres. Thus, for example, the rent cost may be allocated between the cost centres according to the floor areas they occupy. Lighting costs may be allocated according to the number of electric light fittings in each cost centre. Some overhead costs may be able to be directly attributed to one or more cost centres, e.g. materials used in maintenance can be put as an overhead cost to the maintenance cost centre, depreciation of machines used in production can be put as an overhead cost to the production cost centres using those machines.

Table 14.1 indicates how some of the overhead costs might be apportioned between cost centres:

Table 14.1

Overhead item	Total cost	Service cost centres			Producing cost centres		
		Stores	Main-tenance	Per-sonnel	A	B	C
	£	£	£	£	£	£	£
Rent (allocated according to area)	50,000	10,000	5000	5000	10,000	15,000	5000
Light (according to number of light fittings)	10,000	500	500	800	3000	4000	1200
Heat (according to cubic capacity, or perhaps number of radiators)	12,000	500	800	1000	3500	4500	1700
Insurance (according to valuation)	2000	400	100	300	300	500	400
Materials for maintenance	2000	–	2000	–	–	–	–

By taking into account all the overhead cost elements the total overhead costs can be apportioned between the cost centres. Service departments, such as stores, maintenance, personnel, security, etc. are not directly involved with the productive process and as such costs need to be passed onto the buyers of the company's products their overhead costs have to be allocated to the producing cost centres. This allocation can be made in a variety of ways. Thus the overheads of the stores cost centre can be divided between the producing cost centres according to the fraction of the cost of direct materials each centre uses. Maintenance can be divided between the producing cost centres according to the number of labour hours each centre has. Security might be divided between the producing cost centres according to the floor area occupied by them.

The end result of this allocation of the service cost centre overheads is that there is an overhead cost for each producing cost centre and that the total of all these overhead costs is the total overhead cost of the company.

Absorbing the overhead costs

The overhead costs for a particular production cost centre have to be, in some way, allocated to the products produced at that cost centre so that the overheads can be passed on to the purchaser of the product and hence recouped. A variety of methods are used to apportion the overheads among the products, or jobs. Probably the four main methods used are:

1 According to the direct labour costs. The greater the direct labour costs of a product the greater its share of the overheads.

2 According to the direct labour hours. The greater the number of labour hours needed for a product the greater its share of the overheads.

3 According to the machine hours involved. The greater the number of machine hours needed to produce a product the greater its share of the overheads.

4 According to the number of units of product produced. The more units of a particular product produced the greater its share of the overheads.

Where the overheads are apportioned according to the direct labour costs the fraction of the total direct labour costs over some period of time that can be attributed to a particular product is calculated. Thus if the total overhead cost is £50,000 and the total direct labour costs for a particular cost centre are £10,000, for every £1 of direct labour an overhead cost of £5 is to be levied. This amount is known as the *direct labour cost rate*. Thus if a particular product has direct labour costs of £400 against this cost centre then the overhead cost is £2000. This method of apportioning overheads is often used where the production process is labour intensive.

Where the overheads are apportioned according to the direct labour hours the fraction of the total direct labour hours over some period of time that can be attributed to a particular product is calculated. Thus if the total overhead cost is £50,000 and the total direct labour hours for a particular cost centre are 5000 hours then for every hour of direct labour the share of the overhead cost is £10. This is known as the *direct labour hour rate*. Thus if a product has direct labour hours of 50 then the overhead cost is £500.

Where the overheads are apportioned according to the machine hours the overheads that are to be charged against a particular machine or group of machines are calculated and the machine hour rate determined. This is overheads per hour of machine time. The overheads for a particular machine can be calculated on the basis of a fraction of the rents, rates, heating, lighting, etc. according to the fraction of the total area of floor space occupied by the machine, due allowance being made for gangways. In addition specific machine overheads are added, e.g. machine depreciation, maintenance, tooling costs, etc. The total number of machine hours used in the calculation of the machine hour rate is either the number of hours for which the machine is expected to operate or the number of hours which could be operated if it is used at normal capacity. Thus if the overheads are, say, £10,000 and the total number of machine hours 5000 then the machine hour rate is £2. Hence if a particular product requires three hours on this particular machine then the overhead cost is £6. This method of apportioning overheads is often used where the production processes are machine intensive. A high percentage of the overheads in such a case is likely to be due to the depreciation of the machinery and tooling costs.

Where the overheads are apportioned according to the number of units of product produced, the fraction of the total number of units of product produced over some period of time that can be attributed to a particular product is calculated. Thus if the total overhead cost is £50,000 and the total number of units of product produced is 25,000, then the overhead for unit of product is £2.

When standard costing is used a *standard overhead cost rate* is calculated, using whichever of the above methods is most appropriate. The standard overhead cost rate is defined as the rate determined by dividing the expected overhead cost attributable to a particular cost centre by the predetermined quantity of the base, e.g. machine hours, to which the rate is applied. The difference between the standard and historical overhead cost rates is that the standard is calculated in terms of the expected overheads while the historical one is in terms of what has occurred.

Depreciation

Depreciation can be defined as the diminution in the intrinsic value of an asset due to use and the passage of time. Thus a particular machine might have an initial cost of C, this including not only the cost of the machine but its installation and other related costs, and a final scrap value of S. Then the depreciation during the life of that machine is $(C - S)$. If the life of the machine is reckoned as being n years then the average depreciation per year is $(C - S)/n$.

A machine costs, when fully installed, £12,000 and is expected to have a life of five years, at the end of that time having a scrap value of £500. For this particular example the average depreciation is thus

$$\frac{£(12,000 - 500)}{5} = £2300 \text{ per year.}$$

Table 14.2

Year	Value at start of year £	Depreciation £	Value at end of year £
1	12000	2300	9700
2	9700	2300	7400
3	7400	2300	5100
4	5100	2300	2800
5	2800	2300	500

The above method of calculating depreciation per year, known as the *straight line method*, assumes that on item depreciates by equal amounts in each year. An alternative way of calculating depreciation is to assume that a greater amount of depreciation occurs in earlier than later years. Think for example of the depreciation that occurs with a new car. One way of calculating depreciation in this approach is called the *reducing balance method* and provides for depreciation by means of charges calculated as a constant proportion of the balance of the value of the asset after deducting the previously calculated depreciation. Thus for the machine referred to in the above example where the life is reckoned as being five years, we can take 47 per cent of its value as the amount of depreciation each year. This is demonstrated in Table 14.3.

Table 14.3

Year	Value at start of year £	Depreciation £	Value at end of year £
1	12,000	47% of 12,000 = 5640	6360
2	6360	47% of 6360 = 2989	3371
3	3371	47% of 3371 = 1584	1787
4	1787	47% of 1787 = 840	947
5	947	47% of 947 = 445	502

The value at the end of the fifth year is, allowing for rounding errors in the calculations, the scrap value of £500. The value of the percentage to be used in calculating the above depreciations depends on the ratio of the scrap-to-cost value, i.e. $S \div C$, and the number of years n of useful life. The following equation indicates how the percentage r is calculated:

$$r = \left[1 - \left(\frac{S}{C} \right)^{1/n} \right] \times 100\%$$

This gives a value for r which means that at the end of the life the value will be the scrap value.

The above are just two ways depreciation can be calculated and so allowed for in the determination of the value of assets. Other methods are also used. One method involves valuing the assets at the end of each period of time, the depreciation is then the difference between the initial and the end values for that period of time.

Job costing

Job costing involves the allocating of the various cost elements against a job. Each job is considered separately and the material, labour and overhead costs determined. This generally means that a significant clerical effort is required to collect together all the forms used to log the various elements of the job undertaken by different workers and all the materials requisition forms used to extract materials for the job from the store. It is generally a historical system of costing with all the details being gathered after the event. This method is widely used for one-off orders.

The following outlines the types of information gathered and the way the job is costed.

1   A works order is issued. This gives the details of the order and a job number. All future work and materials for the job quote this number.

2   On requiring materials a materials requisition sheet is sent to the materials store. After executing the order the storekeeper passes the sheet to the costing department. On the basis of this information the direct materials cost can be determined.

3   Each worker on completing work on the job completes the relevant part of a job card. When the job is complete the card passes to the costing department. On the basis of this information the direct labour cost can be determined.

4   The costing department then compute the overhead cost and by adding together the direct materials cost, the direct labour cost and the overheads obtain the cost of the job.

Batch costing   May not require

Batch costing is just another form of job costing, however instead of the unit against which the costs are levied being a single job a group or batch of components are considered. Thus the job costing is concerned with the specific order of a customer whereas a batch costing is generally likely to be concerned with a quantity of components being made for the store. The difference is essentially one of making a component against a specific order or making components in anticipation of orders.

The type of documentation used to obtain information for batch costing can be the same as that used for job costing. There may be a major cost item involved in the initial setting of the necessary jigs and tools, this cost then being defrayed over the total number of components produced in the batch. Thus there can be a valid argument for big batches, however against this has to be considered the capital tied up in the stock so produced (see Chapter 16 on inventories).

Process costing   May not require

Process costing is often used where continuous runs of identical products are produced, e.g. mass production, or where the process is continuous, as in the production of chemical or food or drink products. The aim is to produce an average cost of a product. This is done by accumulating the direct materials and labour costs, and the overhead costs and then dividing that sum by the number of units produced during the period of time concerned.

The procedure adopted for process costing is to divide the company into a number of cost centres, and possibly in connection with a production department cost centre into a number of sub-cost centres. The reason for cost centres, and sub-cost centres, is that management consider it necessary to identify the costs, and output, by such centres in order to exercise control effectively. The reason for sub-cost centres in a production department is generally that it is useful to identify costs, and output, in relation to the types of process. Thus there might, for instance, be a cost centre for machining and another one for heat treatment.

For each cost centre the direct materials and direct labour costs for a process are ascertained from records, e.g. material requisition forms and time sheets. Overhead charges are also allocated and so a total cost can be ascertained for a particular period of time for a process. Separate costings are carried out for service and producing cost centres and at the end of the accounting period concerned the costs of the service cost centres are transferred, in some equitable way, to producing cost centres so that the costs can be levied against products and hence passed onto the purchaser of those products.

For the accounting period concerned there need to be records kept of opening stocks, uncompleted units and completed units. Where there are uncompleted units, i.e. work in progress, an estimate needs to be made of the state of these units and their value. Hence the number of equivalent, completed units can be estimated. Uncompleted units in one accounting period will form the opening stocks in the next accounting period. These opening stocks are considered in the same way as the uncompleted units and an estimate made of the equivalent, completed units that are produced in the accounting period concerned. The sum of the completed units and the equivalent completed units in the time gives the effective output from the cost centre concerned.

The above represents a simplified account of process costing, the aim being to indicate the principle rather than the detail of how to carry out such a costing. For more details the reader is referred to specialised texts on cost accounting, e.g. *Cost and management accountancy for students* by J. Batty (Heinemann).

Marginal costing

The conventional methods of dealing with overheads apportions all the overhead costs to the products, as described earlier in this chapter, and is known as absorption costing. Overhead costs however can be considered to be made up of fixed and variable overhead costs. Fixed overhead costs do not vary with output and are incurred in respect to a definite period of time, e.g. security or rent, while variable overhead costs are related to the output, e.g. indirect materials such as cutting oil and the electrical power used by the machines (but probably not the electrical power used for the lighting and heating which is likely to be a fixed overhead). There is thus an argument that only the variable overhead costs should be directly allocated to a product and that the difference between the total cost arrived at with this level of overheads and the selling price should give a return which covers both the fixed overheads and profit.

This method of costing is known as *marginal costing*, the term marginal cost being used for the total cost arrived at by adding together the prime costs, i.e. direct materials and direct labour, and the variable overhead costs. The difference between the value of the sales and the marginal costs is known as the *contribution*. This contribution is used to cover the fixed overhead costs and profit.

Contribution = Sales value − (prime costs + variable overheads)
Profit = Contribution − fixed overheads

Marginal costing can simplify pricing of products in that the price is more directly related to the costs incurred in the production of the product. This is because the calculation of the marginal cost only involves quantities related to the output of the product, and there is no difference in costs due to differences in the quantities produced in different accounting periods. With absorption costing this is not the case since the fixed overheads are spread over the quantity of product produced and so a variable output leads to a variable total cost.

There is also the advantage with marginal costing that it identifies the contribution a product makes and thus decisions can be taken more easily as to whether to continue that line of product. Management can decide, for example, to set the price of a product so that it perhaps makes only a small, or no contribution, and balance this by some other product making a bigger contribution.

The following example illustrates, in very simple terms, the differences between absorption and marginal costing.

Absorption costing:
Direct materials costs   £200
Direct labour cost   £120

The total overheads for that cost centre are £500. The overheads are apportioned among the various products according to the number of machine hours and this results in an allocation of one tenth of the overheads to this particular product. Hence the overheads are £50. Thus the total cost of the product is £370. A profit element of £30 is added to the cost to give a selling price of £400.

Marginal costing:
Direct materials cost   £200
Direct labour cost   £120

The total variable overheads for that cost centre are £120 and the fixed overheads £380. The variable overheads are apportioned among the various products according to the number of machine hours and this results in one tenth of the overheads being allocated to this product, i.e a variable overhead of £12. Thus the total marginal cost is £342. If the sales price is fixed as £400 then the product makes a contribution of £58 which can be used to cover fixed overheads and profit.

Break-even analysis

Break-even analysis can be used to show how revenue and costs relate to provide a profit, or loss, at different volumes of sales and the point, termed the *break-even point*, at which there is neither profit or loss.

Figure 14.1 shows how a break-even chart is constructed. The vertical axis of the chart shows costs and revenue, the horizontal axis shows volume

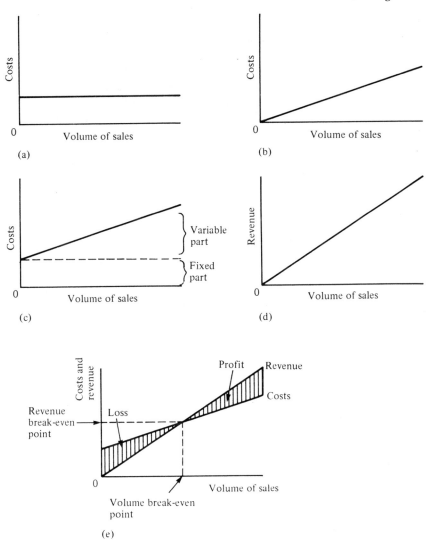

Figure 14.1 *The steps in producing a break-even chart*
(a) *Fixed costs*
(b) *Variable costs*
(c) *Total costs*
(d) *Sales revenue*
(e) *The composite chart*

of sales or volume of production, either being in cash value or number of units. The costs consist of essentially just two elements, fixed costs which are independent of the volume of sales or production and variable costs which depend on the volume. The total cost is the sum of these fixed and variable costs. Hence by combining these a graph can be drawn of costs against volume. As long as there are fixed costs this graph will not pass through the origin, i.e. zero cost-zero volume point, in that there will always be some cost even when the volume sold or produced is zero. On the same chart the graph is drawn of revenue against volume. This graph will pass through the origin in that there is no revenue with no sales or production. The point where these two graphs, cost–volume and revenue–volume, cross is the break-even point. Where the cost–volume graph, at a particular volume, is greater than the revenue–volume graph there is a loss, where the revenue–volume graph is greater than the cost–volume graph there is a profit.

The break even point can be obtained from the chart or by the use of the following equations:

$$\text{Volume break-even point} = \frac{\text{total fixed cost}}{\text{unit selling price} - \text{unit variable cost}}$$

$$\text{Revenue break-even point} = \frac{\text{total fixed cost} \times \text{total revenue}}{\text{total revenue} - \text{total variable cost}}$$

The above equations are just alternate ways of expressing the breakeven point.

To illustrate the use of the above equations consider the situation where the variable cost for a unit is £1 and the unit selling price is £4. If the total

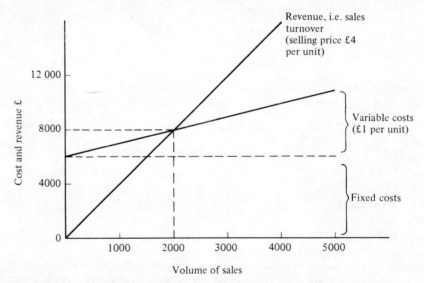

Figure 14.2   *Complete break-even chart*

fixed costs for the product are £6000 then the break-even point is 6000 ÷ (4 − 1) = 2000. This is the number of units that have to be sold before a profit can be made; for sales below 2000 there will be a loss.

If for a sales turnover, i.e. total revenue, of £4000, the total variable costs are £1000 and the total fixed costs £6000 then the break even point is 6000 × 4000 ÷ (4000 − 1000) = £8000. This is what the sales turnover will have to exceed if a profit is to be made.

Figure 14.2 shows the break-even chart for the above data. The profit, or loss at any particular sales volume is the difference between the revenue and the total cost graphs. Thus for the data given in figure 14.2, at a sales volume of 1000 units there is a loss of (£7000 − £4000) = £3000. At a sales volume of 3000 units there is a profit of (£12,000 − £9000) = £3000. The break-even point is 2000 units with a sales turnover (revenue) of £6000. Such profit and loss data as a function of sales volume, can be plotted as another graph (Figure 14.3). This graph shows how the profits and losses vary with the volume of sales.

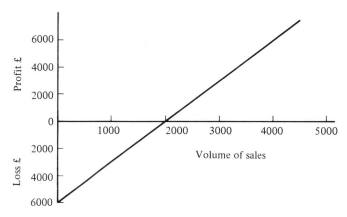

Figure 14.3 *Profit graph relating to Figure 14.2*

Revision questions

1 Distinguish between *standard* and *historical costing*.

2 What are the various elements that constitute the selling price?

3 What is meant by the terms *direct labour costs* and *direct materials costs* and how do they differ from *indirect costs*?

4 How can direct labour and direct materials costs be found for a particular product if historical costing is used?

5 Explain how the direct labour cost is found for a product if standard costing is used.

6   What are *overhead costs*?

7   What is meant by a *cost centre*?

8   With *absorption costing* explain how the overhead costs can be recovered.

9   With absorption costing how are the overheads of service departments recovered?

10   With absorption costing, how can the overheads be allocated to the various products produced at a producing cost centre?

11   What is *depreciation* and how can it be determined if the depreciation is (a) assumed to be constant for each year of the life of a machine and (b) assumed to change by a constant proportion of the balance of the value of the machine each year?

12   Explain how (a) a job, (b) a batch and (c) a process can be costed.

13   What is meant by *marginal costing* and how does it differ from absorption costing?

14   Explain what is meant by *break-even analysis*.

15   Explain how a break-even chart can be plotted.

Assignments and further questions

1   A production department produces three products, *A, B* and *C*, during an accounting period. Calculate the cost for each during this period if the overheads are absorbed according to (a) direct labour costs, (b) machine hours involved.

Costs	Product A	Product B	Product C
Total labour hours	200	800	300
Total machine hours	100	200	600
Direct materials	800	500	600

The labour rate for all the operations is £5 per hour and the total overheads £1200.

2   Calculate the total direct cost for the following product using standard costing.

4 hours process *A*, operator rating 110, labour rate £4.00 per hour
2 hours process *B*, operator rating 100, labour rate £5.00 per hour
3 hours process *C*, operator rating 95, labour rate £4.00 per hour

2.0 kg material *A*, standard material cost £0.40 per kg
1.0 kg material *B*, standard material cost £1.50 per kg
3.5 kg material *C*, standard material cost £2.00 per kg

3 Calculate the total direct cost for the following product.

Process	Cost centre	Labour hours	Machine hours
Machining	A	2.0	2.0
Drilling	A	0.5	0.5
Finishing	B	0.5	4.0
Packing	C	0.5	0

Direct materials cost £25.00

Cost centre *A*, labour rate £5.00 per hour, machine hour rate £10.00
Cost centre *B*, labour rate £4.00 per hour, machine hour rate £3.00
Cost centre *C*, labour rate £3.00 per hour

4 Investigate the methods used in a materials store in some company and report on the documentation used and the way materials are costed.

5 A machine costs, when fully installed, £10,000 and is expected to have a life of six years. At the end of this time it will have a scrap value of £1500. Calculate the value of the machine at the end of each year if the depreciation is to be reckoned according to (a) equal amount per year, (b) the reducing balance method by which a constant proportion of the balance of the value of the asset is deducted each year.

6 Obtain information on the accounting method used to depreciate the value of some asset, quoting not only the method but actual values.

7 A production department in mass producing a product incurs costs of £12,000 for direct materials, £20,000 for direct labour and £15,000 for overheads. If 40,000 units are produced, what is the average cost per unit?

8 How would the answer to Question 7 have to be modified if there had been 500 units at the beginning of the accounting period half-finished and at the end of the period there were 800 units half-finished, the 40,000 representing the units completed? Take it that a half-finished product uses all the materials, as they are required at the beginning of the process, but only half the labour.

9 Using *marginal costing* calculate the contribution the following product makes:

Direct materials cost	£1000
Direct labour cost	£ 800
Fixed overheads	£ 500
Variable overheads	£ 200

10   Write a report arguing the merits of marginal costing in preference to absorption costing.

11   Construct a break-even chart of the following product data and determine the break-even sales volume.

Fixed costs £2000
Variable costs £2 per unit
Revenue £7 per unit

12   Calculate the break-even sales turnover for the following product:

Total fixed costs £8000
Total variable costs £2000
Total sales turnover £13,000

13   A product has fixed costs of £5000 and variable costs of £5 per unit. At present the product is sold for £12 per unit. However it is proposed to reduce the selling price to £11 per unit. What effect will this have on (a) the break-even point and (b) the profit when 1000 units are sold?

14   Plot a profit – sales volume graph for the product given the data in question (a) 11, (b) 12.

15   A company is introducing a new product. The annual capacity of the production department for this product is 35,000 units with fixed costs of £20,000. The variable costs are £3 per unit. Sales are anticipated as being 30,000 units at a selling price of £7 per unit.
(a) What will be the profit at that volume of sales?
(b) Draw profit-sales volume graphs showing how the profit at the above selling price depends on the volume. What is the minimum number of units that must be sold if a profit is to be realised?
(c) What would be the effect on the answer to (b) if the selling price were reduced to £5?
(d) With this reduced selling price what would the number of units that would be needed to be sold to realise the same profit as with the £7 selling price? What comment can you make on this result?

16   The following are the costs that would be incurred for two alternative processes for the production of a hollow thermoplastic container (based on data given in *Manufacturing Technology 4*, by W. Bolton, Butterworths).

Costs	Injection moulding £	Rotational moulding £
Fixed: installation	9000	1000
: die	2000	500
Variable (per unit)		
: indirect labour	0.15	0.30
: power	0.06	0.15
Direct labour (per unit)	0.30	1.40
Direct materials (per unit)	0.40	0.40
Finishing	1.00	0

(a) On the basis of the above costs which process would be the most cost-effective if (i) 1000 (ii) 100,000 units were required?

(b) The injectional moulding process can produce fifty units per hour, the rotational moulding only two per hour. What implication might this have for using the equipment to produce a wider range of goods and so affect the choice of process?

17 The following data refer to three alternative processes by which a gearwheel can be produced (based on data given in *Engineering Materials: An introduction* (The Open University T252 Unit 2). On the basis of the data which process would you propose as the most cost effective if the output required was (a) 100, (b) 10,000 units?

Gravity die casting method, costs per unit
Materials: 10g of aluminium alloy plus 5g scrap, at £1.00 per kg
Special tooling: a die at £500 which has a life of 100,000 gears
Labour: casting 0.010 hours at £4.00 per hour
: finishing 0.001 hours at £4.00 per hour
Overheads to be charged at 200% of labour cost

Pressure die casting method, costs per unit
Materials: 23g of zinc alloy plus 2g scrap, at £0.45 per kg
Special tooling: a die at £4000 which has a life of 100,000 gears
Labour: casting 0.0015 hours at £4.00 per hour
: finishing 0.001 hours at £4.00 per hour
Overheads to be charged at 200% of labour cost

Injection moulding method, costs per unit
Materials: 4g nylon plus 0.4g scrap, at £2.00 per kg
Special tooling: die at £4000 which has a life of 100,000 gears
Labour: 0.006 hours at £4.00 per hour.
Overheads to be charged at 200% of labour cost.

15 Budgetary control

Budgets

The term *budget* is used to describe a plan expressed quantitatively, perhaps in terms of units of production or in financial terms involving revenue and expenditure. Within an organisation there are likely to be a number of budgets. Typically there might be budgets for sales, selling and distribution costs, production, production costs, administration costs, capital expenditure, research and development, etc. The sales budget, for instance, will lay down the plan for sales during perhaps the next year on a month by month basis: how many units of product A, how many of product B, etc. are to be sold in each month. The production budget will be based on the volume of sales predicted by the sales budget and will give the production targets for each month for each product. The production costs budget will follow from the production budget, the output plans being converted into labour, materials and overhead costs.

The purpose of budgets is to enable control to be exercised, i.e. targets are set and then the actual results are compared with them. Thus there is likely to be a budget for each type of function, sales, production, etc., for each department and for each type of cost. This then enables control to be exercised in each of these spheres. These budgets have to be co-ordinated with each other, e.g. the production budget will obviously interlock with the sales budget, if all the different aspects of an organisation are to operate in harmony and with maximum efficiency. For the organisation there will be a master budget which summarises the functional budgets and provides a forecasted profit and loss account and balance sheet.

Constructing a sales budget

For the sales budget to be prepared, forecasts of sales over the budgetary period are required. This period is usually a year, broken down into forecasts by month and by quarter. Because months are of unequal length many organisations divide the year into thirteen four-week periods, in order to make comparision easier.

Forecasts of sales are generally based on information from a variety of sources:

1 Opinions of salespeople and sales managers

Salespeople might be asked to complete a form which lists for each product last year's sales, the average over a number of years, the trend over the last few years and then asks them to complete the column giving their views as to the sales for the next year.

2 Market research

Data might be collected by a market survey in which potential customers are interviewed with regard to their future purchasing intentions. There might be a survey of the sex, income and tastes of potential customers. The pattern of distribution, the different types of outlets, etc. for the products might be investigated. The aim of market research is to show what products might be sold, at what price and in what quantities.

3 General trade data

General trends in trade are likely to depend on the economic and political situation and thus a consideration of government publications and the financial press can provide useful data.

The result of the analysis of the above types of data will be sales forecasts for the various products of the organisation and so a sales budget in terms of the numbers of units of the products. This can then be used as the basis of determining the sales and distribution costs budget. This budget should include all the costs related to distributing and selling the products, e.g. the salaries of the sales office staff and the salespeople, commission given on sales, travelling and subsistence expenses of salespeople, advertising costs, promotion costs such as catalogues and exhibitions, postage, telephone costs, insurance, costs associated with the sales office such as depreciation of furniture and fittings and rent, depreciation of the salesforce's cars, etc. A distinction is generally made between fixed and variable costs, fixed costs being independent of the volume of sales and variable costs dependent on the volume. Thus, in the above list, the salaries of the sales office staff could be fixed costs while the commission given on sales is a variable cost. Some costs might be considered to be semi-variable in that part of them is fixed and part variable, e.g. travelling expenses of the salesteam.

The budget so prepared might just give, for each period, one volume of sales and one set of costs. Such a budget is called a *fixed budget*. An alternative to this is a multi-volume budget where the sales and costs are given for a number of different volumes. Such a budget is known as a *flexible budget*. Table 15.1 outlines such a flexible budget.

Table 15.1

	£	£	£
Sales and distribution budget for year ending ...			
Sales (net)	400,000	410,000	420,000
Fixed costs			
Salaries of office staff	32,000	32,000	32,000
Salary of sales manager	15,000	15,000	15,000
etc.			
	62,000	62,000	62,000
Semi-variable costs			
Salesteam's expenses	18,000	19,000	20,000
Telephone expenses	1100	1300	1500
etc.			
	35,000	39,000	43,000
Variable costs			
Commission	4000	4100	4200
Bad debts	2000	2050	2100
etc.			
	8500	9400	10,300
Grand Totals	105,500	110,400	115,300

A production budget

A production budget in terms of the units of each product to be produced can be constructed from the sales budget. However, not all the information is one-way in that the production department may be constrained in the number of units of each product they can produce and this could therefore affect the sales volume forecasts.

On the basis of a production budget the production costs budget can be prepared. The costs in such a budget are likely to be grouped into direct costs and overheads, with the overheads being subdivided into variable, semi-variable and variable costs. A fixed overhead cost is one which does not depend on the production volume, a variable ones does. A semi-variable cost partly depends on the production volume. Such budgets can be fixed or flexible, a fixed budget being one where only one production volume is considered and a flexible one being where the costs are given for a number of different volumes. Table 15.2 shows, in simplified form, one type of a possible production costs budget.

Table 15.2

| | Percentage of activity | | |
	95%	100%	105%
	£	£	£
Direct costs			
Materials	50,000	55,000	60,000
Labour	90,000	100,000	110,000
	140,000	155,000	170,00
Overheads			
Fixed			
Rent	5000	5000	5000
Insurance	1500	1500	1500
etc.			
Semi-variable			
Electric light	1200	1300	1400
Maintenance	5100	5500	5900
etc.			
Variable			
Electric power	6500	7500	8500
Scrapped output	1000	1100	1200
etc.			
	26,300	28,500	30,100

Cash budgets

A *cash budget* is a forecast of the working capital available in different periods of the year. The working capital consists of cash and other assets which can be quickly turned into cash. This working capital is needed to provide for the day-to-day cash needs of the organisation. For example, wages have to be paid on certain dates in the year, taxation paid, bills for materials met within a reasonable period of time following the invoice, etc. The cash budget is very much affected by all the other budgets in the organisation. Table 15.3 is a simplified version of such a budget.

Table 15.3

	April £	*May* £	*June* £
Income			
Opening balance	55,000	40,000	24,000
Receipts from debtors	69,000	72,000	78,000
Bank interest			8000
Miscellaneous	2000	4000	1000
	126,000	116,000	111,000
Expenditure			
Wages	54,000	54,000	62,000
Materials	16,000	18,500	11,000
Overheads: factory etc.	5500	5500	6500
	86,000	92,000	85,000
Closing balances	40,000	24,000	26,000

The balance sheet

A *balance sheet* is a financial statement showing the assets and liabilities of an organisation, i.e. what it owns and what it owes, at a particular time. On the asset side would be listed the values of all fixed assets, such as buildings, plant, machinery, etc. and current assets. Fixed assets cannot be readily converted back into cash, current assets are those which are cash or are likely to be realised in cash in the near future, e.g. money owed for goods and services already supplied, cash in the bank, stocks of materials and goods, etc. Also on the asset side will be the value of investments held by the organisation, e.g. shares in other companies. Against these assets have to be set the organisation's liabilities. These will include short term liabilities, e.g. bills not yet paid, taxation owed, short term borrowings, etc. The difference between the total assets and the total liabilities is the net value of the company.

The balance sheet also shows the sources of the company's capital. Thus there will be details of the share capital and the company reserves. The total of these will equal the value of the company.

As part of budgetary control an organisation will produce a balance sheet forecast.

Variance

The difference between actual and budgeted performance is known as the *variance*. A negative variance means that the amount indicated is that much under the budgeted amount, a positive variance that it is that much over the budgeted amount. The following illustrates this.

	Budget	Actual	Variance
Materials	£3500	£3700	+ £200
Product A, units	12,000	10,300	− 1700
Overheads	£5200	£5200	zero

The comparision of actual and budgeted amounts and the taking of action consequential on the variances indicated is the essence of budgetary control.

Revision questions

1 What is meant by the term *budget*?

2 Explain what is meant by budgetary control.

3 Explain how a sales budget might be constructed.

4 Explain the difference between *fixed* and *flexible budgets*.

5 Distinguish between fixed, semi-variable and variable costs and give examples of each in connection with a sales and distribution costs budget.

6 What is meant by the term *working capital*?

7 What is a *cash budget*?

8 What is shown by a balance sheet?

9 Explain the term *variance*.

Assignments and further questions

1 Identify the various cost items that could appear in a budget for (a) a sales and distribution department's costs and (b) a production department's costs.

2 Obtain a copy of a budget and identify and explain all the cost items listed.

3 Obtain a company balance sheet and explain the significance of all the items listed in it.

4 Analyse and discuss the significance of the following data relating to a sales and distribution department, presenting it as a budget.

Sales forecast for the year
Product *A*: 140,000 units, product *B*: 132,000 units, product *C*: 36,000 units
Selling prices: *A* £12, *B* £25, *C* £45
Sales costs forecast for the year
Salary of office manager £18,000
Salaries of office staff £52,000
Salaries of salespeople £66,000
Sales promotions and advertising £8000
Sales office post, telephone, etc. expenses £9500
Sales office overheads £5000
Commission £12,000
Allowance for bad debts £20,000
Salesteam's expenses £20,000

5   For the budget arising from the data given in question 4, some variance was found to occur by the end of the year. Produce a table showing the variances in volume and values in the light of the following data.

Product A sales were down by 10%, product B sales were up by 5%, product C sales were down by £2%
Due to one salesman leaving during the year and not being replaced the salaries of the salesforce were down by £5000, all other salaries were as budgeted.
Sales promotion and advertising were increased during the year when the drop in sales became apparent and so an increase by 10% over that budgeted occurred.
Consequential on this increase in promotion the telephone and postal charges incurred by the office increased by 4%
Sales office overheads were as budgeted.
Commission was down by 8% due to the reduction in sales.
Also salespeople's expenses were down by 10%.
Allowance for bad debts was too high and only debts of £12,000 were incurred.

6   The following information was taken from an offer for sale of shares on behalf of Scott Greenham Group PLC. The group is one of the leading specialist lifting contractors and crane hirers in the United Kingdom.
   (a) Explain what they mean by the accounting being prepared under the 'historical cost convention'.
   (b) Depreciation of the tangible fixed assets is said to be on the basis of either straight line or reducing balance. Explain what these terms mean. What will be the depreciation on the freehold land and buildings during the next year if they have a value of £2,015,000 at the end of this year?

(c) In relation to the value of stocks the cost is determined on a first in, first out basis. Explain what this means.

(d) In the financial statements some of the terms are in brackets, e.g. (735). What is the significance of the brackets?

(e) On the basis of an analysis of the presented information write notes describing the trends over the period since 1980 for the group.

A   Accounting policies

(8) The significant accounting policies adopted in arriving at the financial information set out in this report are as follows:–

(a) Accounting convention

The financial statements set out in Section B have been prepared under the historical cost convention as modified by the revaluation of certain freehold land and buildings, the details of which are contained in note 8 in Section B.

(b) Basis of consolidation

The Group profit and loss accounts and balance sheets include the results of companies acquired.or disposed of during the period from the date of their acquisition or up to the date of their disposal. Intra-Group sales and profits are eliminated on consolidation and all sales and profit figures relate to external transactions only.

(c) Foreign currencies

Assets and liabilities expressed in foreign currencies are stated at the closing rate of exchange or where appropriate at the rates at which forward contracts have been entered into. Differences on exchange are dealt with in the profit and loss account.

(d) Turnover

Turnover represents the invoiced amount of sales and services rendered during the period stated net of trade discounts and value added tax.

(e) Stocks

Stocks are stated at the lower of cost and net realisable value. In general, cost is determined on a first in, first out basis. Provision is made where necessary for obsolescent, slow moving and defective stocks.

(f) Tangible fixed assets

Depreciation is calculated to write off the cost or valuation of tangible fixed assets over their expected useful lives and is charged on a weekly basis from the date of commissioning. The principal rates and bases used for this purpose are as follows:

	Rate% *per annum*	*Basis*
Freehold buildings	4	Straight line
Cranes, access platforms and ancillary equipment	5.25	Straight line
Lorries and trailers	15	Straight line
Other motor vehicles	25	Reducing balance

Garage and office equipment   15   Reducing balance
Computer equipment   25   Straight line

Freehold land is not depreciated.

(g) Deferred taxation
Provision is made for deferred taxation under the liability method at the rates of tax for the years in which the liabilities to taxation are expected to arise, except to the extent that any tax reduction can reasonably be expected to continue for the foreseeable future.

(h) Pensions
Contributions to both State and Company pension schemes are charged against profit as incurred. The assets of the Company pension scheme are held by trustees and kept separate from those of the Group.

(11) Balance sheets
The balance sheets of the Group as at 31st March, 1980, 1981, 1982, and 1983, 29th March, 1984 and 4th October, 1984, are set out below:–

							4th October,
		1980	1981	1982	1983	1984	1984
Employment of capital	Notes	£'000	£'000	£'000	£'000	£'000	£'000
Tangible fixed assets							
Freehold land and buildings	8	259	291	633	1,599	2,017	2,015
Cranes, equipment and vehicles		3,000	2,712	9,295	9,666	12,250	12,467
		3,259	3,003	9,928	11,265	14,267	14,482
Current assets							
Stocks		26	73	183	190	192	482
Debtors	9	320	420	2,295	2,083	2,954	3,139
Cash at bank and in hand		353	99	241	15	40	21
		699	592	2,719	2,288	3,186	3,642
Creditors – amounts falling due within one year	10	(735)	(534)	(3,975)	(4,750)	(6,137)	(5,377)
Net current assets (liabilities)		(36)	58	(1,256)	(2,462)	(2,951)	(1,735)
Total assets less current liabilities		3,223	3,061	8,672	8,803	11,316	12,747
Creditors – amounts falling due after more than one year	10	(1,192)	(926)	(2,538)	(1,461)	(2,570)	(2,764)
Provisions for liabilities and charges	11						
Deferred taxation		(1,091)	(1,130)	(4,619)	(4,855)	(3,807)	(4,240)
Other		–	–	(273)	(147)	(99)	(99)
		(1,091)	(1,130)	(4,892)	(5,002)	(3,906)	(4,339)
		940	1,005	1,242	2,340	4,840	5,644

Capital employed							
Share capital	12	100	100	100	100	100	1,600
Revaluation reserve		–	–	–	910	910	–
Retained profits		840	905	1,142	1,330	3,830	4,044
		940	1,005	1,242	2,340	4,840	5,644

Part Five   Technical aspects of production

This part is concerned with production management. The term *operations management* can be defined as the management concerned with the design and operation of systems for manufacture, transport, supply or service, with *production management* being that part concerned with manufacture. However these managers all tend to carry out the same types of tasks; they are managers of an important cost centre in an organisation, they are responsible for planning processes or systems, for planning work and jobs, for operating and controlling the processes or systems. The management of a cost centre is covered in Part Four, the other aspects in this part.

Chapter 16 Production planning and control.   This chapter considers the types of production operation, plant layout, maintenance planning, capacity planning, demand forecasting, aggregate planning, scheduling, inventory management, materials requirements planning, network analysis, progressing and production control.

Chapter 17 Quality control.   This chapter considers quality, its cost, and control. Measurements of variables and attributes, acceptance sampling and process control are considered.

Chapter 18 Workers and production.   Work study, including method study and work measurement, ergonomics, principles of motion economy, payment systems, job evaluation, labour turnover and job design are all considered.

16 Production planning and control

An overview

This chapter is aimed at giving an overview of the key aspects of production planning and control. For more detailed information the reader is referred to more specialist texts, e.g. *Essentials of Production and Operations Management* by R. Wild (Holt, Rinehart and Winston).

In a general sense *production planning and control* can be considered to have a number of facets:

1 Process design. This involves the selection of processes and the layout of the facilities.

2 Capacity planning. This aims to match the level of production operations to the level of demand.

3 Inventory management. This is the management of stocks of raw materials, part-finished goods and finished goods.

4 Scheduling of operations. This is the planning of activities so that the available capacity is efficiently and effectively used.

Types of production operation

As has earlier been indicated in chapter 3, production operations can be classified as:

1 Job or unique product production. This is the production of single unique items, generally to a customer's order and specification.

2 Small batch production. This generally differs little from unique product production, a small batch rather than a single product being produced.

3 Large batch production. This involves the production of large numbers of standard products with the terms mass production, line or flowline production often being used. The products are very often made to stock against future customers' orders.

4 Process production. This term is used to describe the virtually continuous processes used where essentially chemical processes are involved.

The different types of operation have different production implications. Thus an organisation engaging in unique product production, to customers' orders, will require a highly flexible production operation in order to cope with the diversity of products. It will probably also require skilled workers in that only they are likely to be able to cope with constantly changing requirements. An organisation engaged in mass production will however often be producing for stock rather than directly for customers' orders. It will probably have a rigid production system requiring high capital investment in order to produce the standardised products most economically.

Choice of process

Generally the choice of type of production operation will be determined by the product and the industry concerned. The term choice is often likely to be inappropriate in that the type of production operation is likely to be 'obvious'. Thus, for instance, in the case of domestic appliances mass production is almost invariably required because the large quantities to be produced and the economics of such large number production dictate that type of operation. However in the production of large items of machinery or civil engineering the products are generally one-off, against a customer order rather than in anticipation of customer orders, and thus job or unique product production is required.

Products where there is a reasonably constant, high sales volume, where the product design is standard and not changing often and the potential life of the product is long are likely to require large batch production methods in order to be economic.

Plant layout

The term *plant layout* is used to describe the arrangement of the various facilities required in the production process. The prime aim is to arrange the facilities to provide efficient operation. This can be considered to involve designing the layout to achieve:

1 Maximum utilisation of the space, facilities and labour.
2 The minimum manufacturing time.
3 The minimum amount of movement of materials and work-in-progress.
4 Safe operation.
5 A socially acceptable layout for the workmen.

Essentially there are three main systems of production plant layout:

1 Layout by process.
2 Layout by product.
3 Group layout.

Each of the systems has its own characteristics (Figure 16.1) which make it appropriate in some situations. The main factors involved in determing which system might be the most appropriate are the type of production operation involved, e.g. unique product or perhaps mass production, and the range of products that have to be produced.

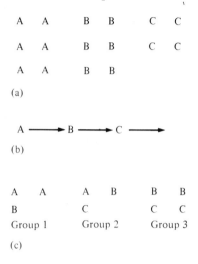

Figure 16.1 *Plant layout*
(a) *Process layout: A is one type of process, e.g. milling, B is another, e.g. drilling, and C another, e.g. grinding. Each product takes its own operational sequence through the processes*
(b) *Product layout: all products follow the same sequence of processes*
(c) *Group layout: a sequence of processes occurring at each group. Products take their own operational sequence between groups but not generally within groups*

With a *process layout* all the plant concerned with a particular process is grouped together. Thus all the milling machines would be together, all the grinding machines together in separate groups, etc. Where unique production is concerned this could be the best layout. It permits great flexibility in scheduling in that the schedule does not have to dictate which machine the workpiece should go to, but just which type of machine. It also gives flexibility in that complex jobs requiring processing through many processes can be dealt with alongside those requiring just a few processes. It is a versatile layout system. However it does have the disadvantage of requiring a lot of travel time between the relevant processes for a workpiece and so does not give the minimum manufacturing time for a particular product. However, because of the diversity of jobs tackled with unique production it is extremely unlikely that any one arrangement of the processes would be capable of giving the minimum manufacturing time for every product.

With *layout by product*, the plant is laid out in the sequence of processes required by a particular product. The production sequence is thus specific to a particular product and so the layout is only suitable where large batches are involved, i.e. mass production. The layout is thus not flexible and adaptation to another product can be expensive. Failure in a particular machine in the production line can lead to a stoppage of the entire line. The workpiece travels from one particular machine to another particular machine and thus if there is a hold-up and the workpiece does not arrive at a machine then that machine is liable to remain idle. The system is thus inflexible, however it does reduce the time wasted by the workpiece in travel between machines and so gives the maximum through-put.

With a variety of products and perhaps small or medium batches, both the process layout and the product layout may be inappropriate, the process layout because too much time would be wasted and the product layout because it could not cope with changes in process sequence. Group layout may be more appropriate in such situations. *Group layout* involves the recognition that many of the products have similarities in their make-up. The range of products is considered and the similarities identified. This leads to an identification of a number of sets of process sequences. Within each set a product layout can be adopted. The result of this is that the layout consists of a number of short production lines, no one line generally being adequate for the manufacture of an entire component. The workpiece is then routed between these different short production lines according to the sequence of processes it requires. This group layout is more flexible than the product layout where a single layout is used and less flexible than the process layout. It does however have the advantage of requiring less travel time for the workpiece than the process layout.

Planning a layout

In planning a layout the main objective is usually to minimise the amount of movement of the workpiece, materials and people, hence a minimisation of cost. In the planning stage this invariably means a minimisation of distance. Visual aids tend to play a significant part in this planning stage, often with models being used and the various paths of the workpieces being indicated. Some computer programs are also available to assist in layout preparation.

A useful chart that can be constructed for a particular layout in order to show the amount of movement is the travel or cross chart. Figure 16.2 shows such a chart. The vertical axis of the chart indicates the starting

From \ To	Stores	Milling	Turning	Assembly	Test	Despatch
Stores		22				
Milling			19	3		
Turning				16		
Assembly					11	
Test			1	2		8
Despatch						

Figure 16.2 *Travel chart*

points for a movement and the horizontal axis the finishing points. The entry made in a particular square refers to the number of items moved. Thus, for example, the chart indicates that 22 items were moved from the store to milling. Numbers appearing above the diagonal indicate the motion of items when following the sequence of operations listed on the chart, numbers below the diagonal occur when the movement is in the opposite direction to the listed sequence.

The comparative size of the numbers appearing in any square indicates the need for those operations to be kept close together if total transit times are to be kept low. Where the number in a square is low, or zero, there is less or no need for those operations to be kept close together.

Maintenance planning

There are essentially two types of maintenance policy that an organisation might adopt:

1 Breakdown maintenance, which involves waiting until the plant fails before repairing it.
2 Preventive maintenance, which involves anticipating breakdown and replacing or adjusting the plant before breakdown occurs.

The decision as to which form of maintenance policy to adopt will probably depend on the relative costs of the two. With breakdown maintenance a factor to be considered is the lost output or the cost of supplementary plant to be used while repairs are being made. A significant factor determining the cost of preventive maintenance is the level of it. Preventive maintenance involves inspection and servicing and the greater the frequency of the inspection the less likely there is to be failure but the greater the cost. Thus generally the level of preventive maintenance is often adjusted so that though there are some failures the cost is not too high.

Preventive maintenance is likely to be more cost effective than breakdown maintenance when:

1 The cost of preventive maintenance is less than the cost of the lost output and repair.
2 Plant failure can cause considerable lost output costs.
3 Plant failure can lead to safety problems.
4 When the failure rate of plant starts to increase rapidly after a period during which it has been relatively low. Anticipating this point can be very cost effective.

When breakdown occurs there is a lost production cost and a repair cost. Such costs can be minimised by:

1 Designing the plant so that repair is facilitated.
2 Designing the layout of the plant so that repair is facilitated.
3 Establishing an efficient repair facility so that repairs are effected rapidly.
4 Providing excess production capacity, i.e. back-up facilities, so that production can continue.
5 Providing buffer stocks so that a production line can still continue.

Capacity planning

The effective management of capacity is one of the most important responsibilities of operations management. The term *capacity* is used to describe the resources available for production purposes, including both facilities and people. The aim of capacity management is to match the level of production operations to the level of demand. The problem however is that the level of demand for which capacity has to be planned is often very uncertain. This uncertainty can result from uncertainty about the number of customer orders likely to be received and the type of resources necessary to meet them; or where production is for stock as opposed to direct customer order, there may be uncertainty about the level of stock necessary in order to meet orders. Demand forecasting is necessary.

Demand forecasting

Decisions regarding the capacity required by an organisation can be made utilising forecasts over a number of different periods of time and of differing degrees of precision. For planning the installation of major capital equipment, perhaps the setting up of a new production line for mass producing cars, a fairly long-term forecast for several years into the future will be required. For capacity decisions involving the allocation of existing machines and labour, short-term forecasts of demand may be required. Short-range forecasts can be fairly accurate and detailed but this is not likely to be true of long term forecasts, such forecasts being easily upset by changes in perhaps the economic or political climate which are difficult to foretell.

A number of different methods can be used for *demand forecasting*, namely:

1 Qualitative forecasting based essentially on gathering the views of people.
2 The analysis of past data and then an extrapolation of past performance into the future (known as time-series forecasting).
3 Relating demand to some other variable and then using predictions of that variable to give, by comparision, demand forecasts, (known as causal forecasting).

Qualitative forecasting can involve market surveys to gather opinions of customers, forecasts developed by panels of experts giving their opinions, salesstaff and sales managers giving their opinions, etc. Forecasts made by individuals on the basis of their experience are however found to give, in general, only poor to fair accuracy, whether short term or long term. Market surveys however can give much better predictions, however the cost of making this type of prediction is much higher than the cost of asking individuals, such as the salespeople, to state their views.

Time-series methods are used to analyse past demand patterns and then project these patterns forward into the future. The basic assumption of this method is that the demand pattern can be broken down into a number of components. Thus, for instance, the demand might vary with time in such a way that it can be considered to have essentially just two components, a level demand with a seasonal pattern superimposed on top of it, as in Figure 16.3, with some random variations. Once the components have been identified they, excepting the random component, are projected forward into the future.

A simple method of carrying out a time-series analysis is to use the *moving-average method*. This assumes that the time series consists of just a level component and a random component. The demand data are available for a number of periods of past time and the average calculated over a number N of past periods.

$$\text{Average} = \frac{D_t + D_{t-1} + D_{t-2} + \ldots}{N}$$

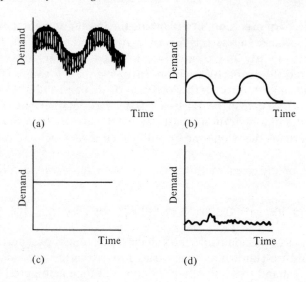

Figure 16.3   *Time-series analysis*

(a)   *The demand pattern*
(b)   *The seasonal component*
(c)   *The level component*
(d)   *A random component*

D_t is the demand for the time t, D_{t-1} is the demand for previous period of time of t minus one time period, D_{t-2} is the demand for the period of time t minus two time periods. On this basis the forecast for the period of time $(t + 1)$, i.e. the next period in the future, is the same as the average obtained for the periods up to time t. As time progresses new demand data are generated and the procedure adopted is to maintain the same N periods of demand in the calculation and let the average move along.

The following is an example to illustrate the moving-average method. A three-period moving average is considered, i.e. $N = 3$.

Past data at time t

Period	March	April	May
Demand	15	17	16

The average is $(15 + 17 + 16) \div 3 = 16$. Thus the forecast for the next period of time, i.e. June, is 16. When the June data are obtained the average is revised and the three period average calculated using the April, May and June data.

Period	April	May	June
Demand	17	16	21

The average is $(17 + 16 + 21) \div 3 = 18$. The forecast for July is thus 18.

The greater the number of periods of time N used in calculating the moving average, the less responsive the average is to changes in demand and the more stable is the value obtained.

With the moving-average method equal emphasis is placed on the demand data for each period, regardless of whether it is a more recent or an earlier period. An alternative method, *exponential smoothing*, places more weight on recent data. How this is done can be illustrated by considering the data used above for the moving-average example. For March, April and May the average is 16. In June the demand is found to be 21. To obtain the forecast for the next period using exponential smoothing we do not consider this demand to be of the same significance as the demand data for March, April or May but, perhaps, we decide it is more significant and weight it. So in the calculation of the forecast for the next month we give it more weighting. The equation used for this is:

$$\text{New average} = \alpha D_t + (1 - \alpha)A_{t-1}$$

where D_t is the demand in period t, A_{t-1} is the average up to and including period $(t - 1)$, i.e. the old average, and α is a weighting constant, sometimes referred to as smoothing constant, that we choose. α has a value between 0 and 1. Thus, if for our example we choose α to be 0.6, then the new average is

$$0.6 \times 21 + (1 - 0.6)16 = 19$$

This is then the forecast for the month of July. More weight has been given to the June data than to the data from the previous months.

An alternative way of weighting data is to use the moving average method but weight each data period differently. Thus

$$\text{average} = \frac{W_1 D_t + W_2 D_{t-1} + W_3 D_{t-2} + \dots}{N}$$

where W_1, W_2, W_3, etc. are weighting factors such that $W_1 + W_2 + W_3 + \dots W_N = 1$. This method has however a disadvantage when compared to the exponential smoothing method in that the entire demand history for N periods must be calculated each time and it requires the adjustment of the weighting factors each time a new period is added. Exponential smoothing is a simpler method.

For long term forecasting both moving averages, either simple or weighted, and exponential smoothing give poor forecasts. However for short term forecasting exponential smoothing can give good results, better than moving averages. Other, more mathematically complex, methods can be used with time series to give better results for short and medium term forecasts.

For many products there can be a close relationship between the demand for them and the sales of other products or general economic indicators or some other factor. For example the demand for car accessories could be related to past sales of cars, the demand for computer games related to the past sales of computers. To use this method of forecasting for a particular product a relationship has to be found with one or more other variables whose fluctuations are afterwards reflected in changes in demand for the product concerned. The method employed is to collect data for the demand for the product and values of the other variables and then look for relationships between them. A relationship between the demand and some variable can be expressed by what is known as a *simple regression* equation; where the demand is related to more than one variable then *multiple regression* is involved.

To illustrate the methods employed, consider the relationship between the demand for a car accessory and past sales of cars. The data might be:

Month	Car accessory sales	Car sales
1	800	1200
2	850	1250
3	870	1400
4	930	2100
5	1210	4000

A relationship exists between car accessory sales in any one month A_t and the car sales in the previous month C_{t-1}. The following is the relationship

$$A_t = 0.4C_{t-1} + 370$$

This is the regression equation (it is the standard straight line equation between two variables y and x of $y = mx + c$). Now if in any one month the car sales are, say, 5200 then the equation can be used to make a prediction of the number of car accessories that are likely to be demanded the next month, in this case

$$A_t = 0.4 \times 5200 + 370$$
$$= 2450$$

The above is an artificial case invented for the purpose of illustrating the method; in practice the data points would not precisely fit the relationship and there would be some scatter.

Aggregate planning

The term *aggregate* is used to indicate that the capacity planning under this heading is not concerned with details of individual products nor with details of scheduling plant and personnel but with the overall output required, i.e. all the product demands aggregrated or collected together. Aggregate planning is usually concerned with medium term planning, i.e. plans up to one or two years in the future. Such planning is a comparision between the capacity available and what the demands will require. It is assumed, since only medium term planning is involved, that there can be no major new capacity within such a time and that the demand has to be met from using or adjusting existing capacity.

Aggregate planning can be considered to involve the following sequence of operations.

1 Forecast demand for the products over the time concerned.

2 Express the demands for the different products in some common capacity-related units. This is necessary if all the demands are to be aggregated together. Thus a brewery might use litres of beer as its aggregated capacity measure, despite producing a variety of beers in a variety of different volume containers. Volume is often used in process production where chemical processes are involved. In a highly mechanised production department machine hours might be used.

3 Produce an aggregated demand.

4 Consider the demand data and how best the capacity can be utilised to achieve those demands. There are essentially three ways this can be done: chase demand, level capacity or a mixed plan. With *chase demand* the output is directly linked to the demand and as demand changes so there will have to be capacity changes. *Level capacity* involves smoothing out the demand fluctuations and maintaining a level use of capacity over the time concerned (Figure 16.4). This can be done by, perhaps, producing for stock during low demand periods and making use of that stock during high demand periods. Another

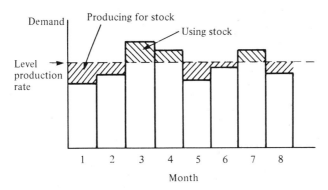

Figure 16.4 *A level-capacity production plan*

possibility is to allow a backlog of orders to develop at high demand periods. A *mixed plan* involves a mixture of chase demand, at perhaps the main peak and troughs of demand, with a level capacity approach to most of the demand.

5 Consider what changes in capacity will be needed and how they can be obtained. This might involve hiring and firing employees, using overtime or lay-offs, producing for stock or utilising stocks, subcontracting, buying-in, adjusting the demand by changing the price or advertising, allowing backlogs to develop. etc.

6 Finally put it all together as an aggregrate plan.

Scheduling

Capacity and aggregate planning are concerned with establishing what resources are likely to be required, *scheduling* is concerned with the planning of activities to make the most effective and efficient use of available resources. Thus capacity and aggregate planning can be considered as determining the resources that should be required for scheduling and thus scheduling can be considered to be the last aspect in the sequence of decision making concerned with production planning.

Where an assembly line is being used and there is just one product made by that line then there is no scheduling problem, the output being determined completely by the design of the line. However, where more than one product is made by the line, e.g. it might be that the line makes a variety of models of the same basic product, then there is a scheduling problem. Each product is generally made in batches, with a changeover to the next product involving costs associated with perhaps setting up or even retooling. The problem then becomes the determination of the most economic batch size. The production of small batches means fewer stocks to be held but more frequent resetting and associated costs, large batches however mean more stocks to be held but less frequent resetting and so over a period of time lower resetting costs. The problem is thus one of inventory management.

Inventory management

An *inventory* can be defined as the stock of material used to facilitate production or meet customer demand. Thus inventories can include raw materials, work in process and finished goods. A stock of finished goods can provide a way of meeting fluctuations in demand without having to change production capacity, i.e. accommodate short-term differences between demand and production output rate. Work in process stocks can be used to accommodate fluctuations in input and output rates of the various production stages. A stock of raw materials can be used to protect

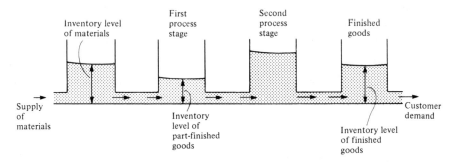

Figure 16.5   *Inventory management*

against uncertainties in the supply of the materials and also to permit fluctuations in the demand for the materials from the production stages that follow. A simple way of describing the above in terms of a model is shown in Figure 16.5. The size of the inventory is represented by the level of water in a tank, the tank having an input and an output. If the input and output rates are the same then the inventory level remains constant. If however there is a change in one then the inventory level can either rise or fall to accommodate the fluctuation and still give the required output. The existence of the inventories thus enables the production manager to maintain an even rate of production flow.

Among the principal advantages for an organisation holding inventories is that it enables them to:

1   In the case of a raw materials inventory:
    (a) Accommodate fluctuations in the supply of the materials.
    (b) Provide strategic stocks for materials that might for some reason become in short supply.
    (c) Take advantages of quantity discounts.
    (d) Guard against anticipated price increases.
    (e) Accommodate fluctuations in the demand for materials for the production processes.

2   In the case of work-in-progress inventories:
    (a) Decouple the different stages of production and so enable a more even rate of production flow to be maintained.
    (b) Give greater flexibility in production scheduling.
    (c) Improve the utilisation of plant and labour.
    (d) Assist in coping with plant breakdown and maintain a production flow.

3   In the case of finished goods:
    (a) Achieve a steady supply to customers though the production may be intermittent.

(b) Cope with fluctuations in demand without making changes in the rate of production.

(c) Achieve a supply to customers if plant breaks down or some other factor stops production.

(d) Be able to supply customers off-the-shelf without delay.

Inventories incur costs. These can be considered under the following headings:

1   Item cost.

2   Ordering costs. In the case of raw materials there will be a cost associated with the replenishment of stocks, the cost including such items as the paperwork, transportation, etc.

3   Holding costs. This cost is associated with the keeping of items in inventory for a period of time and includes the costs associated with storage, e.g. the facilities and insurance, costs associated with obsolence, deterioration and loss of items, and the costs of the capital tied up in the inventories, such capital not therefore being available for other purposes.

There is also another cost factor that has to be considered in relation to inventories and that is the cost of running out of stock, showing itself as a hold up in production or sales. This is referred to as a stockout cost.

Organisations tend to need inventories and since inventories cost money there is the obvious question – what is the right amount of inventory? An inventory holding in an item in excess of what is required is effectively money earning no useful return. An inventory holding inadequate to what is required can cost money in, for example, lost production, i.e. the stockout cost. The control of inventories is thus vital.

Control of inventories

A vital factor in the control of inventories is whether the demand for a particular inventory is independent or dependent. An *independent demand* is where it is independent of the production operations but depends only on external factors. Thus the demand for finished goods is independent. *Dependent demand* is where it is related to the demand for another item and is not independent of production operations. Thus the demand for part-finished items is determined by the demand for the finished goods and so is a dependent demand. The type of control system used will depend on whether the demand for the inventory is dependent or independent and as an organisation is likely to have inventories which fall into both categories then more than one type of control system will have to be employed.

Inventory control for independent demand is based on forecasts, often evolving from past demand. The questions that have to be considered in relation to such inventory control are – when should an order be placed to replenish the inventory and how much should be ordered? One method could be to reorder whenever the inventory falls to a particular level. The term *two-bin system* is used for this method. This is because we can consider the inventory to consist of two bins, with one bin containing items which are issued while the second bin remains sealed. When the items in the first bin have all been issued an order is placed for fresh stock and the second bin opened. This bin should contain enough items to last out until a new delivery of items occurs. The term *single-bin* system could be used for a method whereby the inventory is allowed to run down to zero before an order is placed, i.e. there is nothing kept in a second bin to cover the time taken for the new stock to be delivered. An alternative to methods involving ordering when the inventory reaches a particular level, even if the level is zero, is to order at fixed time intervals. Such orders are generally placed so as to bring the inventory up to a particular level.

Figure 16.6 illustrates the differences in these two approaches. For convenience it has been assumed for the figures that restocking is instantaneous following ordering.

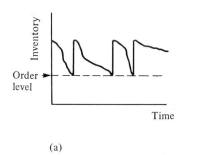 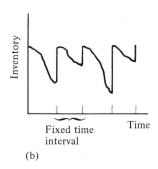

Figure 16.6
(a) *Inventory replenishment at a fixed level*
(b) *Inventory replenishment at fixed time intervals*

Inventory control with independent demand is generally concerned with batch ordering and the minimising of the total variable costs, i.e. the minimisation of the total of the holding and ordering costs. Figure 16.7 shows how these costs might vary with the size of batch ordered. The batch order size at the minimum total cost is called the *economic order quantity* (EOQ). Various equations have been developed for calculating the economic order quantity and tables and charts to enable these equations to be easily used are available.

The following shows how an equation is developed and the conditions pertaining to its use. With the two-bin method, a constant demand, the items ordered or produced in batches are all put into the inventory at one time, there is a constant and known time from order to delivery, and no

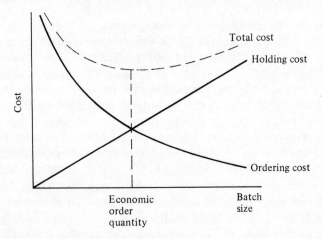

Figure 16.7   *Economic order quantity*

stockouts and the inventory level will vary with time in the way shown in Figure 16.8. The quantity ordered each time and put into the inventory is Q. This then results in an average inventory level of $\frac{1}{2}Q$. If c is the unit cost of the item then the average cost of the inventory is $\frac{1}{2}Qc$. If C is the carrying cost rate per unit time, i.e. effectively the rate of interest lost on the capital, then the holding cost for that time is $\frac{1}{2}QcC$. This is the equation of the holding cost line in Figure 16.7. If the consumption rate per unit time is r then the number of items consumed in that unit time will be r/Q. If the cost of placing an order or setting up production is C_s, then the ordering cost in that time is rC_s/Q. This is the equation of the ordering cost line in Figure 16.7. Hence as the total cost is the sum of the holding cost and the ordering cost:

$$\text{Total cost per unit time } C_t = \frac{1}{2}QcC + rC_s/Q$$

The minimum value of this total cost can be obtained by using calculus or by realising that the minimum occurs when the holding cost equals the ordering cost, i.e.

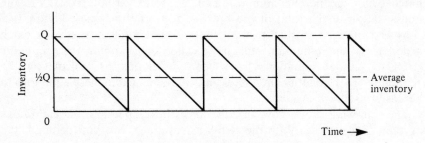

Figure 16.8   *Inventory levels vary with time*

$$\tfrac{1}{2}QcC = rC_s/Q$$

Hence

$$Q^2 = \frac{2rC_s}{cC}$$

This is the economic order quantity, hence:

$$EOQ = \sqrt{\frac{2rC_s}{cC}}$$

To illustrate the use of the above equation, consider a company which makes an item for which the yearly sales are forecast at 200, each item costing £150. The carrying-cost rate per year is 25% and the cost of setting up for production is £1000. If we assume that there is a constant demand and we can use the above equation then the economic order quantity is:

$$EOQ = \sqrt{\left(\frac{2 \times 200 \times 1000}{150 \times 0.25}\right)}$$
$$= 103$$

Thus the company should produce the items in batches of 103 if costs are to be kept to a minimum. The cost, over the above the production cost of the item, for such batch sizes is, using the earlier equation for C_t:

Total cost per year $C_t = \tfrac{1}{2} \times 103 \times 150 \times 0.25 + 200 \times 1000/103$
$$= £3873$$

In this example the order has effectively been considered to be from the sales department for its inventory of finished goods to the production department. A similar approach can be used for a production department ordering raw materials.

In the above equations it was assumed that all the items would be delivered into inventory at the same time. The equations are however modified if the items are delivered into stock continually throughout the

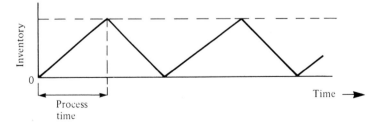

Figure 16.9 *Inventory levels with continual stock delivery*

process period, as illustrated by Figure 16.9. The average inventory is then $\frac{1}{2}Q(1 - r/q)$, where r is consumption rate per unit of time and q the process rate per unit of time. Thus:

$$C_t = \tfrac{1}{2}QcC(1 - r/q) + rC_s/Q$$

and, as before

$$EOQ = \sqrt{\left(\frac{2rC_s}{cC(1 - r/q)}\right)}$$

Another factor that can be taken into account is the holding of buffer stocks. In Figures 16.8 and 16.9 the inventory is shown as falling to zero. If there is a buffer stock level B then, as shown in Figure 16.10, the effect is to increase the average inventory to $(B + \frac{1}{2}Q)$ and so the total cost per unit time to:

$$C_t = (B + \tfrac{1}{2}Q)cC + rC_s/Q$$

In calculating the minimum cost the term involving B has no effect on the value and thus the economic order quantity is unchanged, as:

$$EOQ = \sqrt{\frac{2rC_s}{cC}}$$

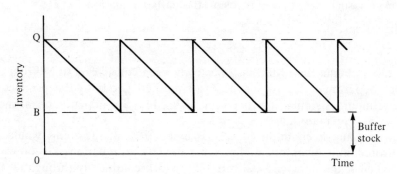

Figure 16.10   *Effect of buffer stocks on the inventory*

Scheduling for batch processing

In the previous section of this chapter the size of a production batch to meet a constant demand was considered and the optimum batch size determined where there was to be minimum cost, the term economic order quantity being used for this optimum batch size. However if an organisation is producing more than one product on the same machines there can be a clash of requirements, unless the different batches occur in sequence. This is often not the case and the situation might be like that described in Figure 16.11 where the required process times for two products overlap. A technique that can be used to deal with scheduling in such situations is the line of balance technique. This technique is considered later in this chapter.

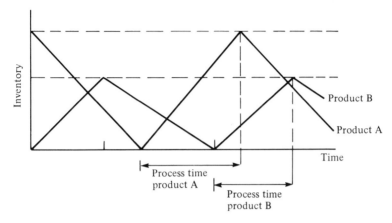

Figure 16.11   *Process time for two products may overlap*

Materials requirements planning

Where items are assembled in batches, certain components will be required at particular times to suit the batch assembly schedule. Thus to maintain an even production flow inventories of these items are likely to be held. The demand for these items is dependent, i.e. not subject to market forces but dependent on the demand for other items in the production operations. For example, the drilling operation for a particular product cannot take place until the machining operation is complete. Thus to avoid the drill operators running out of work if there is a delay in the machining, inventories of machined parts can be held. The level of this inventory depends on the demand generated by the drill operators, not on any market forces. *Materials requirements planning* (MRP) is concerned with ensuring that items are available when required and also that unnecessarily high inventory levels are not held.

Figure 16.12 shows the essential features of a materials requirements planning system. The purpose of the MRP system is to co-ordinate the entire planning operation and produce purchase orders and production orders at the appropriate times and in the appropriate quantities. Inputs to the system are details of the materials (resulting from the design data), a master schedule giving details of the quantities and types of products

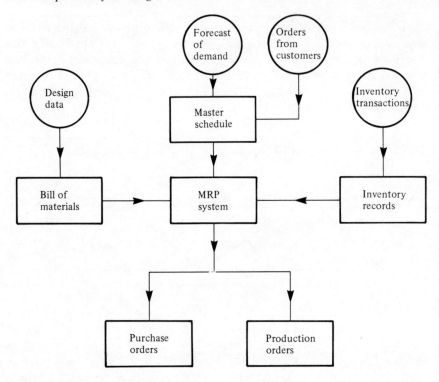

Figure 16.12   *Essential features of a materials requirements planning (MRP) system*

required in each time period, and inventory records giving the current inventory levels and details of ordering procedures. There is also feedback of information to the system on how it is functioning and hence the possibility of changes being made in plans. The system is almost invariably run on a computer, the MRP system being essentially the computer program.

Schedules and loads

The term *job schedule* is used for a schedule that has been prepared for a single job. It will show the start and finish times for each activity involved in that job. A bar chart, sometimes referred to as a *Gannt chart*, can be used to show the schedule. The vertical axis of such a chart, see Figure 16.13, shows the activities and the horizontal axis time. The planned operations and their times are shown in the form of bars, the beginning of the bar indicating the start time and the end of the bar the finish time. Thus, for example, activity *B* is planned to start at the beginning of week 2 and finish half way through week 4. Activity *A* might be the designing,

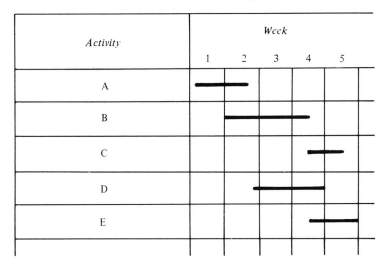

Figure 16.13 *A schedule*

activity *B* the process planning, activity *C* the setting up, etc.

The term factory or *production schedule* is used where the schedule simultaneously considers a number of jobs. A bar chart can be used, as before, and in that case activity A might refer to product *A*, activity *B* to product *B*, etc. Production schedules and job schedules obviously interact.

Another form of schedule is the one that indicates for each work centre their work. The term *load* is used for the work assigned to a particular work centre, perhaps a particular machine, and the term *loading* to describe the working out of the anticipated load profile for a work centre. Loading indicates the utilisation that it being planned for a work centre. There is an obvious interaction between such load schedules and both production and job schedules.

Network analysis

In both planning and scheduling activities a technique that is widely used is *network analysis*. Such a method can show the interdependencies and relationships between activities. The following represents the various stages in carrying out such an analysis in its simplest form:

1 Identify all the activities involved.

2 Construct a network diagram where each of these activities is repre-sented by an arrow and the arrangement of the arrows represents the order in which the activities will occur and their interdependence. At the start and finish of each arrow a small circle is drawn to indicate an 'event', i.e. the start or completion of the activity. Any number of

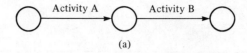

(a)

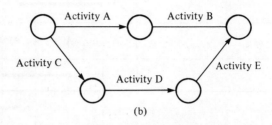

(b)

Figure 16.14
(a) *Sequential activities: B cannot occur until A is complete*
(b) *Parallel activities: C, D and E can occur without relationship to A and B*

activities can go into or out of an event. Activities occurring in the same linear path are sequential and thus directly dependent on each other, activities on different paths are termed parallel activities and can therefore take place at the same time. Figure 16.14 illustrates these principles.

3   Estimate the time taken for each activity and insert the times alongside the appropriate arrows.

4   Examine the various paths through the network and compute for each activity the earliest start time and the latest finish time.

5   Further analysis can then lead to the identification of the critical path, this being defined as the longest time path through the network. It is this path which determines the completion time and the activities along that path are critical since any delays in them will increase the overall time and delay the completion.

The above outlines the basic steps in carrying out network analysis. One type of activity that was not mentioned above is the *dummy activity*. Dummy activities consume no time and may be used to indicate a dependence or to avoid having more than one activity with the same beginning and end events. Dotted lines are used for the arrows representing dummy activities, as in Figure 16.15.

To illustrate this network analysis approach consider the following example, making a cup of coffee.

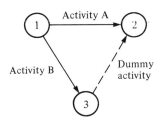

Figure 16.15 *Dummy activities: no time spent going from event 3 to event 2*

Activity	Activities on which dependent
A Fill kettle with water	–
B Plug kettle into mains	A
C Water heats up	B
D Pour hot water onto coffee in cup	C, G
E Get cup and saucer	–
F Get coffee	–
G Put coffee in cup	E, F
H Take cup with coffee to kettle	G
I Get milk	–
J Add milk to hot coffee	D, I
K Get sugar	–
L Put sugar in hot, milky coffee.	J

Figure 16.16 shows the network for the coffee making. Event 1 is where it all starts, event 12 where it finishes. An event marks the completion or start of an activity or activities. Thus, for example, event 4 is the completion of the activities of the water heating up and taking the cup with coffee to the kettle and the start of the activity of pouring the hot water onto the coffee in the cup. It is sometimes easier to draw a network by starting from the end and working backwards.

The numbers written under each arrow are the times taken for the activities, in this case in seconds (s). Thus, for example, activity A which is the filling of the kettle with water takes 25 s.

The earliest start time for each activity is calculated from the beginning of the network by adding together all the preceding activity durations. Where two or more activities lead into one event then the last of the activities to finish determines the start time for the subsequent activity. This is because this activity cannot start until all the activities leading to this event have been completed. Thus for event 3 the earliest start time is 25 + 3 = 28 s. For event 4 there are two paths to that event, one having a

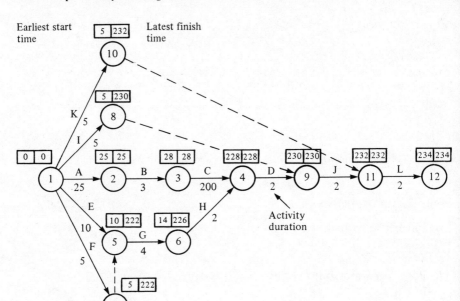

Figure 16.16   *Making a cup of coffee*

total duration of 25 + 3 + 200 = 228 s and the other 10 + 4 + 2 = 16 s. Hence the earliest start time is 228 s. The earliest start times are shown on the network as the first of the two times in the rectangular boxes.

The latest finishing time is calculated from the end of the network by subtracting activity durations from the project finish time. Where two or more activities stem from one event the earliest of the times determines the latest finishing time for the previous activities. Thus for event 11 the latest finishing time is 234 – 2 = 232 s. For event 10 the latest finishing time is 232 – 0 = 232 s.

From the above information a number of other times can be calculated. Thus the earliest finish time for any activity is the sum of the earliest start time of the activity and its duration. Hence for activity H the earliest finish time is 14 + 2 = 16 s. The latest start time for any activity is the latest finish time for that activity minus its duration. Thus for activity H the latest start time is 228 – 2 = 226 s.

The earliest finish time for any activity, or the entire project, is determined by the longest time path through the network to that event. Thus the earliest finish time for activity *D* is determined by the path through activities *A*, *B*, *C* and not the path through *E*, *G*, *H*. Therefore the shorter time path will have more time available to it than is required. The time available for an activity is the latest finish time minus the earliest start time. Thus for activity *H* the time available is 228 – 14 = 214 s. The actual time required is 2 s, thus there is $214 - 2 = 212$ s spare, this spare time being referred to as the *total float*.

The total float is the amount of time by which an activity can slip without causing any change in the total time required for the project. However it should be noted that if there is slippage in the time for activity E in that path, E, G, H then the time available for slippage in activity H will be reduced.

The critical path through the network is the longest time path. For the coffee making it is A, B, C, D, J, L. It is the path with minimum total float. Any delay in the activities along this path will delay the completion of the project. A delay along any other path will just use up some of the total float associated with that path.

Progressing

The term *progressing* is used to describe the checking that production is going to plan and the taking of remedial action where it is not. The terms *progress chaser* or *expeditor* are used for the individuals whose job it is to carry out this work.

Information on the progress of production is obtained in a number of ways. For example there might be counting or recording devices attached to machines. There are the operator's work record, a sheet on which an operator lists all the jobs he or she has done, and job cards, which are the instructions to an operator as to what jobs to do and which are filled in when jobs are completed. In addition there is much information to be obtained by progress chasers just walking round the production facilities and observing.

Production delays can occur for a wide variety of reasons, the following being some of them:

1 **Personnel.** There might be absenteeism, disputes, high labour turn-over, inadequately skilled operators, etc.

2 **Machines.** There might be breakdowns, tool problems, loading errors, etc.

3 **Materials.** Materials might be delivered late or of the wrong quality, there might be handling problems in the stores, etc.

4 **Design.** There might be design errors or perhaps an accuracy specified which presents production problems.

5 **Planning.** The plans might have been too optimistic or have errors.

6 **The customer.** The customer might make changes to the specification or delivery dates.

Progress information can be presented on the Gannt chart (Figure 16.17). As well as showing the planned times (as earlier shown in Figure 16.13) it can also show the progress towards meeting those plans. Thus if we wanted to consider progress at the end of the fourth day for the example given: Activity *A* is complete, Activity *B* is also complete – ahead of schedule, Activity *C* is still occurring but progress is ahead of schedule in that more is completed than was expected, activity *D* is behind schedule in that not as much has been completed as was planned.

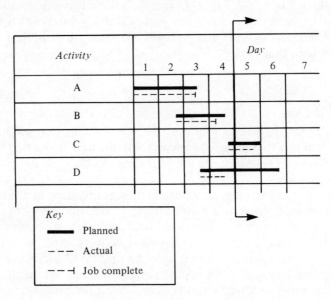

Figure 16.17   *Presenting progress information using a Gannt chart*

Production control

Where mass production is involved and there is a small range of products, *production control* is often mainly concerned with ensuring that inventories are maintained at the appropriate levels. This is a simpler situation than one where jobbing or small batch production is involved. Such situations involve a great number of variables, generally a wide range of products and often flexible plant. Progress chasing plays a big role in such situations.

Production control can be fairly straightforward if for each operation a batch is kept intact, the entire batch finishing one operation before moving on to the next operation. However this can result in a longer throughput time and inefficient use of plant. For this reason *batch splitting* is often used. In this, part of the batch is undergoing one operation while another part is undergoing a different operation. This, while decreasing throughput time and increasing the efficiency of plant usage it does make it more difficult to ascertain whether the entire batch is proceeding to plan. A technique that can be used is the *line of balance* technique.

To illustrate the use of this technique, consider a simple product which has just four operations A, B, C and D performed sequentially on it. Operation A takes 2 days, operation B 3 days, operation C 1 day and the final operation D 2 days. This is a total time of 8 days. Suppose that the delivery requirements are 20 units per day, starting after the 8th day, i.e. the batch has been split. To meet this we must have 20 units through operation D by the end of the 8th day. Because operation C has a lead time over operation D of 2 days sufficient units should have been completed through this operation at day 8 to meet the delivery schedules for both the 8th and 9th days, i.e. a total of 40 units. These are the cumulative completions by that 8th day.

For operation B the lead time over operation D is 3 days. Hence at day 8 we must have a cumulative completion for process B of 60 units, to meet the deliveries for days 8, 9 and 10. For operation A the lead time over operation D is 6 days. Hence the cumulative completion for process A must be 120 units, to meet deliveries for days 8, 9, 10, 11, 12 and 13. We can represent this days as a histogram, Figure 16.18.

Control over actual production at the various operations is obtained by comparing the histogram of actual progress with the line representing the planned progress histogram, the line being referred to as the line of

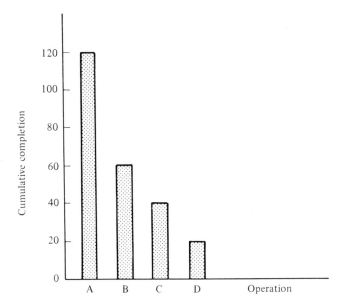

Figure 16.18   *The planned completions*

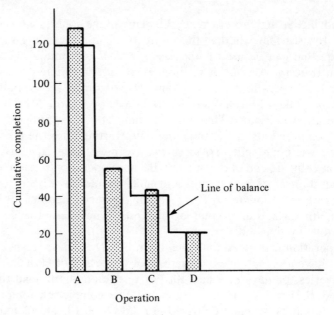

Figure 16.19   *A progress chart*

balance. Figure 16.19 shows such a comparison. Thus, for this example, cumulative completions from operation *A* are ahead of schedule, from operation *B* behind schedule.

Revision questions

1 Explain the differences between *job, small-batch, large-batch* and *process production.*

2 What type of product is likely to be produced by (a) job and (b) mass production?

3 What criteria are likely to be involved in the design of a plant layout?

4 Explain the differences between plant layouts by (a) process, (b) product and (c) group?

5 Which type of layout is likely to be the most efficient for (a) job production, (b) mass production?

6 Explain the significance of a travel chart.

7 Explain the difference between *breakdown maintenance* and *preventive maintenance.*

8 Under what circumstances is preventive maintenance likely to be more cost effective than breakdown maintenance?

9 What is meant by capacity planning?

10 Explain what is meant by demand forecasting by (a) qualitative means, (b) time-series, and (c) causal methods.

11 Explain the principle of the *moving-average method* of demand forecasting.

12 How does the *exponential smoothing method* of forecasting differ in principle from the moving-average method?

13 Explain how causal methods of forecasting can be done using a *regression equation*.

14 What is meant by *aggregate planning*?

15 What is meant by *inventory management*?

16 What are the principal advantages to an organisation of holding inventories in (a) raw materials, (b) part finished goods and (c) finished goods?

17 What are the main types of costs that inventories can incur?

18 Inventory control can be considered in terms of *dependent* or *independent demand*. Explain these terms.

19 What is meant by the *two-bin system* of inventory control?

20 Derive the equation for the economic order quantity, $EOQ = \sqrt{(2rC_s/cC)}$, explaining the terms and the assumptions made.

21 Explain what is meant by the *economic order quantity*.

22 What is meant by the term *materials requirements planning*?

23 Explain the purpose of a Gannt chart and describe its form.

24 What is meant by *loading*?

25 Explain the significance of the following in relation to a network diagram, (a) an arrow, (b) a circle, (c) a dotted line arrow.

26 Define the following terms, (a) earliest start time, (b) latest finishing time, (c) earliest finish time, (d) latest start time, (e) total float, (f) critical path.

27 What is meant by *progressing*?

28 What is the function of a *progress chaser*?

29 What is meant by *batch splitting* and what are the reasons for doing it?

30   Explain how the *line of balance method* can be used for production control where there is batch splitting.

Assignments and further questions

1   Investigate a plant layout in some company and comment on it in relation to the types of product that are produced.

2   The following is a travel chart that has been produced over a period of one month. Comment on the layout of the production facilities and suggest on improvement, giving the new travel chart for your proposal.

From \ To	Stores	Turning	Milling	Grinding	Assembly	Testing
Stores		20	25	2	2	1
Turning			18			
Milling				16	24	
Grinding					15	
Assembly						38
Testing				5	3	

3   Discuss the relationship that should exist between marketing and production stategies.

4   For each of the following present arguments for a type of production operation and a form of layout.
(a) Domestic vacuum cleaners.
(b) Furniture.
(c) Specialist machine tools made to order.
(d) A popular car model.

5   Compare line with small batch production processes, considering such factors as efficiency, flexibility, capital investment, labour skills, type of product, control and planning.

6   Present a reasoned argument for your proposal for a maintenance plan for (a) electric light bulbs throughout the company, (b) machines in a job production situation, (c) machines in a line production situation.

7   Discuss the relative merits, and problems, associated with the following methods of demand forecasting, (a) qualitative forecasting using the opinions of salesmen, (b) qualitative forecasting using market surveys, (c) the moving average method, (d) the weighted moving average method, (e) exponential smoothing, (f) causal methods and the development of a regression equation.

8 The following data show the monthly demand for a product. Use (a) five-period moving average method, (b) exponential smoothing with a weighting factor of 0.7 for the last month, to obtain forecasts of the demand in the next month.

Month	Jan	Feb	Mar	Apr	May	June	July
Demand	550	650	600	750	900	800	600

9 For the product data given in the previous question the demand in the month of August was found to be 500. Using the same methods as in that question, forecast the demand for September.

10 The following data show the number of breakdowns to which the service engineers have been called during the last few months. Prepare (a) a three-period moving average forecast for the next month, (b) a three-period weighted moving average forecast for the next month if $w_1 = 0.5$, $w_2 = 0.3$ and $w_3 = 0.2$.

Month	Jan	Feb	Mar	Apr	May	June
Breakdowns	52	65	60	70	65	80

11 Obtain some sales data for a product over a period of time and devise a forecasting method for use with it. Present reasoned arguments for your choice of method.

12 The sales manager believes that the demand per month for photographic film is related to the number of fine Sundays in the month. He therefore collects data for a number of months. Is his belief justified and if so what is the regression equation?

Number of fine Sundays	0	1	2	3	4	5
Sales in thousands	3	5	7	9	11	13

13 A hotel manager wants an aggregate plan. Based on the following data produce one. No changes are expected year by year.

Month	Jan	Feb	Mar	Apr	May	Jun	Jly	Aug	Sept	Oct	Nov	Dec
Room demand	15	15	25	30	35	50	50	50	45	35	15	30

The manager requires one employee for each 10 rooms used, each being paid £500 per month. There is the possibility of overtime, up to 20% at time-and-a-half. Temporary staff can be hired at a cost of £300 per month. To fire an employee would cost £1000, to fire a temporary worker has zero cost.

14 The following is a forecast of the number of units production department will have to produce.

Week	1	2	3	4	5	6	7	8
Units	3500	2500	2500	3500	5000	6500	5000	5000

Produce a level capacity aggregate plan.

15 Determine the economic order quantity to be ordered in each of the following situations, assuming that the demand for the inventory is independent and constant, delivery being in complete batches.
(a) Demand per year 4000, price per unit £20, carrying cost rate per year 30%, ordering cost per unit £10.
(b) Demand per year 20,000, price per unit £12, carrying cost per unit per year £0.50, ordering cost per unit £10.

16 A company makes a furniture item for which the yearly sales are fairly constant at 800, each item costing £250. How many of these items should be made in a batch if the carrying cost rate per year is 20% and the cost of setting up production £500?

17 Draw a Gannt chart for the operations giving the following data.

Activity	Activities on which dependent	Duration in days
A Obtaining materials	–	0.5
B Machining	A	1.5
C Drilling	B	1.0
D Grinding	C	1.0
E Testing	D	0.5

18 Draw a Gannt chart for the project giving the following data

Activity	Activities on which dependent	Duration in days
A	–	2
B	A	1
C	B	3
D	A	2
E	D	3
F	C, E	2
G	F	1

19 Draw a network for the project described in question 18 (a) What is

the critical path? (b) What is the minimum project completion time?

20 Draw a network for the following project, identifying earliest start and latest finish times for each event and determining the critical path.

Activity	Activities on which dependent	Duration in days
A	–	4
B	–	2
C	A	1
D	C	5
E	B	1
F	D, E	3
G	F	1
H	F	3
I	G, H	2

21 Draw a network for the following project, identifying the earliest start and latest finish times for each event. Determine the total floats and the critical path. Comment on the significance of this path and the floats.

Activity	Activities on which dependent	Duration in hours
A	–	1
B	–	2
C	–	3
D	A	2
E	C	2
F	B, D, E	3
G	C,	2
H	F, G	1

17 Quality control

Quality

The *quality* of a product can be defined as its fitness for the purpose for which it was required. The term quality should not be considered as implying that a product is highly priced, highly valued, high precision, etc., quality is a measure of whether a product is up to standard, what the customer wanted, what was designed, etc. Any product, however lowly, can be of the right quality if it is what was required.

There are a number of aspects in the production of a product at which quality can be considered, namely:

1 Design quality.   This is the degree to which the design specification of a product satisfies the customer's design requirements.

2 Manufacture quality.   This is the degree to which the manufactured product conforms to the design specifications.

3 Product quality.   This embraces both the design and manufacture quality and is the degree to which the product satisfies the customer's requirements.

Linked with the concept of quality is reliability in that generally a high quality product is more likely to be reliable than a low quality product. Reliability can be defined as the ability of a product to function as required, where required, when required and for as long as is required.

The cost of quality

The cost of quality can be considered to be made of two components, *control costs* and *failure costs*.

1 Control costs

These are the costs concerned with ensuring that products are of the required quality. This can be considered as being made up of two elements, *prevention* and *appraisal costs*. Prevention costs are those associated with those activities designed to prevent poor quality products being produced, e.g. training, and appraisal costs are those associated with inspection of the products in order to remove those that are not of the quality required by the customer.

2 Failure costs

These are the costs associated with the product failing to meet the required quality, either during the production process or after the product has been received by the customer. The cost incurred as a result of failure to meet the required quality during the production process includes such costs as those of the cost of the labour and materials for a product which cannot be sold, the costs of reworking the product to bring it up to quality, etc. The cost incurred as a result of failure after the product has been received by the customer includes the cost of refunds, repairing or replacing the product, the cost of dealing with complaints, etc.

The more money that is spent on prevention the fewer will be the number of failures, either during production or after the customer has received the product. The more money that is spent on appraisal the fewer will be the number of failures, either after the customer has received the product or during manufacture if appraisal occurs at a number of points in the manufacturing process. Thus, the higher the cost of control the fewer the failures.

The greater the number of failures, either during production or after the customer has received the product, the greater the failure costs. Thus the greater the money devoted to control the smaller the cost of failures.

Figure 17.1 shows, in a simplified way, how both the control and the failure costs might vary with the number of failures. Adding together these two costs gives the total cost of quality, this showing a minimum value at

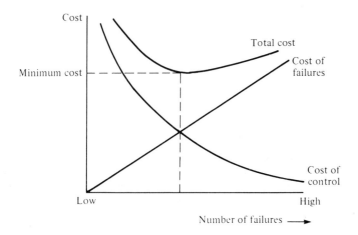

Figure 17.1 *The cost of quality*

some particular number of failures. Thus the total cost of quality can be minimised if a certain number of failures are accepted as occurring.

Quality control

Inspection is a necessary feature of any quality control system. The critical points in a manufacturing process where inspection can most effectively occur are:

1 Incoming materials.   Are the materials in accord with the specifications? Are bought-in parts to the required specifications? Checking at this stage can eliminate materials of the wrong specification and avoid an entire batch of products later in the manufacturing process failing to be of the right quality.

2 In-process.   This is inspection of work in process. The identification of failures part way through the manufacturing process can be less costly than identifying them only at the end.

3 Finished product.   This is the final inspection prior to sale to a customer.

The type of measurement to be made at each inspection determines the type of quality control to be exercised. There are essentially just two types of measurement, namely:

1 A measurement of variables.   A product may have some property that varies, e.g. chemical composition, length, hardness, etc. The inspection can then be of this variable. *Control by variables* is the term used.

2 A measurement of attributes.   A product may have some attribute which is either right or wrong, e.g. an item fits into a hole or it does not, the colour is red or it is white. The inspection can then be based on acceptance or rejection techniques. *Control by attributes* is the term used.

When to inspect and what to measure at the inspection are two key features of any quality control system. The third feature is concerned with how much inspection. The choice is between an inspection involving every item being inspected or one involving an inspection of just a sample. The greater the number of items inspected the greater the cost but the less the chance that a customer will receive a defective item. There is also the point that inspection, for some items, might cause damage or even complete destruction, e.g. electrical fuses, and so inspection of just a sample is all that is possible. Statistical methods are thus widely used to determine not only how many items to inspect but also what deductions can be made from the results with regard to the entire batch of items from which the sample was taken.

Two types of statistical methods are used:

1 Acceptance sampling. A random sample is taken from a batch and on the basis of an inspection of that sample the entire batch is either accepted or rejected.

2 Process control. This involves inspection of items during the production process with a view to determining how the process is proceeding, e.g. whether a machine is developing a fault.

With both statistical methods the inspection method used could be either by variables or attributes.

Acceptance sampling

Acceptance sampling involves taking a random sample from a batch of products or materials and on the basis of inspecting that sample, very often by attributes, either rejecting or accepting the entire batch. There are a number of different ways we can take samples but for the moment consider just a single sample to be taken. Thus if there is a batch size of, say, 100 then we might consider taking a sample of 10 and inspecting them. Suppose we find 1 defective item in that 10, i.e. 10% of the sample is defective. Does this mean that 10% of the entire batch is defective? Or could it be less than 10%, or perhaps more? If we had taken 10 samples of 10 items, would we have obtained 10% defective in each sample?

The answers to these questions depend on the laws of probability. In fact, if there were 10 defective items in 100, i.e. 10% defective, then there is, in taking a sample of 10 from the 100, a 35% chance that we will find a sample with no defective items, a 39% chance of a sample with 1 defective item and a 26% chance we will find a sample with more than 1 defective item. If we had been rejecting, on the basis of the sample, any batch where the inspection revealed more than 1 defective item in 10 then there would have been a 26% chance that the sample taken would have been pessimistic and the entire batch would have been rejected. There would, conversely, have been a 74% chance that we would have obtained a sample with no or just one defective item and so rightly accepted the batch.

If we take a sample size of 10 and an acceptance plan that we will accept the batch if the sample contains one or less defective items, then a graph can be drawn relating the chance of accepting a batch with the actual percentage of defective items in the batch. Such a graph is known as the *operating characteristic*, Figure 17.2 showing the one for this data. Hence, using the graph, we can determine that if the actual percentage of defective items in the batch was 10% then there would be a 74% chance we would have accepted the batch on the basis of our acceptance plan. However, the operating characteristic does tell us that the acceptance plan could result in

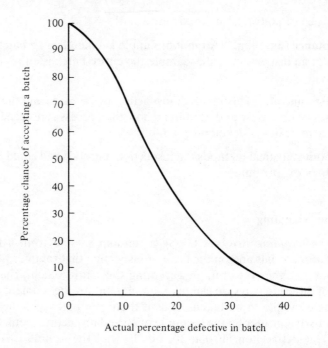

Figure 17.2   *An operating characteristic when sample size is 10 and number of defectives in sample is 1 or less*

our accepting batches with percentages of defective items greater or less than 10%. For example there is a chance of about 15% that the actual percentage of defective items in the batch would be 30%.

The operating characteristic curve depends on the size of the sample and the acceptance plan adopted. Tables and charts are available to enable the operating characteristic to be drawn for different sample sizes and different acceptance plans. Figure 17.3 shows the operating characteristic when the sample size is 10 but the acceptance plan is that a batch will be accepted if the sample contains two or less defective items. Compare this graph with that in Figure 17.2. Now, if the actual percentage of defective items is 10% there is a 93% chance we would have accepted the batch. The chance of the batch having 30% defective items is however 38%. Thus this acceptance plan where the number of defective items can be as high as 2 leads us to accept batches which can have considerably higher percentage of defective items than the plan where we only accepted if the sample contained one or less defective items.

The lower the number of defective items in a sample which results in acceptance of a batch the tighter the inspection. Similarly, the bigger the size of the sample the tighter the inspection (Figure 17.4). The tighter the inspection the smaller is the chance that the sampling will result in a batch

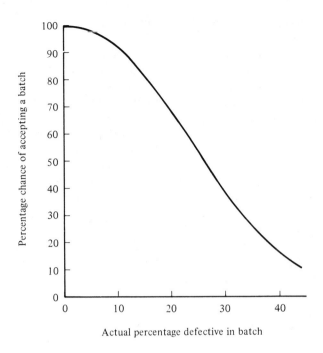

Figure 17.3   *An operating characteristic when sample size is 10 and number of defectives in sample is 2 or less*

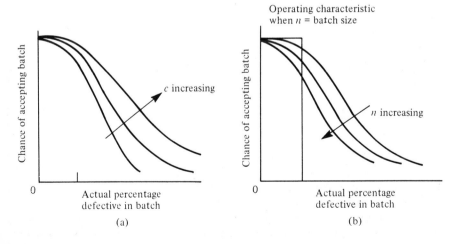

Figure 17.4
(a)   *A constant sample size (n)*
(b)   *A constant number of defectives in sample (c)*

that should have been rejected being accepted.

The term *acceptable quality level* (AQL) defines the highest percentage of rejects in a batch which the receiver of the goods will accept. Thus we might, for instance, have an AQL of 10%. This would mean that the receiver of the goods would want there to be a sampling plan which ends up rejecting all batches with more than 10% defective items. However this can only be such a certainty if all the items in the batch are inspected, i.e. a 100% sample. Any sample which is less than 100% will mean there is some chance that a batch with more than 10% defective items will get through.

The term *lot tolerance percentage defective* (LTPD) defines the percentage of defective items which is unacceptable to the receiver of the goods. This is the percentage value above which we want to be almost certain that no batch will get through the inspection stage and be accepted.

An operating characteristic and hence a sampling plan can be derived from a specification of the acceptable quality level and the lot tolerance percentage defective. Figure 17.5 shows an operating characteristic and these two points. Typically the AQL is around 1% or 2% and the LTPD about 10%. Such values give an operating characteristic where the chance of accepting a batch with the AQL is about 99.5% and the chance of accepting a batch with the LTPD is about 5%.

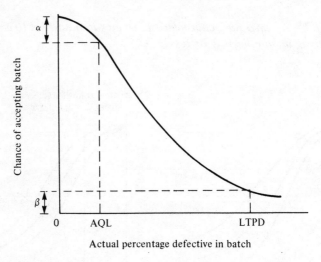

Figure 17.5 *Operating characteristic showing AQL and LTPD*

The customer, i.e. consumer, wants to have a low chance of accepting batches including too many defective items and thus wants a low value of β, the term indicated in Figure 17.5. The term β is called the consumer's risk. The producer wants to have as low a chance of rejecting a batch containing an acceptable number of defective items, i.e. α as low as possible. The term α is called the producer's risk.

Thus by specifying the AQL and LTPD, and hence also α and β, an operating characteristic can be derived and a sampling plan determined.

In the discussion so far concerning acceptance sampling a decision whether to accept or reject a batch has been made on the basis of a single random sample taken from a batch. Other sampling methods however can be used. *Double sampling* involves the following sequence:

1 A random sample is taken from the batch and inspected.
2 If the number of defective items is less than or equal to some acceptance number c_1 then the entire batch is accepted with no further sample being taken.
3 If the number of defective items is greater than some acceptance number c_2 then the entire batch is rejected with no further sample being taken.
4 If the number of defective items is between c_1 and c_2 then a second sample is taken and inspected. If the number of defective items in this sample plus the number found in the first sample is greater than c_2 then the batch is rejected, below c_2 it is accepted.

Double sampling involves two samples possibly being taken, *multiple sampling* is a similar process with more than two samples possibly being taken. Double and multiple sampling allows smaller-sized samples to be taken than would be the case with single sampling.

Process control

No matter how carefully controlled a manufacturing process is or however skilled the operators are the items produced will show variations. In any process there is invariably some inherent variability. Thus, for example, with a machine filling containers, exactly the same weight of material will not be put in each container; some variation in the weight will occur. Generally this variation will occur around some average value. *Process control* is concerned with establishing the degree of variation that is inevitable with a process, any variation which is then greater than this natural variation can be attributed to other causes and remedies sought to bring the production back within the natural variation.

Variations can thus be considered as falling into two categories:

1 Due to the inherent variability of a process, such variations being in a random manner about some average value.
2 Due to some specific reason, such as tool wear, operator error, faulty material, etc.

The variations resulting from the inherent variability of the process occur randomly and can be described by a *frequency distribution* curve, the curve often describing what is termed a *normal distribution*. To illustrate what is meant by a frequency distribution, consider a rod being machined to some particular length. Inspection of the machined lengths will indicate some variability and, if this is due purely to the inherent variability of the process, these variations will be randomly scattered about some mean. We might thus have, when a sample of 40 rods is measured:

> 1 rod with length in the range 99.86 to 99.90 mm
> 7 rods with lengths in the range 99.91 to 99.95 mm
> 12 rods with lengths in the range 99.96 to 100.00 mm
> 11 rods with lengths in the range 100.01 to 100.05 mm
> 8 rods with lengths in the range 100.06 to 100.10 mm
> 1 rod with length in the range 100.11 to 100.15 mm

The number of rods within a particular length interval is called the frequency. Figure 17.6 shows the histogram produced by plotting this data. With larger amounts of data the histogram would be smoothed out to give a graph like that shown in Figure 17.7, this graph being the frequency distribution. The bell shape of this graph is a very common form of distribution that occurs when the variations are due to the inherent variability of a process, this type of distribution being referred to as the normal distribution.

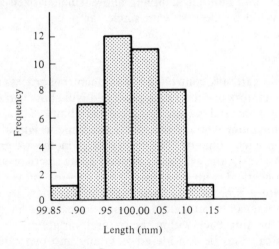

Figure 17.6 *Length distribution histogram*

With a normal distribution the curve is symmetrical about the average value of the variable, the length in Figure 17.7. With a normal distribution, regardless of the variable or the frequency values, the shape is always the same and thus equations developed for the curve can be applied to all processes that give this type of distribution. On this basis *control charts* have been developed. They aim to determine whether inspection data fits the distribution pattern that could be expected of the random variations of a process or whether it does not fit and so there is some fault in the process.

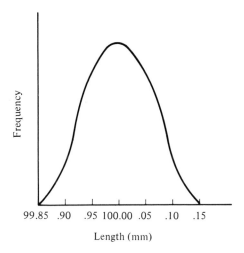

Figure 17.7 *Frequency distribution of length*

There are two types of control chart: an average or mean chart and a range chart. The data for both charts are obtained by taking a sample and inspecting them. In the case of a control chart for variables, the variable is measured for each item in the sample. Thus there might be, for a length variable, lengths of:

$$10.1, 10.0, 10.2, 10.2, 10.0 \text{ mm}$$

The average, or mean, length is given by summing the lengths and then dividing by the number of items, i.e. $50.5 \div 5 = 10.1$ mm. The range for that sample is the difference between the greatest and the smallest values, i.e. $10.2 - 10.0 = 0.2$ mm. These calculations are repeated for each sample and the average and range values plotted on the appropriate control charts, as in Figure 17.8.

The average control chart shows lines representing the *design limits* and the *control limits*. The design limits are those imposed by the design of the item concerned. The control limits are drawn so that they would only be exceeded once in every 40 times if random variations are occurring, their positions being determined by the properties of the normal distribution. The range control chart shows just a control limit, this line is drawn so that it is only expected to be exceeded once in every thousand times if random variations are occurring.

If the control charts indicate samples are going beyond the control limits

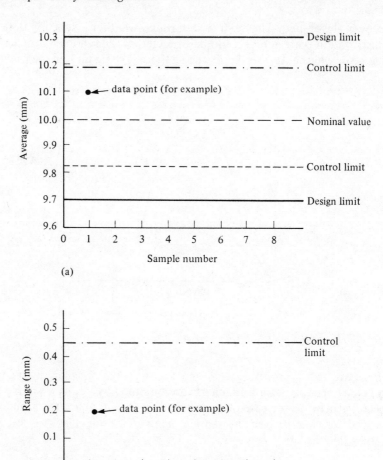

Figure 17.8
(a) *Average control chart for controlling to a design limit*
(b) *Range control chart*

more than can be expected by random chance, then the deduction made is that there is some other effect causing it. Thus there might be, for example:

1 The average chart goes out of limit for hardness measurements – the reason being perhaps that the components were in the furnace for the wrong period of time or the furnace temperature was incorrect.

2 The average chart goes suddenly out of limit for length of a machined

component – the reason being perhaps that the machine jammed and so altered its setting or a new operator started or there was a change in properties of the materials being machined.

3   The average chart drifts out of limit for length of a machined component – the reason being perhaps tool wear or the tool moving out of alignment.

4   The range chart goes out of limit for hardness measurements – the reason being perhaps that the batch was of variable quality before the heat treatment or there was an uneven temperature distribution in the furnace.

5   The range chart goes out of limit for length for a machined component – the reason being perhaps that play is occurring in a bearing or the material being machined is of variable quality.

Some control charts are used not in relation to some design limit but to control to the best that a process is capable of. For this the average control chart is drawn with two pairs of control limits, called action and warning limits. The *action limits* are drawn either side of the average of all, or a large number, of samples so that there is only a 1 in 1000 chance they will be exceeded for a process conforming to the normal distribution. The *warning limits* are drawn either side of the average so that there is only a 1 in 40 chance they will be exceeded. Figure 17.9 shows such a chart. the range chart is drawn as before (Figure 17.8(b)).

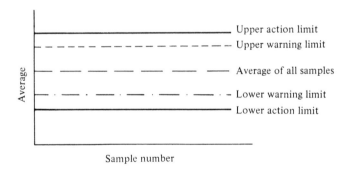

Figure 17.9   *Average control chart for process capability*

Control charts so far considered refer to control involving inspection of variables. Where the inspection is of attributes the charts are similar to those already described but have a vertical axis of either number of defects or proportion or percentage of defective items (see Figures 17.12 and 17.13 in the later discussion on control limits).

Control limits

The following explains how the control limits used with control charts can be determined. The methods used depend on whether the control is by variables or attributes, and also whether the control is to design specifications or the capability of the process.

1 Control limits to design specifications

(a) Inspect ten or more samples.
(b) Calculate the range for each sample.
(c) Calculate the average range.
(d) Multiply the average range by the appropriate value of the factor $A''_{0.025}$, the value depending on the size of sample used. The factor is for a chance of 25 in 1000, or 1 in 40.

Sample size	4	5	6	7	8
$A''_{0.025}$	1.02	1.95	0.90	0.87	0.84

(e) Draw control limits on the average control chart a distance equal to the product obtained in (d) inwards from each design limit (Figure 17.10).
(f) The control limit for the range control chart is the product of the average range and the appropriate value of the factor $D'_{0.001}$, the value depending on the size of sample used. The factor is for a chance of 1 in 1000.

Sample size	4	5	6	7	8
$D'_{0.001}$	2.57	2.34	2.21	2.11	2.04

(g) Draw on the range control chart the limit a distance equal to the product obtained in (f) above the zero range value.

2 Control limits for process capability

(a) Inspect ten or more samples.
(b) Calculate the range for each sample.
(c) Calculate the average range.
(d) Multiply the average range by the appropriate value of the factor $A'_{0.025}$, the value depending on the size of sample used. The factor is for a chance of 25 in 1000, or 1 in 40.

Sample size	4	5	6	7	8
$A'_{0.025}$	0.48	0.38	0.32	0.27	0.24

(e) Calculate the average for each sample.
(f) Calculate the average of the averages.
(g) One warning control limit on the average control chart is obtained by adding to this average of the averages the value of the product obtained in (d), the other warning limit by subtracting (Figure 17.11).

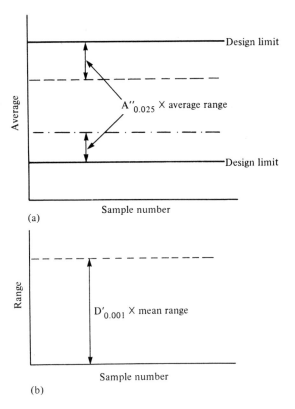

Figure 17.10 *Charts to design limits*
(a) *Average control chart control limits*
(b) *Range control chart control limit*

(h) Multiply the average range by the appropriate value of the factor $A'_{0.001}$, the value depending on the size of the sample used. The factor is for a chance of 1 in 1000.

Sample size	4	5	6	7	8
$A'_{0.001}$	0.75	0.59	0.50	0.43	0.38

(i) One action control limit on the average control chart is obtained by adding to the average of the averages (f) the value of the product obtained in (h), the other by subtracting.

(j) For the range control chart the action control limit is obtained by multiplying the average range (c) by the appropriate value of the factor $D'_{0.001}$, the value depending on the size of the sample used. The factor is for a chance of 1 in 1000 and values are given in the sequence for the calculation of control limits to design specifications.

(k) For the range control chart the warning control limit is obtained by

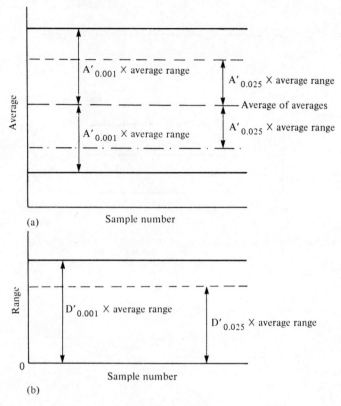

Figure 17.11 *Charts to process capability*
(a) *Average control chart control limits*
(b) *Range control chart control limit*

multiplying the average range (c) by the appropriate value of the factor $D'_{0.025}$, the value depending on the size of the sample used. The factor is for a chance of 25 in 1000, or 1 in 40.

Sample size	4	5	6	7	8
$D'_{0.025}$	1.93	1.81	1.72	1.66	1.62

3 Control limits for attributes with number defective

(a) Inspect ten or more samples and ascertain the number defective in each sample.
(b) Calculate the average number of defective items per sample ($\bar{c}$).
(c) Calculate the standard deviation L, where

$$L = \sqrt{\{\bar{c}\,[1 - (\bar{c}/n)]\}}$$

n is the sample size.

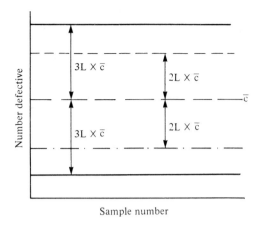

Figure 17.12 *Control limits for attributes with number defective*

(d) The action limit is obtained by adding $3L$ to $\bar{c}$, the other by subtracting (Figure 17.12).

(e) One warning limit is obtained by adding $2L$ to $\bar{c}$, the other by subtracting.

4 Control limits for attributes with percentage defective.

(a) Inspect 10 or more samples and ascertain the number defective in each sample.

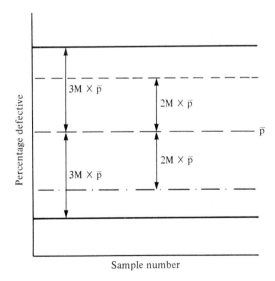

Figure 17.13 *Control limits for attributes with percentage defective*

(b) Calculate the percentage defective in each sample.
(c) Calculate the average percentage defective ($\bar{p}$).
(d) Calculate the average sample size ($\bar{n}$).
(e) Calculate the standard deviation M, where

$$M = \sqrt{[\bar{p}(100 - \bar{p})/\bar{n}]}$$

(f) One action limit is obtained by adding *3M* to $\bar{p}$, the other by subtracting (Figure 17.13).
(g) One warning limit is obtained by adding *2M* to $\bar{p}$, the other by subtracting.

Revision questions

1   What is meant by the term *quality* in the manufacturing industry?

2   What is meant by *reliability*?

3   Describe the components making up the cost of quality.

4   At what points in the manufacturing process can inspection most effectively occur?

5   Explain the difference between the measurement of variables and of attributes.

6   Explain the difference between *acceptance sampling* and *process control*.

7   Sketch an operating characteristic curve and explain its significance.

8   Define the terms *acceptable quality level, lot tolerance percentage defective, consumer's risk, producer's risk*.

9   Explain how double sampling varies from single sampling and its possible advantage.

10   What are the two types of control chart used with control by variables?

11   What is the average value and the range for the following inspection data:

Length/mm   80.2   79.9   80.0   80.1   80.1   79.9

12   How do action limits differ from warning limits on control charts?

Assignments and further questions

1   For some product or products produced by a company, establish the various points at which inspections occur and critically comment on the justification for inspections at those points.

2 Write a report arguing the case for some particular level of inspection and hence quality control. In your report consider both control and failure costs.

3 Present a case for acceptance sampling and indicate the factors that will determine the size of sample taken.

4 The following data relate to quality control with variables to process capability. Construct the quality control charts with the appropriate control limits. Each sample consists of four items.

Sample number	1	2	3	4	5	6	7	8	9	10
Lengths (mm)	10.1	10.1	9.9	10.0	9.9	10.2	10.0	9.9	9.9	10.0
	9.9	10.1	10.0	9.8	9.9	10.0	9.9	9.9	10.0	10.1
	10.0	10.0	10.1	10.0	10.0	10.1	10.0	10.0	9.9	9.9
	10.0	9.9	10.0	10.0	10.1	9.9	10.1	10.0	9.8	10.1

5 For the quality control of the items giving the data quoted in the previous question, the following results were obtained. Comment on their significance.

Sample number	11	12	13
Lengths (mm)	10.1	10.2	10.1
	10.0	10.1	10.2
	10.1	10.2	10.3
	10.2	10.1	10.1

6 The following data relate to quality control by attributes. Construct the quality control chart with the appropriate control limits. Each sample consists of ten items.

Sample number	1	2	3	4	5	6	7	8	9	10
No. defective	2	2	1	3	2	2	1	0	2	1

7 For the quality control of the items giving the data quoted in the previous question, the following results were obtained. Comment on their significance.

Sample number	11	12	13
No. defective	2	3	3

8 Devise a quality control system for letters typed in a typing pool.

18   Workers and production

Work study

The term *work study* is used to describe the scientific study of work, the term *time and motion study* being used in America. The aims of work study can be considered to include:

1   Making the most effective use of economic resources, i.e. people, machines, space, capital, that are available.
2   Establishing the most economical way of doing a job, making this then the standard method.
3   Establishing the time required for a suitably trained worker to do this standard job when working at a defined level of performance, this then becoming the standard time for the job.
4   Improving planning and control as a result of using standard methods and times.

Work study embraces method study and work measurement. *Method study* is the systematic recording and critical examination of existing and proposed ways of doing work, as a means of developing and applying easier and more effective methods and reducing costs. *Work measurement* is the application of techniques designed to establish the time for a qualified worker to carry out a specified job at a defined level of performance.

Method study

Method study is concerned with finding the best way to do jobs. Seven steps have been identified.

1   Select

Select the job to be investigated. The most appropriate jobs are those where significant savings might be produced as the result of the investigation, e.g. where bottlenecks exist in the production process. Thus not all jobs merit being investigated, the cost saving would not be worthwhile in view of the expense of the investigation.

2 *Record*

Observe the job and record all aspects of it. Many techniques exist for recording existing work methods. One method is a flow diagram. This shows the locations of specific activities carried out by workers, their sequence, and the routes followed by the workers, materials and equipment. Figure 18.1 shows an example of such a chart (a travel chart, as in Figure 16.2 might also be used).

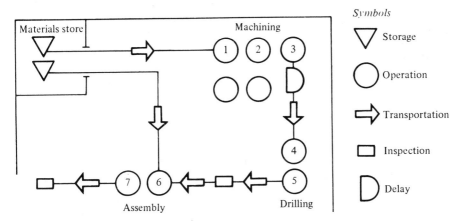

Figure 18.1 *Method study flow diagram*

Another method is a process chart. A variety of types of process charts are used. For example there might be an outline process chart giving an overall view of the sequence of processes used for a particular product, another process chart might give the sequence of events associated with a particular worker, another process chart might give the record of all the events associated with material. Figure 18.2 shows an example. Another method of recording a job involves the use of photography, either still or cine, and video.

3 *Analyse*

Study the record with a view to determining the best method.

4 *Develop*

Develop from the analysis the most efficient or optimum method.

5 *Define*

Describe the new method that has been developed.

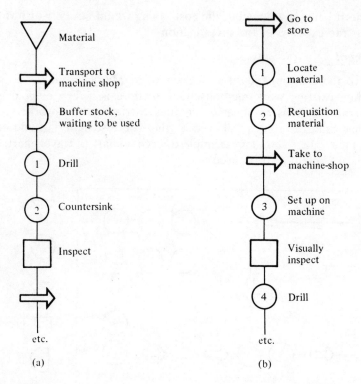

Figure 18.2
(a) *Outline process chart*
(b) *Worker process chart*

6 Install

Set up this method as the standard practice, retraining workers, providing appropriate equipment, materials, etc.

7 Maintain

Ensure that the new method continues to be used, reviewing its operation periodically.

The above sequence has been written to fit an existing job where improvement is desired. If a new job is involved the sequence is the same but rather than existing practice being recorded a record is made of a number of alternative methods tried for the job in order that the optimum one can be selected.

Work measurement

The main objective of work measurement can be considered to be the establishment of standard times for jobs. The *standard time* is defined as the time needed for a qualified and trained worker to carry out the job at a defined level of performance. Standard times are used in the costing of jobs (see Chapter 14), production planning, determining the manning required for a job, incentive payments for workers, etc.

The methods used for work measurement can be classified into two categories: *direct* and *indirect work measurement*. Within each category there are a number of different methods that can be used.

1 Direct work measurement

(a) Time study
This method requires an investigator to record directly the times, and rates of working, for each element of a job. The instrument generally used is the stopwatch. The rating is an estimation by the investigator of the general tempo of the work and involves a consideration of such factors as speed of movement and effectiveness of the worker. The basic times of each element are calculated from

$$\text{basic time} = \text{observed time} \times \frac{\text{observed rating}}{\text{standard rating}}$$

The standard rating is the performance expected from an average qualified and motivated worker working at a natural rate. The basic times for all the elements are added up and when combined with an allowance, for such things as relaxation, a standard time is obtained.

(b) Activity sampling
Time study while appropriate for defined, short-cycle, repetitive work is not so appropriate for long irregular-cycle work, for instance, the amount of time supervisors spend on paperwork. For such situations *activity sampling* can be used. This involves determining the percentage of time spent on a particular activity and is determined from a large number of instantaneous observations made over a period of time, each observation recording what is happening at that instant. The percentage of observations recorded for a particular activity is a measure of the percentage of time during which that activity occurs.

2 Indirect work measurement

(a) Synthetic timing
Many jobs are likely to contain a number of elements common to other jobs. Thus by breaking a job into its constituent elements a time can be obtained for the job on the basis of a knowledge of the times needed for these elements in other situations.

(b) Predetermined motion time systems (PMTS)
This method involves the breaking down of a job into its basic human

motions, the times for these motions being obtained from tables. Basic human motions are such things as reaching, moving, turning, grasping, releasing, eye travel, etc. With each such motion there is further subdivision to quantify, for instance, the type of reaching motion involved, e.g. reaching for an object in a fixed location, reaching for an object jumbled up with other objects, etc. In order to determine the time of a job a considerable amount of detailed information is required.

(c) Analytical timing
Standard times are determined using the data available for some of the elements in a job and the other elements are estimated on the basis of experience. This method is often used for non-repetitive work, e.g. maintenance.

Ergonomics

Ergonomics is the study of humans in the working situation. The design of a machine or a work station that has to be operated by a human being must take account of the characteristics of the human being. The man-machine interface has to be considered. It has been said that the controls of a lathe are situated in such a way that the ideal operator to interface with them would be 1.37 m ($4\frac{1}{2}$ ft) tall, 0.61 m (2 ft) across the shoulders and have an arm span of 2.35 m (8 ft). Since this is not the description of the average man most men will not find the controls convenient to use and this can cause fatigue as well as generally increasing the time to carry out a job with the lathe.

Using controls, reading displays, and environmental factors, such as noise, are all factors that have to be considered in the man-machine interface. Thus, for example, in considering the type of control to be used consideration should be given to the speed, accuracy and range of use that the operator will be involved in. A lever is capable of fast operation but gives poor accuracy and a poor range. A handwheel however is not capable of high speed but can give good accuracy and a fair range. A push button gives high speed but is completely unsuitable for anything other than an on-off control, thus providing no accuracy or range.

With displays a wide variety of forms are possible, e.g lights which are either on or off, the position of a switch, pointers on dials, dials moving past pointers and counters. The characteristics of these various forms of display need to be considered. If an operator needs to see at a glance whether the power is on or off then a warning light would be better than a pointer moving across a scale since time is needed to read this form of display. Counters enable quantitative readings to be taken without ambiguity, this not being true of pointers on dials, but such a display is not very good for checking purposes. With a pointer on a dial marks can be put on the dial to indicate crucial values and so checking values is better with a pointer on a dial than a counter.

The three main environmental factors that can affect workers are illumination, noise and the climate. If these are not at acceptable levels then fatigue, discomfort and possibly physical damage can occur. All have an effect on worker performance. An adequate lighting system should provide:

1 Sufficient brightness for the job concerned, fine work requiring higher levels than coarse work.
2 Uniform illumination.
3 Some contrast between the brightness of the job and the background. This can aid the eye to detect detail.
4 No glare, e.g. unwanted reflections from polished or glass surfaces. This can, for instance, make it very difficult to read meters.

Noise can have not only a nuisance value but cause interference with communications, produce stress and hearing damage. Noise levels can be controlled by putting barriers between workers and the source, providing protective devices for workers, e.g. ear plugs or muffs, controlling the source of the noise or rearranging the locations of the workers and the noise sources.

The climate experienced by a worker depends on factors such as:

1 The air temperature.
2 Air movement.
3 Relative humidity.
4 Air pollution.

While workers are highly adapatable to such environmental factors, fatigue, discomfort and poor performance are obvious consequences of a poor working climate.

Principles of motion economy

In order both to reduce fatigue and to keep motion to a minimum a number of principles of *motion economy* have been derived from observations of workers. The following is one version of these principles, the original list produced by Gilbreth having been modified by later researchers.

Use of the human body

1 The two hands should preferably begin as well as complete their motions at the same time.

2 The two hands should not be idle at the same time except during rest periods.

3 The motion of the arms should be in opposite directions and symmetrical directions, instead of in the same direction, and should be made simultaneously.

4 Continuous curved motions are preferable to straight-line motions involving sudden and sharp changes in direction.

5 Hand, arm and body movements should be confined to the lowest possible classification with which it is possible to perform the task. The following list gives the classification with the lowest, i.e. least tiring and most economical, movements first.
   (a) Finger motions.
   (b) Finger and wrist motions.
   (c) Finger, wrist and lower arm motions.
   (d) Finger, wrist, lower and upper arm motions.
   (e) Finger, wrist, lower and upper arm and shoulder motions.

6 Momentum should be employed to assist the worker wherever possible, and it should be reduced to a minimum if it must be overcome by muscular effort.

7 Ballistic movements are faster, easier, and more accurate than restricted (fixation) or 'controlled' movements.

8 Work should be arranged to permit natural and habitual movements.

9 The need to fix and focus the eyes on an object should be minimized and when necessary the occasions should occur as close together as possible.

Arrangement of the work place

10 There should be a definite and fixed place for all tools and materials.

11 All tools, equipment and materials should be located as close to the point of use as possible.

12 Gravity-fed bins and containers should be used to deliver the material as close to the point of assembly in use as possible.

13 Drop deliveries, whereby the worker may deliver the finished article without moving to dispose it, should be used wherever possible.

14 Tools, equipment and materials should be located to permit the best sequence of motions.

15 All materials and tools should be located within the normal group area.

16   Illumination levels and brightness contrasts between objects and the surroundings should be arranged to avoid or alleviate visual fatigue.

17   Noise and vibration should be minimized.

18   The height of the workplace and the seating should enable comfortable sitting or standing during work.

19   Seating should permit good posture and adequate coverage of the work area.

20   All work activities should permit the worker to adopt several different but equally healthy and safe, postures without reducing his or her capability to do the work.

Design of tools and equipment

21   Clamps, jigs or fixtures rather than hands should be used to hold work.

22   Two or more tools should be combined wherever possible.

23   Tools and materials should be pre-positioned wherever possible.

24   The loads should be distributed among the limbs according to their capacities.

25   Wheels, levers, switches, etc. should be located in such positions that the operator can manipulate them with the least change in body position.

Payment systems

Employees in an organisation can receive payment for:

1   Fulfilling a function, e.g being production manager. Such payment is likely to be a fixed wage with regular reviews and increments.

2   For attendance, i.e. a wage related to a specific number of hours worked. With such a system overtime payments are possible. This would not be the case where the payments were for fulfilling a function.

3   By results. There are a number of methods used: piece work where the payment is per unit completed; differential piece work where there are different piece-work payments for different levels of production, e.g. a basic wage up to a certain number of units produced and then a bonus system of extra payment per unit produced above that basic level; multi-factor schemes where payments are related to a number of factors, e.g. output, quality, material untilisation.

There are a number of different ways by which employees can receive remuneration for their efforts, for example:

1   As a salary, i.e. payment at regular intervals.
2   As an hourly rate, i.e. payment according to how many hours worked.
3   As bonuses, i.e. lump sums often related to either company or individual performance, perhaps a profit sharing scheme.
4   As a rate per job, e.g. piece rates.
5   As commission on sales.
6   As tips.
7   As benefits, e.g. a pension or use of a company car.

The objectives of any payment system might include:

1   To enable an employee to earn a good and reasonable wage.
2   To reward and encourage high-quality work.
3   To encourage employees to use their initiative.
4   To encourage employees to develop better methods of working.
5   To reward and encourage high levels of output.
6   To be understandable and acceptable to employees.
7   To pay equitable sums to different individuals.

The above, based on objectives given in A. Bowey, *Handbook of salary and wage systems* (Gower, 1975), are just a few of the possible objectives. If, for example, the primary objective is to reward and encourage high levels of output then some form of piece-work payment might be appropriate. If, however, the main objective is to reward and encourage high-quality work then piece-work payments might be highly inappropriate. The questions that have to be considered in relation to any wage system is to what extent an incentive payment system is required and, if so, what form it should take.

Job evaluation

The term *job evaluation* is used to describe the methods used to establish the relative value of a job so that jobs can be ranked for a pay structure. Job evaluation is not concerned with particular individual employees doing a job but the relative value of the job in terms of its demands, requirements for intellectual abilities, expertise, experience, training, qualifications, etc.

There is no one method of job evaluation. Four main methods are used, namely:

1   **Job ranking.**   Each job is considered as a whole and ranked in relation with other jobs in the organisation.

2   **Job classification.**   A hypothetical job scale is determined and the existing jobs allocated to grades on that scale.

3   Points evaluation.   This method is the most common and involves the assignment of points to various factors of a job, in other words whole jobs are not compared but facets of jobs.

4   Factor comparison.   This is an extension of the points evaluation method.

In the *job ranking method*, jobs are compared with each other on the basis of difficulty, importance to the organisation, responsibilities, etc. Such comparisons are made on the basis of job descriptions that have been prepared for each job. The end position is that jobs are grouped together with roughly the same degree of difficulty, importance, etc. and a grade can then be assigned to each job and hence a pay scale. Such a method is simple, straightforward, relatively cheap and flexible, but it has the disadvantage of relying heavily on the judgement of those carrying out the ranking.

With *job classification*, as with ranking, the job is considered as a whole and allocated to a point or grade on a scale. The decision as to where on the scale to put a job is based on a consideration of its value to the organisation and its relation to the descriptions specified for the grades on the scale. Thus, for example, grade 1 might be: jobs involving tasks where no previous experience or special skill is required, a straightforward job where each task is allocated individually and closely supervised. Grade 2 might then be: jobs involving tasks requiring some simple initial training, involving only straightforward tasks where procedures are specified and a range of tasks are allocated and closely supervised. Higher grades would involve less routine tasks, more skills required and at higher grades a degree of responsibility.

The most common method is *points evaluation*. Unlike job classification or ranking, this method relies upon the identification of elements or factors of a job rather than the job as a whole. Points are allocated to the various levels within each factor. A job is thus evaluated by determining what factors it contains and the levels associated with each factor. The points total is then converted into a wage rate. For example, the factors used might be skill, effort, responsibility and job conditions. Within each factor there will be sub-factors. Thus, for instance, in skill there might be education, experience, initiative and ingenuity. For each sub-factor there could be five levels. Thus experience might have: *level 1* up to six months' experience – 20 points; *level 2* more than six months and up to 1 year's experience – 40 points; *level 3* more than 1 year and up to 3 years' experience – 60 points; *level 4* more than 3 years' and up to 5 years' experience – 80 points; *level 5* more than 5 years' experience – 100 points.

Factor comparision involves the selection of a number of key jobs, for which the view is that they are correctly paid, and then other jobs are compared with these in terms of factors which are common to all of them.

The factors usually used are mental requirements, skill requirements, physical requirements, responsibilities, and working conditions. The procedure adopted is that a key job is considered and the wage paid allocated to the individual factors. Thus, for example, if the hourly rate for key job X is £4.00, then this sum might be allocated as: mental requirements £1.30, skill requirements £1.10, physical requirements £0.40, responsibilities £1.00, working conditions £0.20. This procedure is then repeated for all the key jobs, generally 15 to 20. From this a rank order of jobs, in terms of money values, can be obtained for each factor.

Finally, after any inconsistencies have been resolved, a rank order in terms of money is established and then used for evaluating other jobs. Each job is broken down into its factors and compared with the key jobs and so a money value is assigned to them. Thus, for example, job Y might involve less mental requirements than job X and on consideration of the other key jobs on the scale allocated a money value of £0.60. The skill requirements might also be less than X and allocated a money value of £0.50. The physical requirements might be greater than X and so a money value of £1.00 allocated. Responsibilities might be very low, thus a money value of £0.20 allocated but working conditions such that a money value of £1.00 is required. The total is £3.30 and so this becomes the hourly rate for job Y.

Labour turnover

Labour turnover (LTO) describes the total movement of employees in and out of an organisation in a particular period of time. The following are some of the terms used, expressed as percentages, in describing labour turnover.

$$\text{Separation rate} = \frac{\text{total number of leavers in period}}{\text{average number of persons employed in period}} \times 100$$

The above is sometimes referred to as the *crude LTO rate* since it includes all separations, whether voluntary or not. A more useful term is the quit rate.

$$\text{Quit rate} = \frac{\text{total number of voluntary leavers in period}}{\text{average number of persons employed in period}} \times 100$$

Neither the separation rate nor the quit rate distinguish between the loss of newly engaged and long-term employees. For example, in the above formulas a person who left after just one day's work would be just as significant as one who had been employed for years with the organisation. This can be avoided by using the long-service stability index.

$$\frac{\textit{Long-service}}{\textit{stability index}} = \frac{\text{total no. employees with}}{\text{average no. employees at start of period}} \times 100$$

Another term, which focuses on the turnover in the first year of employement, is the fringe turnover rate.

$$\frac{\textit{Fringe turnover}}{\textit{rate}} = \frac{\text{no. employees joining/leaving within 1 year}}{\text{average no. employees in 1 year}} \times 100$$

Another way of monitoring employees joining an organisation is the new starter survival index.

$$\frac{\textit{New starter}}{\textit{survival index}} = \frac{\text{no. employees still employed after 1 year}}{\text{no. joining at beginning of year}} \times 100$$

The period used for the new starter survival index can be 2, 3, 4, etc. years, as also can be the other terms. Another way of monitoring is to use a concept borrowed from nuclear physics – half life.

$$\textit{Half life survival index} = \frac{\text{time elapsed before a group of entrants is}}{\text{reduced to one half its original number.}}$$

Labour turnover data is found to differ for the sexes (being higher for women); the different age groups (being higher for the lower age groups); the type of work undertaken (being higher for unskilled than skilled); the length of service (being higher among newcomers than those with long periods of service with the organisation). Labour turnover also depends on the local employment situation.

There are a number of causes of labour turnover, some which the organisation could avoid, if it wanted, and others which are unavoidable. Avoidable causes are pay, working conditions, lack of promotion, job dissatisfaction, etc. Unavoidable causes are illness, death, marriage, pregnancy, housing problems, transport problems, etc. In addition, labour turnover can be caused by the organisation discharging employees by virtue of disciplinary action, redundancy, or their just being unsuitable for the job.

While a low labour turnover can present some problems to an organisation, e.g. an ageing work force which means a large turnover at retirement age and no employees with recent knowledge of the 'outside' world, a high labour turnover leads to significant costs. The following are some of the costs involved:

1   The cost of the time while new employees are being trained.
2   The cost of lost production time, while the job is vacant and while the new employee is being trained.
3   The cost of extra supervision required for new employees.

4　The cost of poor quality products produced initially by new employees.
5　The costs of recruitment and selection.

Job design

Job design and redesign involves the consideration of individual tasks or activities and bringing them together into a job which is assigned to an individual worker or group of workers. There are a number of different ways this problem has, and is being, approached. One approach is that of scientific management, as developed by F. W. Taylor (see Chapter 4). In relation to job design, this approach leads to:

1　A separation of those engaged in mental and manual work.
2　The maximum decomposition of work tasks so that any one job consists of a very small number of tasks or activities.
3　The minimisation of the skill requirements of any task or activity.
4　No consideration of psychological or social factors, i.e. no consideration of the worker as a human but rather as a machine.
5　The assumption that workers work purely for financial reward.

A consequence of adopting such an approach can be considered to be the system established by Henry Ford for the mass production of cars, the famous Model T. This system had four basic elements:

1　The product was standardised. This meant not only the car itself but the components used in the car. Thus a car was not made by making separately all the pieces for the particular car concerned so that they only ended up fitting that one car. Components were standardised so that any one of a batch of components could be used in any one of the cars.

2　Flow-line production methods were used, i.e. the assembly line, with each worker tied to a particular job in a particular position along the line.

3　An extensive use of machine tools. This made many of the jobs semi-automatic and de-skilled many jobs.

4　The use of the principles of scientific managment, e.g. the maximum decomposition of work tasks.

Job design was thus not influenced by any real consideration of the individual workers' abilities or indeed any consideration of the worker as being an individual. More recent considerations of job design have, however, involved a consideration of the worker as an individual and how to make best use of the abilities of individual workers. An example of such a development is the work of Herzberg (see Chapter 5) in 1959 when he, and his co-workers, considered the factors which lead to job satisfaction and dissatisfaction, motivator and hygiene factors. Motivator factors are achievement, recognition, the work itself, responsibility and advancement. Hygiene factors, those leading to dissatisfaction, are company policy and administration, supervision, salary, interpersonal relations and working conditions. Getting hygiene factors right can get rid of dissatisfaction but it does not lead to motivation; for that the motivator factors must be right. Increasing the motivator factors was called job enrichment.

Job enrichment can involve:

1   Combining tasks to give greater skill variety.
2   Forming natural work units so that the unit can develop an identity.
3   Increasing job responsibilities and autonomy.

The aim of job enrichment is to give:

1   Workers higher internally generated work motivation.
2   Workers higher satisfaction with the work.
3   The organisation higher quality work performance.
4   The organisation lower absenteeism and turnover.

Other ways of job design that have been developed are job rotation and job enlargement. *Job rotation* describes the procedure by which workers in a group can change their jobs with other workers at prescribed times or when freely chosen. The prime aim of this is to reduce the strain and monotony that can occur with a worker carrying out the same job every day. *Job enlargement* describes the procedure by which several similar work steps or tasks are joined together to increase the scope of the work.

New technology

The term *new technology* is generally applied to the wide range of equipment based on the use of microelectronics and associated software. Information technology is one aspect of this, that involving microelectronics data handling with modern communication facilities. The microelectronics revolution can be considered to have its roots in the developments in physics which led to the invention of the transistor in 1948. In the early 1960s, transistors, resistors, and other circuit components with their interconnections started to be produced as a complete circuit inside just one small chip of silicon. By 1970 the possible number of circuit components in a single chip had risen to about 1000, by 1976 it was 32,000. The microelectronics revolution had arrived.

Microelectronics have the following consequences for equipment:

1   It allows for compactness.
2   It is cheap.

3   It can operate at high speed.
4   It is reliable and accurate.
5   It has low energy consumption.

In the case of information technology the consequences is that information can be collected, collated, stored and accessed with a very high speed.

The following are just a few examples of the applications of new technology:

1   Computer-aided design (CAD) and computer-aided manufacture (CAM).
2   Computerised stock control and warehousing.
3   Word processing and electronic filing.
4   Computerised information systems.
5   Electronic mail and facsmile transmission.

A consequence of such applications is the move to the automated factory, the automated office, etc.; a move to a reduction in the role of humans and an increase in the role of machines. The introduction of new technology has resulted in many instances in a de-skilling of the work of humans.

The introduction by management of new technology is generally welcomed because they envisage:

1   Reducing operating costs.
2   Improving efficiency.
3   Increasing flexibility.
4   Increasing the quality and consistency of production.
5   Improving control over production operations.

A reduction in operating costs and improvement in efficiency may occur by the replacement of humans by machines, e.g. automatic spot welding with cars, of perhaps the improved capabilities of the machines, e.g. word processing. Improved stock control can also result in a reduction in operating costs. The improvement in control and greater flexibility can be obtained by computerised scheduling.

Revision questions

1   What is meant by the terms work study, method study and work measurement?

2   Describe the seven steps necessary in method study.

3   Distinguish between a flow diagram and a process chart in method study.

4   Define basic time and standard rating.

5 Explain the principles of (a) time study, (b) activity sampling, (c) synthetic timing, (d) predetermined motion time systems, (e) analytical timing, methods of work measurement.

6 Explain the term ergonomics.

7 List some of the factors that have to be considered in the design of a control to be operated by a human.

8 List five forms of display.

9 What are the three main environmental factors that can affect workers?

10 What is meant by the principles of motion economy?

11 List the main ways employees can receive remuneration.

12 List some of the objectives of any payment system.

13 What are the four main methods used for job evaluation and what is the purpose of such evaluation?

14 Explain the points evaluation method used for job evaluation.

15 Explain the terms separation rate, quit rate, long-service stability index and fringe turnover rate and explain how the information they each give differs.

16 What are some of the costs incurred as a result of labour turnover?

17 What is meant by job design, job enrichment, job enlargement and job rotation?

Assignments and further questions

1 Draw a flow diagram for some operation, either in an organisation or perhaps in your home, e.g. making a cup of coffee. Analyse the diagram and consider an optimum flow.

2 Draw an outline process chart for some operation, either in an organisation or perhaps in your home, e.g cutting the grass.

3 Figure 18.3 shows a schematic diagram of a motor-car assembly line (reproduced with permission from the Open University Technology: A Second Level Course, Systems Behaviour Module 3).
(a) Draw a possible flow diagram.
(b) Draw an outline process chart.

4 Carry out a time study of a job being undertaken, e.g a typist typing a letter, somebody in your home peeling potatoes. Ascertain a standard time for the job.

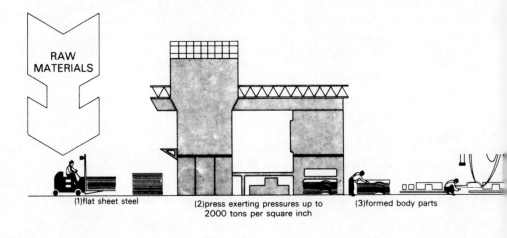

(1)flat sheet steel

(2)press exerting pressures up to 2000 tons per square inch

(3)formed body parts

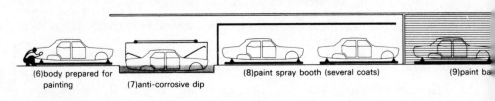

(6)body prepared for painting

(7)anti-corrosive dip

(8)paint spray booth (several coats)

(9)paint ba

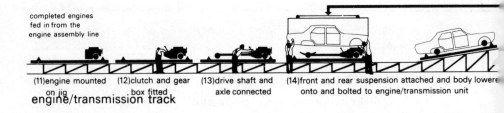

completed engines fed in from the engine assembly line

(11)engine mounted on jig

engine/transmission track

(12)clutch and gear box fitted

(13)drive shaft and axle connected

(14)front and rear suspension attached and body lowere onto and bolted to engine/transmission unit

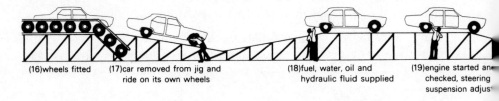

(16)wheels fitted

(17)car removed from jig and ride on its own wheels

(18)fuel, water, oil and hydraulic fluid supplied

(19)engine started an checked, steering suspension adjus

Figure 18.3   *Schematic diagram of the motor-car assembly line*
By permission of The Open University from T241, *Edition 2.1, Module 3,*
Figure 20 (Open University 1977)

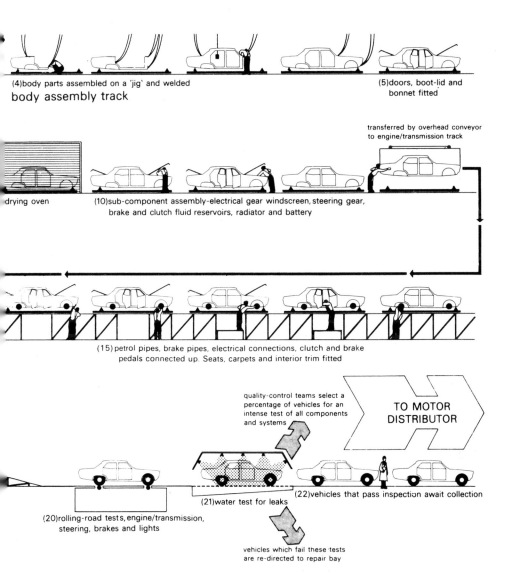

(4)body parts assembled on a 'jig' and welded
body assembly track

(5)doors, boot-lid and bonnet fitted

transferred by overhead conveyor to engine/transmission track

drying oven

(10)sub-component assembly-electrical gear windscreen, steering gear, brake and clutch fluid reservoirs, radiator and battery

(15)petrol pipes, brake pipes, electrical connections, clutch and brake pedals connected up. Seats, carpets and interior trim fitted

quality-control teams select a percentage of vehicles for an intense test of all components and systems

TO MOTOR DISTRIBUTOR

(21)water test for leaks

(22)vehicles that pass inspection await collection

(20)rolling-road tests, engine/transmission, steering, brakes and lights

vehicles which fail these tests are re-directed to repair bay

5   A small company making one-off or small batches of items has never bothered with any work measurement, basing its charges to customers and the rates it pays its workers on the manager's experience. Write a report to the manager giving the advantages, limitations, possible problems that might be encountered, a possible method or methods that might be used, etc. if work measurement were to be used. Also consider the cost factor.

6   The supervisor of the typing pool is considering an incentive pay system. Suggest a work measurement method that might be used in such a situation.

7   Consider the ergonomics of some human-operated machine, e.g. a lathe, a domestic electric cooker, a car or a motorbike. Consider the controls and the reading displays. List the types occuring and consider whether they are the most appropriate for the activity concerned. Also consider the location of the controls and displays. Hence write a report on the ergonomics of the machine concerned.

8   Write a critical analysis of the different types of reading displays and the various situations under which they are most appropriate.

9   For the assembly line described in Figure 18.3, critically comment on the illumination, noise and climate factors that are required, or might occur, at different parts of the line.

10   Analyse some task carried out by a worker, e.g. somebody engaged in an assembly job or perhaps a typist, and comment on the motions involved in terms of the principles of motion economy.

11   Describe the various payment systems employed in some organisation.

12   Investigate the points evaluation method and produce a report indicating how it might be operated in your company.

13   Write a report advocating job enrichment for a particular group of workers. In your report discuss the advantages, and possible disadvantages, and how it might be organised.

14   Write a report indicating the possible consequences of new technology in some particular industry or company.

Index